Development Policies and Poverty Alleviation in Bangladesh

Development Policies and Poverty Alleviation in Bangladesh

Pk. Md. Motiur Rahman

SERIALS PUBLICATIONS
New Delhi

First Published–2005

ISBN: 81-86771-69-7

SERIALS PUBLICATIONS

4, B.S.S. Hall, Khyber Pass Market,
Civil Lines, Delhi–110054 (India)
Phone: 23245225
Fax: 91-11-23272135
e-mail: serials@satyam.net.in

Branch Office

4830/24, Prahlad Street, Ansari Road,
Darya Ganj, New Delhi-110002 (India)

Printed at : R.K. Offset Process, Delhi-32

PRINTED IN INDIA

This book is Dedicated to my Departed Father and Mother

Preface

A large share of population in Bangladesh suffers from poverty and thus various development policies and programs have been taken by Government Organisations (GOs) and Non-Government Organisations (NGOs) for Poverty alleviation. There is a need for in-depth studies on how and to what extent development policies and programs can help poverty reduction. This study is primarily based on the analysis of secondary data, policies taken in different Five Year Plans, thought-provoking published and un-unpublished papers as well as individual studies done for poverty situation analysis.

Development policies for poverty alleviation have been discussed in Chapter 1. Chapter 2 deals with unseen and unknown aspects of poverty. Development plan objectives and plan outlay for poverty alleviation have been discussed in Chapters 3 and 4 respectively. Chapter 5 traces the major socio-economic performance. A brief review of targeted public policies and expenditure have been presented in Chapter 6, while Chapter 7 is concerned with NGOs programs for poverty alleviation. Chapter 8 is devoted to the study of safety net programs for poverty alleviation. Microfinance activities taken by the formal sector Finance Institutions have been outlined in Chapter 9. A profile of agricultural growth performance has been outlined in Chapter 10, while Chapter 11 has been devoted to statistical evaluation of regional disparity in socio-economic development. The last Chapter presents the main conclusions on and strategies for poverty alleviation.

I am particularly thankful to Professor Muzaffer Ahmad of the Institute of Business Administration (IBA), University of Dhaka, for his kind interest and encouragement in writing this book. I am very happy to put on record my thanks to my young colleagues Ms. Tamanna Howlader and Mr. Israt Raihan for their help during writing of this book. Thanks are due to Mr. Md. Abdul Aziz who bears the brunt of typing the manuscript. I humbly dedicate this book to the fond memory of my departed father and mother.

Finally, I shall be happy if this book is of any help to those who seek a way towards poverty alleviation.

Pk. M.M.Rahman
Institute of Statistical Research
And Training (ISRT)
University of Dhaka
Dhaka
BANGLADESH

Contents

1

Development Policies for Poverty Alleviation

Conceptual Issues of Poverty

Bangladesh is one of the poorest countries in the world with about 130 million people in an area of only 144 thousand sq. km. and with a per capita income of US$386. The land-man ratio (per capita cultivated area) is of about 0.14 acres per person, which is on historical decline. The total civilian labour force of the country was estimated at 56 million in 1995-96. Of this, 45.8 million was in the rural areas and about 63 per cent of the total rural labour force was engaged in agriculture sector. The rural society is highly differentiated with rich land owners at the top and the landless labourers at the bottom, while owner cultivators and sharecroppers come in between. Besides these, there are other social groups such as literate and illiterate, artisans and wage labourers, self-employed and unemployed etc. Poverty strikes unevenly among these social groups and it is thus rooted in economic, political and social processes and is the outcome of multidimensional factors which interact with each other and reinforce each other in such a way that exacerbate the deprivation of the poor.

The causes of poverty are, however, much more complex and no single factor is sufficient to understand and explain the dynamics of process of poverty. A large number of interlinked factors are considered as determinants of poverty. They are high population growth, low economic growth, low resource endowment, illiteracy, low per capita income, technological backwardness etc. Besides these visible factors of poverty, there are many invisible factors which are rooted in a complex web of social, political and natural factors. Poverty in Bangladesh is both a rural and urban phenomena, but the extent of rural poverty is more alarming and its dimensions are quite different from those of urban poverty. Millions of landless, marginal and small farm households suffer from unemployment, impoverishment and poverty. Rural women also account for a high disproportionate share of poverty and malnutrition. They often lack adequate food and shelter, education and health, employment opportunity etc. On the other hand, economic shocks arising from natural calamities, illness, insecurity, dowry, malnutrition etc., are common phenomena which constitute a severe barrier to economic graduation but these factors rather graduate income erosion of the poor. Poverty may, therefore, be conceptualized in three broad ways: these are (a) intrinsic poverty which is characterized by lack of basic needs due to poor resource endowment and technological backwardness, (b) induced poverty which results from inequality in distribution of income productive assets, exploitation of ignorance or weakness and (c) emergency poverty which is brought about by temporary circumstances such as natural disasters like drought, flood, earthquakes etc. Thus any attempt for poverty reduction involves multi-dimensional and intersectoral efforts which focus on addressing a number of issues such as high economic growth with social justice, high investment in social sectors for accelerating human capital formation, promotion of income and employment for the vulnerable groups.

Development: Policy Issues

In a broad sense, development is defined as the overall well being of the entire population. Thus development agenda goes beyond income and encompasses healthy living, equity, empowerment, participation, security and social cohesion. The national development goals are, therefore, to increase economic growth with social justice, improve human resources, empower the poor and create employment opportunity for them and consequently to reduce poverty.

The recent literature on poverty has caused rethinking of development policies appropriate for poverty alleviation in developing countries including Bangladesh. The outcome, as reflected in the literature on development policies, has been essentially to focus greater attention than before on reduction of poverty, since the developing countries are plagued with continued mass poverty. It is now realised that alleviation of poverty should be fundamental to development policies. Within the overall development framework, the goals of development policies should be to attain development that promotes better quality of life, improves participation of the poor people in the development process, mitigates inequalities and facilitates income and employment generation of the poor, particularly women and other traditionally excluded groups. In the last two decades there has been noticeable socio-economic progress in the country. Per capita income, life expectancy, literacy, infant and child mortality, maternal mortality, empowerment of women, primary and secondary enrolment etc. have increased significantly. But inspite of the significant level of progress in these areas, the proportion of poor did not reduce significantly and proportion of rural population living in absolute poverty is still large.

The government of Bangladesh has been taking a number of macro and microeconomic policies for poverty alleviation. Among others, the structural adjustment policy which involves denationalization and privatization of financial institutions, reduction in aggregate public expenditure, withdrawal of subsidies for food, agricultural inputs such as ferilizer and irrigation equipment etc. is important. This policy was adopted with assistance from the International Monetary Fund (IMF) and the World Bank (WB) [Hossain, M. and Sen, B. (1992)]. The structural adjustment Programme was started in 1986 with the hope that it would accelerate economic growth, maintain macroeconomic stability, reduce inflation rate and the overall economic benefits would then "trickle down" to the poor thus raising their standard of living. But it is difficult to assess precisely how benefits accrued from structural adjustment are distributed among different social and economic groups and to determine the net impact on the welfare of the poor. Thus the structural adjustment programme has recognized the need for microeconomic programmes for the poor who are not generally benefited from the growth process.

Besides structural adjustment programmes, the government of Bangladesh emphasizes on four broad policies for poverty alleviation. These policies are (i) raising economic growth through sectoral development such as agricultural, industrial, infrastructure development, etc. (ii) developing human resources and capabilities of the poor via education, health and family welfare, social welfare, nutrition etc. (iii) providing microcredit, and (iv) providing social security and safety net to the poor.

Policy Framework for Poverty Alleviation

Policies for poverty alleviation can be broadly classified into two categories, viz. (i) indirect policies, and (ii) direct policies. The indirect policies are designed to achieve objectives other than poverty alleviation, but nevertheless may have a substantial impact on the welfare of the poor. These policies include both long-term and short-run macroeconomic policies. The long-term policies lead to sectoral growth, increased demand for labour, greater socio-economic development etc. while the short-run macroeconomic policies include fiscal, monetary exchange rate, agriculture, industry, education, health, social welfare, etc. These macro policies are target neutral and provide benefits to all groups of people along with the poor group through trickle-down process. For instance, high economic growth may benefit the poor through increasing employment opportunity, social welfare, infrastructure development etc. But an important limitation of indirect policies for poverty alleviation is that in the absence of policies relating to social justice, high economic growth alone may not alleviate poverty adequately. This is because the growth process sometimes bypasses certain segments of the population if equitable distribution of income and assets is not ensured.

The macroeconomic policies described above are, thus, important for poverty alleviation, but they are by no means adequate to remove poverty completely from the society. Microlevel policies and specific target interventions such as group-based lending for microenterprises, skill development training, women and youth development etc. are also important for poverty alleviation in regions with high population density, landlessness and inequality in income distribution. Targeted policies lead to increase in productive capacity of the target group through human resource or skill development, access to credit and creation of self-employment opportunities. For instance, women development through free education and skill development training along with access to credit, not only reduces fertility and improves child welfare and nutrition, but also improves the income earning capacity of the poor women and provides safety net in time of economic crisis. The direct intervention policies adopted are target group oriented and extend immediate help to the poor and are designed to benefit the underprivileged and disadvantaged groups which are generally bypassed by the indirect policies. Examples of direct interventions for poverty alleviation are Vulnerable Group Development (VGD), Food for Works (FFW), Free Education for girl's up to class X, rural credit, food for education at the primary level etc. However, the direct policy is not a substitute for indirect policy. Rather, they are complementary to each other.

Poverty Alleviation: Policy Frames in the Plans

From the emergence of Bangladesh, the problem of poverty caught the attention of successive governments and different policies were framed to solve the problem. During the last three decades, a variety of policy measures have been suggested to stimulate greater employment and income-earning opportunities among the poor. In successive five-year development plans, various policy measures were designed to address this issue. Moreover, there has been a gradual shift in the objectives of development policies with regard to poverty alleviation from one plan to another.

In 1973, the First Five Year Plan (FFYP: 1973-78) was formulated and the main objectives of the plan were to rehabilitate people affected during the war of liberation, construct shattered physical infrastructures and create a framework wherein common people could be provided with basic needs. Although no specific policies were formulated in the name of poverty alleviation in the first plan, an attempt was made to undertake land reform policy to protect the interests of the landless poor, reduce the burden of land tax on small farmers and to support prices of major crops. The general pattern established in the FFYP was changed in the Two-Year Plan (TYP: 1978-80). For instance, there was a shift of policies in the FFYP from rehabilitation and social welfare to skill development and self-employment.

The Second Five Year Plan (SFYP: 1980-85) also aimed at reducing poverty through participation of the rural poor in the development process. The policies of the SFYP shifted further to human resources development through the provision of adequate facilities for non-formal, vocational education and training so as to undertake a more comprehensive approach for poverty alleviation. Another important objective of the SFYP was to reduce poverty through participation of rural poor within an expanded programme of area development. In this plan period too, land reforms were undertaken to protect the interests of landless labourers, tenants and small farmers. But certain constraints impeded the implementation of the land reform measures and institution development in this respect.

The Third Five Year Plan (TFYP: 1985-90) gave due importance to poverty alleviation by ensuring greater access of the rural poor to means of production by extending facilities in agriculture, physical infrastructure and social services sectors. The prime objective of the plan was to generate employment and increase income of the rural poor through vocational/trade skill development training, rural development, organising two-tier cooperative etc. Its main purpose was to raise labour incomes, thereby improving the standard of living of the poor. Keeping poverty alleviation in view, several projects were undertaken by the government all over the country [Huda, S.A.T.M.(1993)]. The plan also took special measures to protect the interest of the rural poor from the domination of the rural rich by organising the two-tier cooperative system.

The Fourth Five Year Plan (FFYP: 1990-95) put particular emphasis on poverty alleviation. In this plan specific attention was given to rural development and promotion of women participation in the development process. The government categorically attached top priority in the plan to poverty alleviation programmes and involved commercial banks in providing credit particularly to the poorer section of the rural population.

In the late 1980s, emphasis was given to microcredit programmes for the poor and to give it further support, Palli Karma Sahayak Foundation (PKSF) was set up in May 1990 as a non-profit organisation. The foundation was established for undertaking nationwide programmes for mobilizing micro-credit programmes, and to implement and carry out efficient anti-poverty programmes. It also adopted the strategy of organizing the rural poor into savings groups and created opportunities for income generation for them by providing collateral free microcredit through the NGOs termed as partner organizations (POs). Moreover in 1990, the task force recommended providing around Tk.18070.0 million annually for implementing poverty alleviation programmes in the country (Huda, S.A. TM (1993). P.194].

Recognizing the importance and intensity of the problem of rural poverty, the Government has attached top priority to poverty alleviation in the Fifth Five-Year Plan (FFYP: 1997/98-2001/02). The goals for poverty alleviation have been well articulated in determining all development policies and keeping poverty alleviation as the primary goal, the FFYP draws upon the pro-poor plan objectives. The aim of the pro-poor plan objectives is to improve the economic conditions of the poor and human resource development.

Besides these, four special programmes have been undertaken for the hardcore poor and disadvantaged groups to provide economic security and to address specific constraints and vulnerability. These are (a) Boyoska Vata (old age pension), (b) Grihayan Tahbil (Housing Fund) (c) Asrayan (shelter for the homeless), and (d) Karma Sangsthan Bank (Employment Bank). All these programmes have been designed for poverty alleviation of the landless and homeless people, distressed widows and poor women abandoned by their husbands by providing shelter, training for skill development and microcredit for income generating activities. The Employment Bank is a statutory public bank and it provides credits to unemployed youth for creating productive self employment opportunities. The major breakthrough was achieved by promoting the role of NGOs in the field of skill training and development, empowerment, microcredit, self-employment opportunity, income generating activities etc. to supplement the government programmes for poverty alleviation.

Major Programmes for Poverty Alleviation

Bangladesh has implemented and is still in the process of implementating various anti-poverty programmes in rural areas. It is not possible to discuss all the programmes and their impact on the rural people in this section.

Major programmes and projects related to poverty alleviation have been implemented by the GOs and NGOs among which (i) Land Reforms, (ii) Safety net, (iii) Integrated Rural Development, (iv) Targeted Micro Credit, (v) Employment Generation, (vi) Co-operatives, (vii) Women and Youth development etc. are important. The GO and NGO projects together have covered upto June 99 more than 11 million clienteles of which about 2.36 million have been covered by Grameen Bank (GB), another 2.71 million by BRAC, about 1.40 million by Proshika, 1.07 million by ASA, 3.52 million by other NGOs and more than 1 million by the Ministries/ agencies [BER (2000), P.116]. However, a brief account of these programmes are narrated below.

Land Reforms

In a predominantly rural and agro-based economy like Bangladesh, the distribution of ownership and access to productive assets (land) as well as opportunities for productive employment for the landless, have significant impact on reduction of rural poverty.

Land reform policy is important to protect the interest of landless labourers and pure tenants in terms of access to land asset and other related factors. Over the last three decades, several measures have been taken to establish the right of the landless families over land and to alleviate poverty. To make the land reform policy effective, initiatives were taken to distribute khas lands among the landless poor to strengthen their economic and social power for the rehabilitation of assetless and landless families. But despite having the good intentions, the existing power structure precludes the possibility of implementing effective land reforms. Since land is the most important asset in an agrarian economy, its effective implementation is likely to have an effect on income accruing from land. But the programme of land reforms has proved to be mere political slogans with feeble commitment at the implementation level.

Safety-Net

Non-monetised food distribution through Food for Works programmes (FWP), Vulnerable Group Development (VGD) programmes, Gratuitous Relief (GR), Test Relief (TR), Vulnerable Group Feeding (VGF), School Feeding etc. have been considered as a part of safety net programme for the rural economy which is characterised by mass poverty and unemployment. However, the food distribution programmes are very much present in the country and about Tk.9610.3 million in 1995-96, Tk.13975.7 million in 1997-78 and Tk.15360.0 million in 1999-2000 were distributed for safety net programmes [BER (2000), P.111]. But its coverage is limited and depends largely on the availability of food supply by donor agencies.

Integrated Rural Development

The Bangladesh Rural Development Board (BRDB) under the Ministry of Local Government and Rural

Development (LGRD) is a specialised public agency designed to promote integrated rural development and poverty alleviation. Most of the BRDB's programmes and projects are designed and focussed on poverty alleviation. For instance, Rural Development projects at different phases, Skill Development Training projects, Rural Poor-Cooperative project etc. capture the major component of poverty alleviation. But the limitation of the rural development programmes or projects is that a large number of ultra poor are by-passed and these programmes generally suffer from sustainability problems.

Employment generation through infrastructure development activities is another important policy of the government for poverty alleviation. In view of this, the government has created the Local Government Engineering Department (LGED) under the Rural Development and Institution (RD&I) sector. It is one of the prime Engineering Departments to undertake rural development projects for employment generation and poverty alleviation.

Targeted Micro Credit

The targeted microcredit programmes mostly taken up by the NGOs have become an important element of poverty alleviation strategy in rural Bangladesh. It aims at improving socio-economic status of the poor through different income generating activities and by providing safety-net for the rural poor when they are most vulnerable to "shocks" that could lead to destitution. Most of the credit programmes have concentrated on the rural poor women, except agricultural credit given by the specialized banks and scheduled banks. Besides NGOs, several Ministries/agencies including BRDB and banks have been giving collateral free loans to the poor for various microenterprises which constitute small businesses and shops, cottage industries, transport service, fish cultivation, poultry, cow/goat rearing etc.

Employment Generation Programme

Intensification of agriculture, increase in the number of processing units, and other non-farm activities are the programmes for employment generation of the rural poor. Public works programmes in the recent years have been considered as a part of policy measures for employment generation. Given the magnitude of unemployment and underemployment particularly in agriculture, manufacturing industries and other sectors, the public works programme serves as an effective instrument for employment generation and increasing purchasing power of the poor. The Rural Works Programme (RWP) - Food for Works, Test Relief, Road Maintenance etc. designed to provide infrastructure in the form of irrigation, drainage and roads are the most important employment generation programmes for the rural poor especially during slack seasons in agriculture. Besides employment, these programmes have multiplier effect on the income. But these programmes largely depend on donor agencies and suffer from the problems of sustainability.

Co-Operatives

Under the Poverty Alleviation and Rural Development Programme, BRDB is organising farmers, women and the assetless in cooperatives at the grass-root level. It has gradually realized that cooperatives at the village level are a source of strength and a mechanism of capacity building for the assetless rural poor and cooperatives work as local level institution. The targeted beneficiaries are organised into formal co-operative societies called "Bittoheen Samabaya Samiti (BSS), Mohila Bittaheen Samabaya Samiti (MBSS) and Krishak Samabaya Societies (KSS). These village level cooperatives are federated into Thana Bittoheen Central Cooperative Association (TBCCA). Formation of these cooperatives facilitates support services in terms of skill development, credit and input services to the members in different farm and non-farm activities to earn their livelihood. The cooperatives encourage the disadvantaged group of people to participate in the development process of the country. But despite having large coverage of cooperatives, they are not successful in poverty alleviation and cooperatives can not single handedly bring about rural development due to weak base of grass-root level institutions.

Women and Youth Development

The Ministry of Women's Affairs and other ministries such as Social Welfare, Education, Health and Population Control have taken up several programmes to bring women into the mainstream of development process. Among the programmes, Skill Development Training, Women's Credit, Poverty Alleviation, Support Services and Special Women's programme are notable. The aim of these programmes is to create awareness among the women about the development process with a view to enhancing their capacity to mobilise and administer resources for development thereby improving their socio-economic conditions. Considering youth as a most directive source of development, the Department of Youth and Development under the Ministry of Youth and Sports has taken up a number of programmes with a view to engaging the youth in national development stream. Programmes both for women and youth development are important for poverty alleviation because these programmes have ample scope for employment opportunities. But given the ambitious nature of the above strategy for poverty alleviation, the impact of the efforts have been limited as seen from different results.

Objectives of the Study

The main objective of the study is to assess and examine the development policies and programmes for poverty alleviation in rural Bangladesh. Other specific objectives are delineated to cover the following aspects:

(i) To investigate development objectives in different five year plans for poverty alleviation;

(ii) To examine plan outlay for poverty alleviation;

(iii) To assess economic performance and reduction of poverty;

(iv) To examine public policies and public expenditure for poverty alleviation;

(v) To highlight the roles of NGOs for poverty alleviation;

(vi) To illustrate the food aided programmes for poverty alleviation;

(vii) To examine the role of financial institutions for poverty alleviation;

(viii) To identify level, determinants and differentials of poverty in different districts etc.

Organisation of the Study

This study has been arranged in 12 Chapters. The first chapter is an introductory one, which gives a brief description of the background of the study. The objectives of the study have also been highlighted in this chapter.

Chapter 2 deals with unseen and unknown aspects of poverty. The vicious circle of poverty has also been described in this chapter.

Chapter 3 examines the development plan objectives and plan outlay by public and private sectors. Sectoral allocation as well as ADP allocation to social sectors has been described in this chapter.

Chapter 4 analyses the main development plan outlay for poverty alleviation. Public expenditures and its share of GNP in social sectors under different plans have also been discussed in chapter 4.

Chapter 5 describes the public policies and expenditures for poverty alleviation. Economic performance and their impacts on poverty alleviation have been highlighted in this chapter.

Chapter 6 deals with public policies and spending for poverty alleviation. Different targeted programmes and projects undertaken by the Government have also been discussed in this chapter.

Chapter 7 examines the role of non-government organisations (NGOs) in poverty alleviation. Different targeted programmes and projects including microcredit programmes undertaken by the NGOs are also the main concerned of this chapter.

Chapter 8 highlights the food-aided safety net programmes for social development and poverty alleviation of the target groups.

Chapter 9 describes the role of microfinance institutions in poverty alleviation. Linkage effects between institutional credits and agricultural growth have been analysed in this chapter.

Chapter 10 analyses the growth performance of agricultural production, acreage and per acre yield. Distribution of landholding, normative measures of landholding inequality and relationships between landholding size and poverty have been discussed in this chapter.

Chapter 11 provides an integrated picture of socio-economic development for sixty four districts with the help of composite index. The statistical evaluation which enables us to present an overall view of development and gives an understanding of the factors related to poverty reduction has also been included in this chapter.

Chapter 12 includes conclusion and specific strategies for socio-economic development for poverty alleviation.

Appendix 1.1

Number of General and BRDB Co-operatives in Bangladesh (as on September 1999) by Division and Type of Cooperatives

Type of Societies	*Dhaka Division*	*Chittagong Division*	*Rajshahi Division*	*Khulna Division*	*Total*
A. Secondary Societies (General):					
1. General Cooperative Bank	17	19	16	22	74
2. General Fishermen's Cooperatives	28	34	10	16	88
3. Central Weavers' Cooperatives	21	8	11	10	50
4. Central Sugarcane Growers' Cooperatives	1	-	8	3	12
5. Central Women's Cooperatives	15	7	9	6	37
6. Others	54	34	38	32	158
Sub-total (A)	136	102	92	89	419
B. Secondary Societies (BRDB):					
1. Thana Central Coop. Association	121	121	115	90	447
2. Central Bittaheen Cooperatives	47	17	86	86	236
3. Others	4	2	1	4	11
Sub-total (B)	172	140	202	180	694
Grand total of Secondary Societies (A+B)	308	242	294	269	1113

C. Primary Societies (General):					
1. Land Mortgage Coop. Bank	16	8	16	17	57
2. Union Multipurpose Co-operative	959	799	948	860	3566
3. Krishi Samabay Samity	5997	2723	3700	4115	16535
4. Fishermen's Society	825	1214	580	741	3360
5. Weavers' Cooperatives	778	184	316	314	1592
6. Sugarcane Growers' Cooperatives	58	1	418	116	593
7. Women's Co-operatives	318	151	173	138	780
8. Milk Producers' Co-operatives	127	-	177	1	305
9. Auto-rickshaw Society	249	141	50	34	474
10. Others	6907	3960	3717	3801	18385
Sub-total (C)	16234	9181	10095	10137	45647
D. Primary Societies (BRDB):					
1. Krishi Samabaya Samity	17870	10344	17434	11788	57436
2. Women's Cooperatives	2531	1695	1646	1844	7716
3. Bittaheen Men's Cooperatives	3421	2728	4746	3342	14237
4. Bittaheen Women's Cooperatives	3809	1828	7851	8090	21578
Sub-total (D)	27631	16595	31677	25077	100967
Grand total of Primary Societies (C+D)	43865	25776	41772	35214	146614

(Appendix 1.1 Cont...)

Appendix 1.1

Savings Deposit of General and BRDB Co-operatives Members in Bangladesh (as on September 1999) by Division and Type of Cooperatives

(in lakh Tk.)

Type of Societies	*Dhaka Division*	*Chittagong Division*	*Rajshahi Division*	*Khulna Division*	*Total*
A. Secondary Societies: (General):					
1. General Cooperative Bank	124.88	201.58	80.20	128.82	535.48
2. General Fishermen's Cooperatives	12.49	13.69	4.15	12.81	43.14
3. Central Weavers' Cooperatives	37.72	31.44	14.83	45.17	129.16
4. Central Sugarcane Growers' Cooperatives	7.34	-	25.29	17.92	50.55
5. Central Women's Cooperatives	0.63	1.66	0.60	0.04	2.93
6. Others	27.39	104.54	10.62	48.59	191.14
Sub-total (A)	210.45	352.91	135.69	253.35	952.40
B. Secondary Societies (BRDB):					
1. Thana Central Coop. Association	1882.70	1756.88	2246.40	1284.56	7170.54
2. Central Bittaheen Cooperatives	682.13	319.12	1998.60	2222.56	5122.41
3. Others	0.03	-	-	-	0.03
Sub-total (B)	2564.86	2076.00	4245.00	3507.12	12492.98
Grand-total of Secondary Societies (A+B)	2775.31	2428.91	4380.69	3760.47	13345.38

C.	**Primary Societies (General):**					
1.	Land Mortgage Coop. Bank	15.45	8.05	14.55	7.66	45.71
2.	Union Multipurpose Co-operative	41.73	101.35	45.46	82.87	271.41
3.	Fishermen's Cooperative	54.37	142.51	20.76	36.30	253.94
4.	Krishi Samabay Samity	95.89	79.37	65.36	72.38	313.00
5.	Weavers' Cooperatives	23.20	21.39	14.11	37.15	95.85
6.	Sugarcane Growers' Cooperatives	1.03	0.02	22.67	18.33	42.05
7.	Women's Cooperatives	16.25	14.85	10.92	11.53	53.55
8.	Milk Producers' Cooperatives	6.33	-	8.68	0.08	15.09
9.	Auto-rickshaw Society	90.30	277.65	5.48	4.57	378.00
10.	Others	5667.28	1526.20	904.18	976.79	9074.45
Sub-total (C)		6011.83	2171.39	1112.17	1247.66	10543.05
D.	**Primary Societies (BRDB):**					
1.	Krishi Samabaya Samity	1403.59	1164.02	1774.69	945.79	5288.09
2.	Women's Cooperatives	323.16	270.39	377.18	328.20	1298.93
3.	Bittaheen Men's Cooperatives	270.48	307.66	659.11	466.66	1703.91
4.	Bittaheen Women's Cooperatives	582.96	339.78	1540.95	1790.60	4254.29
Sub-total (D)		2580.19	2081.85	4351.93	3531.25	12545.22
Grand Total of Primary Societies (C+D)		8592.02	4253.24	5464.10	4778.91	23088.27

(Appendix 1.1 Cont...)

Appendix 1.1

Number of General and BRDB Co-operatives Member in Bangladesh (as on September 1999) by Division and Type of Cooperatives

Type of Societies	*Dhaka Division*	*Chittagong Division*	*Rajshahi Division*	*Khulna Division*	*Total*
A. Secondary Societies (General):					
1. General Cooperative Bank	8828	4847	4425	6010	24110
2. General Fishermen's Cooperatives	711	1168	434	580	2893
3. Central Weavers' Cooperatives	804	225	310	250	1589
4. Central Sugarcane Growers' Cooperatives	58	-	410	110	578
5. Central Women's Cooperatives	224	90	123	57	494
6. Others	3093	4342	1806	2185	11426
Sub-total (A)	13718	10672	7508	9192	41090
B. Secondary Societies (BRDB):					
1. Thana Central Coop. Association	22543	14642	20201	14222	71608
2. Central Bittaheen Cooperatives	5081	1907	11476	10735	29199
3. Others	74	32	12	48	166
Sub-total (B)	27698	16581	31689	25005	100973
Grand total of Secondary Societies (A+B)	41416	27253	39197	34197	142063

C. Primary Societies (General):					
1. Land Mortgage Coop. Bank	12068	14159	15409	22531	64167
2. Union Multipurpose Co-operative	296032	239727	285323	369518	1190600
3. Krishi Samabay Samity	92319	144240	64307	75870	376736
4. Fishermen's Society	265703	127977	234801	181152	809633
5. Weavers' Cooperatives	171803	49116	60474	42921	324314
6. Sugarcane Growers' Cooperatives	12157	41	53232	42257	107687
7. Women's Co-operatives	19998	-	14773	284	35055
8. Milk Producers' Co-operatives	15359	5345	7708	8242	36754
9. Auto-rickshaw Society	9577	7937	1317	1775	20606
10. Others	444375	396265	168809	209277	1218726
Sub-total (C)	1339391	984807	906253	953827	4184278
D. Primary Societies (BRDB):					
1. Krishi Samabaya Samity	607289	443786	713341	396042	2160458
2. Women's Cooperatives	82924	49257	56174	54989	243344
3. Bittaheen Men's Cooperatives	101218	86990	131861	101719	421788
4. Bittaheen Women's Cooperatives	102015	59260	199086	209840	570201
Sub-total (D)	893446	639293	1100462	762590	3395791
Grand total of Primary Societies (C+D)	2232837	1624100	2006715	1716417	7580069

(Appendix 1.1 Cont...)

Appendix 1.1

Share Capital of Memebrs (as on September 1999) by Division and Type of Society

(in lakh Tk.)

Type of Societies	*Dhaka Division*	*Chittagong Division*	*Rajshahi Division*	*Khulna Division*	*Total*
A. Secondary Societies: (General):					
1. General Cooperative Bank	137.13	188.17	120.19	153.37	598.86
2. General Fishermen's Cooperatives	3.07	13.89	0.82	5.96	23.74
3. Central Weavers' Cooperatives	25.52	25.84	6.62	9.09	65.07
4. Central Sugarcane Growers' Cooperatives	2.99	-	27.18	13.83	44.00
5. Central Women's Cooperatives	0.36	0.10	0.51	0.14	1.11
6. Others	37.74	54.16	17.04	23.53	132.51
Sub-total (A)	204.81	282.16	172.39	205.93	865.29
B. Secondary Societies (BRDB):					
1. Thana Central Coop. Association	1327.04	916.53	1451.23	731.49	4426.03
2. Central Bittaheen Cooperatives	132.75	54.93	488.72	565.22	1241.62
3. Others	0.03	0.15	-	-	0.18
Sub-total (B)	1459.82	971.61	1939.95	1296.45	5667.83
Grand-total of Secondary Societies (A+B)	1664.63	1253.77	2112.34	1502.38	6533.12

C. Primary Societies (General):					
1. Land Mortgage Coop. Bank	24.29	28.69	38.27	47.43	138.68
2. Union Multipurpose Co-operative	70.69	121.13	75.52	115.39	382.37
3. Fishermen's Cooperative	21.01	67.88	14.98	17.87	121.74
4. Krishi Samabay Samity	113.03	100.83	95.17	112.45	421.48
5. Weavers' Cooperatives	18.85	24.75	13.20	13.09	69.89
6. Sugarcane Growers' Cooperatives	4.72	0.05	31.17	23.47	59.41
7. Women's Cooperatives	4.53	-	14.86	0.14	19.53
8. Milk Producers' Cooperatives	6.33	7.56	5.36	2.73	21.98
9. Auto-rickshaw Society	67.55	79.98	5.44	4.76	157.73
10. Others	2785.48	864.03	465.84	444.16	4559.51
Sub-total (C)	3116.48	1294.90	759.81	781.49	5952.68
D. Primary Societies (BRDB):					
1. Krishi Samabaya Samity	1047.63	687.70	1209.44	612.47	3557.24
2. Women's Cooperatives	124.49	128.04	189.12	119.39	561.04
3. Bittaheen Men's Cooperatives	156.52	133.05	217.63	169.20	676.40
4. Bittaheen Women's Cooperatives	118.94	91.03	328.15	422.12	960.24
Sub-total (D)	1447.58	1039.82	1944.34	1323.18	5754.92
Grand Total of Primary Societies (C+D)	4564.06	2334.72	2704.15	2104.67	11707.60

Source: Habibullah, M., Cooperative Academy, Kotbari, Comilla.

2

Unseen and Unknown Aspects of Poverty

Households Environment

If we examine the poor households and their environment we can observe that they have few assets, small shelter made of straw and bamboo, mud, grass etc. These households have no sanitary toilet and source of safe drinking water of their own. The landholding size is small which does not assure or barely assures subsistence living. The poor households have no livestock or have only small stock such as hen, ducks, goats etc. The small flow of commodities and cash to the poor is inadequate for better living. They have little or no control over productive assets and thus they have no power to bargain on the only asset which they possess – labour [Chambers, R. (1984)]. These unseen aspects of poverty may be substantiated by Table 2.1 which shows that almost 50 per cent of the rural poor households have straw roofs and only 6 per cent have roofs made of brick/ cement. The average floor space of rural poor household was estimated at 229 sq.ft., while the same for non-poor household was 303 sq.ft. About 12 per cent of the poor households had sanitary and slab-latrine facilities for hygienic disposal of excreta. This figure for non-poor households was about 28 per cent. The proportion of poor households using open space for disposal of excreta was estimated at 42 per cent, while this figure was 21 per cent for non-poor households [Table 2.2]. Only 4 per cent

Table 2.1: Roof Materials and Average Floor Space of Main Living Unit

Roof materials	*Households*			
	Poor		*Well-off*	
	%	*average floor space (sq.ft.)*	%	*average floor space (sq. ft.)*
Brick/Cement	198	6.07	409	7.38
C.I. Sheet	243	38.32	312	59.54
Tiles	164	1.60	185	1.83
Bamboo/wood	204	2.20	257	3.50
Straw	217	49.07	266	24.36
Leaves	131	0.73	252	1.17
Others	270	2.01	318	2.22
Total	229	100.00	303	100.00

Source: Rural Poverty Monitoring Survey, December 1995, BBS.

Table 2.2: Households by Types of Toilet Facility

Toilet facility	*% Household*	
	Poor	*Well-off*
Sanitary	3.47	9.59
Slab-latrine	8.82	18.52
Katcha	43.62	49.36
Open space	42.01	20.79
Others	2.07	1.71
Total	100.00	100.00

Source: Rural Poverty Monitoring Survey, December 1995, BBS.

of the poor households had electricity as source of lighting whereas 15 per cent of the non-poor households used electricity for lighting. The proportion of poor households that used kerosene as source of lighting was about 96 per cent, while this figure was 84 per cent for non-poor households [Table 2.3]. The poor household have larger household size compared to non-poor. According to the Poverty Monitoring Survey (PMS) conducted by the BBS in 1998, the average household size in rural areas in the poor household was estimated at about 4.7 persons as against 4.4 persons in the non-poor household [BBS (2000)].

Table 2.3: Source of Lighting for Households

Sources	*% Households*	
	Poor	*Well-off*
Electricity	3.74	15.15
Kerosene	96.06	84.46
Others	0.20	0.39
Total	100.00	100.00

Source: Rural Poverty Monitoring Survey, December 1995, BBS.

A house with mud walls and a straw roofs is easily damaged by storm and floods and needs repairing every year, which involves big amount of money. If money is borrowed to finance repairing of house, interest payments and other obligations add to the impoverishment and deepen the vulnerability. The poor suffer more than non-poor from adverse natural shocks and they have fewer options for coping with shocks, because they own the fewest resources for dealing with natural shocks. Family members living in a house without safe drinking water, sanitary toilet facilities and sufficient floor space are more likely to contact with several diseases such as diarrhoea, malaria, worm disease and other infectious diseases which need hard cash for treatment. This type of expenditure may be the most common trigger for sales of land and livestock of the poor people for their survival. Most rural households are poorly ventilated and being made of materials such as jute, bamboo and mud, the conditions are often damp and clammy, particularly during the wet season. Pathogens of major diseases, such as tuberculosis, thrive in such conditions and therefore people living in these households often become bedridden with various illness. The poor are more susceptible due to undernourishment and low immunity in their bodies. Thus, poor living conditions contribute to income erosion and low productivity by affecting the health and working capacity of the rural poor.

Vicious Circle of Poverty

There are many causes of poverty and no single cause is sufficient to explain how poverty occurs. A large number of visible interlinked factors are responsible for existence and persistence of poverty. Among the visible factors low economic growth, low resource endowment, technological backwardness, unemployment, low human capital etc. are important. But poverty goes beyond these factors and encompasses many other invisible features such as illiteracy, physical weakness, vulnerability, isolation and powerlessness. These invisible interlocking disadvantages trap the common people in deprivation which may be described as a vicious circle of poverty. Poverty is the main determinant of these disadvantages. The strength of interlinkage of poverty and their disadvantages are briefly illustrated below:

Illiteracy

Lack of education is one of the many links that lead to poverty through factors such as inability to acquire remunerative employment, loans from the government and failure to invest in productive activities. Illiterate people generally do not have access to resources from the state because they have no contact with political leaders, officials, and extension workers. They are unable to cope with crisis caused by accident, crop failure, floods, draught and sickness. Poverty is the main determinant of illiteracy. The poor people cannot afford the cost of schooling for their children. Even if children are sent to school, they are likely to dropout after a few months and join as child labourers in the labour market with low wages and unfavourable terms and conditions. Illiterate people find it difficult to familiarize with new technologies and services resulting in low labour productivity. Consequently, their demand and mobility in the labour market is very low. These disadvantages in turn lead to poverty, isolation, vulnerability, and powerlessness. The average year of schooling has highly significant coefficient (-0.2462) in estimated logit equation which explains the lower chance of being poor for a household with higher education level. On the other hand, the likelihood of being poor is higher for a household with lower education level [Table 2.4].

Table 2.4: Logistic Regression of Poverty Status for Rural Households in Bangladesh

Variables	*Estimated co-efficient*	*Odds ratio*
1. Household head characteristics:		
(a) Occupation status (OCCUPSTAT)		
(i) Service[a]	-	-
(ii) Business	-0.2415	0.785
(iii) Agriculture	1.1338**	3.107
(iv) Labourer	1.663**	3.210
(b) Age of head of household (AGEH)		
(i) Age under 30	0.0335	2.454
(ii) Age 30-49[a]	-	-
(iii) Age 49 and above	-0.7621**	0.467

2. Household Charactistics:		
(a) Household Size (HS)		
(i) Less than 5	-0.9133**	0.401
(ii) 5-6[a]	-	-
(iii) Above 6	0.8975**	2.454
(b) % of female members in the household (PFM)	0.8975**	1.157
(c) Dependency ratio/household (DEPDR)	0.0429**	1.044
(d) Average Year of Schooling/household (AYORS)	0.2462**	0.782
(e) Agricultural landholding size (AGLANDS)	-0.6797**	0.507
3. Village Characteristics:		
(a) Distance of village from upazila (DIST)	0.1314**	1.140
(b) Households under rural development (VURDP)	-0.1378	0.871
(c) Households not under rural development (VNOTURDP)[a]	-	-
4. Geographical Region:		
(i) Dhaka Division	0.5528*	1.738
(ii) Chittagong Division[a]	-	-
(iii) Khulna Division	0.9666**	2.526
(iv) Rajshahi Division	1.0629**	2.895
5. Intercept	-1.4955	-
-log likelihood	851.5574	
Model chi-square	1224.74	
R^2	0.4074	

a Reference group

* P<0.001

** P<0.0001

P Indicate the significance level of the test H_0: $\theta_j=0$ against H_A: $\theta_j \neq 0$.

Source: Rahman, Pk. M. (1994): Poverty Issues in Rural Bangladesh, UPL, Dhaka.

Isolation

Isolation means detached from the society, community and outside world. A household may be isolated due to remoteness, poor communication and lack of other physical infrastructures. However, an individual may become isolated due to illiteracy, poverty, sickness, powerlessness etc. Social and economic services usually do not reach people living in remote areas, and people who are illiterate and unaware of economic development activities. Isolated people are often ignorant about different physical and social aspects of life and they are not well informed about events of development and economic activities beyond their friends, neighbour and own locality. Children from remote area cannot attend schools for education and remain illiterate and thus their mobility in the labour market is limited. As a result of isolation, remote people are deprived of benefits of road communication, growth centres, health services, and extension services of agriculture. The distance coefficient in logit equation provides some illustration of the importance of location of households from development centre. The regression coefficient (0.1314) for distance of village from upazila in logit equation explains that households located remote from upazila are more likely to be living in poverty [Table 2.4]. The incidence of poverty is considerably greater in remote and less urbanized areas (having fewer employment and income generating opportunities). Thus, isolation creates poverty and vulnerability.

Physical Weakness

Inadequate consumption of food and lack of health services leads to physical weakness of a person. Physically weakness leads to deprivation and contributes to poverty in several ways. A weak labourer has lower productivity and wage because he is unable to toil and work long hours. Due to physical weakness, he cannot travel in search of better jobs and opportunities for higher earning and often he has to withdraw from work due to poor health resulting in income erosion. Hungry and sick people have little or no strength to protest against the injustice made by the powerful elite of the society and state. Loss of labour and earning power of an adult brought on by physical weakness reduces or stops the flow of income and food into the poor household. All these disadvantages accentuate isolation, vulnerability, powerlessness and consequently poverty. Conversely, those disadvantages also contribute to physical weakness due to insufficient food, lack of road communication and other social services.

Vulnerability

Poverty, weakness, illiteracy and isolation create vulnerability which make poor people poorer. Vulnerability relates to poverty through distress sales or mortgaging of productive assets such as land, livestock, trees, future labour and standing crop particularly during natural calamities. Famine, floods, drought, river erosion, crop failure and sickness are the worst times for the vulnerable and poor people. According to Rural Poverty Monitoring Survey 1998, the crisis due to death of main income earner was faced by 13 per cent of the poor households. The poor households which reported facing crisis due to large medical expenses, crop failure and river erosion were 16 per cent, 37 per cent and 4 per cent respectively [Table 2.5]. Poverty also accentuates vulnerability and they are linked with each other through inability of the poor and vulnerable to cope with crisis during economic shocks and contingencies. Deprivation is a web in which poverty and vulnerability are interlocked. In most societies, the vulnerable class of people have inferior status and they are shy to ask officials and extension workers for help. Vulnerable people become poorer by loss of assets. For small needs, they take loans from neighbours, relatives, moneylenders, landlords, and patrons at usurious terms, while they sell their capital assets or surrender livestock, standing crops, tools etc. to buy food for survival. Loss of capital assets is accepted as the way for survival.

Table 2.5: Per centage of Households Affected by Different Crises, April 1998

Crisis	*% of crises affected households*		
	All	*Poor*	*Well-off*
Death of main income earner	12.5	12.7	12.3
Large scale medical expense	24.0	15.9	29.7
Unnatural death of family member	1.3	2.1	0.7
Theft/Dacoity	1.8	1.5	1.9
Loss of crops	35.8	36.5	35.3
Eviction from land	1.5	2.1	1.1
Theft of cow	0.4	0.5	0.4
Death of bovine animal	1.1	0.5	1.9
Loss of property by natural calamities	1.0	-	1.9
Litigation	1.5	1.6	1.5
River erosion	2.4	4.2	1.1
Payment of dowry	4.8	3.7	5.6
Others	11.8	18.5	7.1
Total	100.0	100.0	100.0

Source: BBS (1998): Rural Poverty Monitoring Survey, Ministry of Planning.

Powerlessness

Poverty, vulnerability, isolation and illiteracy are the syndrome of powerlessness. Powerless people are often ignored and easily exploited by the powerful elite of the society because they are ignorant about their right in resources, law, system and negotiating terms. They are generally illiterate and thus their voice is feeble and their status in the society is low for which they are deprived by the state, community and law enforcing agencies. As their position in the society is weak, they are weak in negotiating terms for selling their labour, produce and assets and they become easy victims of predation by the powerful elite, landlords, moneylenders and merchants. Powerless people have no influence on the government in providing pro-poor services for them and their localities. These disadvantages are linked with poverty through inability to buy adequate food and to derive benefits from social services. Linking these six disadvantages gives thirty possible causal relations, which in their negative forms interlink like a web to make poor people poorer [Figure 2.1].

The earlier national development goals were mainly centered around higher economic growth, higher per capita income, human resources development, employment generation etc. But policy makers gave little attention to redress unseen causes of poverty such as illiteracy, isolation, vulnerability, physical weakness and powerlessness. Poverty has many dimensions including inadequate consumption of food, but these features are important determinants of poverty. Thus where there is wide-spread poverty, national planning, policies and rural development programmes are essential to remove these disadvantages from the society. It is observed that households located in the village under rural development programmes (VURDP) have lower per

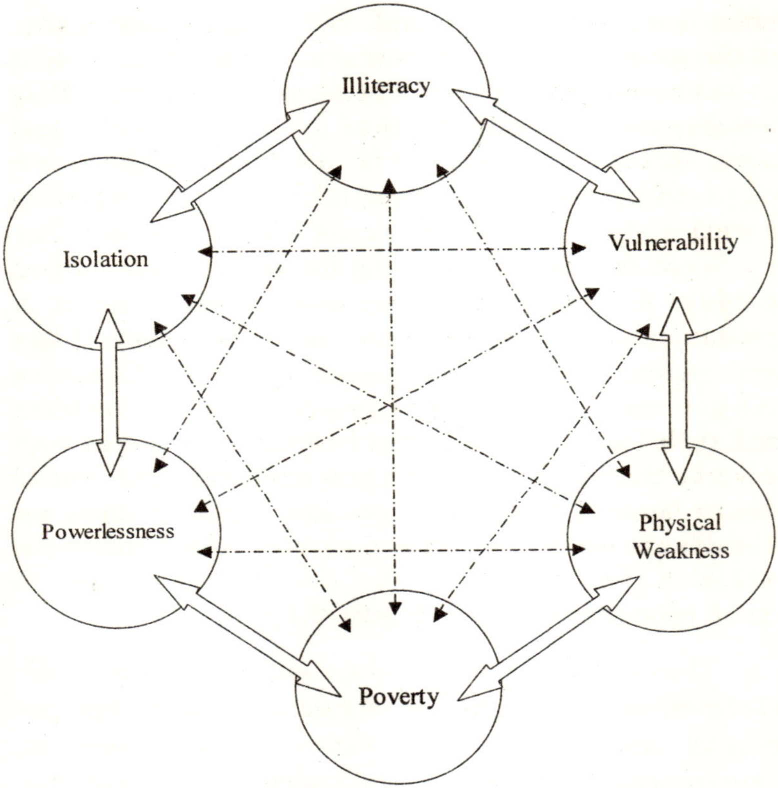

Figure 2.1: Poverty Trap

centage of poor as compared to the households located outside the VURDP. The coefficient (-0.1378) for VURDP explains that households located in VURDP have lower chance to live in poverty, while households located outside the VURDP are more likely to be living in poverty [Table 4.2]. These phenomena referred above suggest that human resource development through education infrastructure development and rural development efforts must be directed towards target groups with appropriate policies programmes for poverty alleviation. In the following chapters, the past and present policies and programmes are briefly examined and surveyed.

3

Poverty and Development Plan Objectives

Introduction

Bangladesh has had a long experience of planning at the national level since its liberation in 1971. It has already implemented five FiveYear Plans and a Two Year Plan with a plan holiday during fiscal 1995-96 and 1996-97. It has completed the First Five Year Plan (1973-78), Two Year Plan (1978-80), Second Five Year Plan (1980-85), Third Five Year Plan (1985-90) and Fourth Five Year Plan (1990-95). But poverty is still widespread in Bangladesh as reflected by the low per capita GNP, low economic growth and low level of consumption. Social problems such as malnutrition, unemployment and illiteracy have also been faced by Bangladesh since long past. The central objective of almost all the plans is to raise the standard of living of the common masses. As poverty is the most pressing problem in the rural areas of Bangladesh, all the plan documents set "poverty alleviation measures" as one of the major development objectives. The recent Fifth Five Year Plan is no exception. This plan too has documented various objectives for socio-economic development and poverty alleviation. In this chapter we examine the direct and indirect potential roles assigned to development objectives in different Five Year Plans for poverty alleviation.

Development Objectives Of Different Five Year Plans

First Five Year Plan

In the situation of a war-ravaged economy in the wake of the Liberation War of 1971, the First Five Year Plan (FFYP) was prepared to give a new sense of direction in promoting economic growth, reducing poverty and ensuring social justice. However, the more specific development objectives of FFYP (1973-78) were:

(i) to increase output of major sectors like agriculture, industry etc. and complete reconstruction work;

(ii) to raise per capita income at a modest rate of 2.5% per annum and adopt policies to ensure equitable distribution of income;

(iii) to increase output of essential commodities to meet the basic needs of the masses and to make them available to common people at reasonable prices;

(iv) to alleviate poverty through expansion of employment opportunities, increase in the rate of growth of GDP to the extent of 5.5% and equitable distribution of income;

(v) to mobilize labour in the informal and non-monetised sectors in order to increase output, income and employment opportunities;

(vi) to accelerate development expenditure, particularly in social sector such as education, health, housing, sanitation and safe drinking water;

(vii) to transform institutional and technological base of agriculture in order to attain self-sufficiency in foodgrains;

(viii) to reduce dependency on food aid and;

(ix) to reconstruct the shattered infrastructure.

It appears that the FFYP was more concerned with the increase in GDP growth through increase in output of the most labour-intensive sectors of the economy particularly agriculture and industry than with poverty reduction. Moreover, the plan's targets for GDP growth, output, employment, income etc. remained largely unrealized as the necessary action programmes could not be undertaken due to shortage of adequate domestic and external resources. Besides a dearth of resources, there was lack of adequate institutional support, skilled manpower, favourable weather condition etc. As a result, a great majority of the development objectives could not be fulfilled.

Two Year Plan

The Two Year Plan was initiated and formulated in 1978 after the FFYP to complete as many of the on-going projects as possible with the available resources before embarking upon a new Five Year Plan. The main objectives of the TYP were to attain an annual GDP growth rate of 5.6 per cent and per capita income of 2.8 per cent. However, the other central development objectives of the TYP were

(i) to increase rate of growth of GDP;

(ii) to accelerate employment opportunities and increase rural productivity;

(iii) to reduce poverty by expanding employment generation for the poor, improving income distribution and promoting social justice;

(iv) to achieve self-sufficiency in foodgrains;

(v) to reduce population growth rate;

(vi) to improve provisions for basic needs, and;

(vii) to reduce dependence on foreign assistance for development.

If we compare the plan objectives of FFYP with those of TYP, it will be observed that none of the objectives were new except that in the name of poverty alleviation, expansion of employment and improvement of distribution had been substituted by the idea of social welfare. Moreover, none of the poverty-focused objectives such as equitable distribution of income, employment generation etc. were achieved during the FFYP and TYP periods. The annual growth rate of GDP during the TYP was estimated to be 5.0 per cent as against 5.6 per cent envisaged.

Second Five Year Plan

The Second Five Year Plan (SFYP) continued more or less in the same vein and the objectives of the plan were formulated in the context of acute problems of poverty, unemployment, illiteracy and malnutrition of the rural masses. The main poverty-focused development objectives of this plan included large expansion of employment opportunities, reduction of inequalities, adequate supply of basic needs, reduction of illiteracy etc. However, the listed objectives of the SFYP were

(i) to bring about equitable growth for ensuring improvement in the standard of living through adequate supply of basic needs such as foods, safe drinking water, clothes, primary healthcare, education, housing etc.;

(ii) to achieve self-sufficiency in foodgrains;

(iii) to expand gainful employment opportunities in order to increase income, to fulfil basic needs at an affordable price and to share the benefits of economic growth;

(iv) to reduce poverty by a significant level through growth of income, employment and efficient utilization of land, water and human resource;

(v) to reduce population growth rate;

(vi) to achieve self-reliance through mobilization of domestic resources;

(vii) to eliminate illiteracy and achieve universal primary education;

(viii) to promote participation of people in the development processes, and;

(ix) to accelerate the pace of economic development.

The objectives of expansion of employment opportunities, economic growth, reduction of population growth, utilization of resources, such as, land, water, and human resources and achievement of self-reliance continued to have important positions in SFYP. Elimination of illiteracy and participation of people in the development processes were recognized for the first time in the SFYP.

Third Five Year Plan

Like the earlier development plans, the Third Five Year Plan (TFYP) too visualized the needs for reducing poverty by ensuring better access for the rural poor to the means of production through provision of facilities in such areas as development of agriculture, basic physical infrastructure and social services. Poverty alleviation and improvement of income and employment opportunities in rural areas were the major thrust of the TFYP. Decentralization of the public administration to Upazila and strengthening of local administration structure by a larger allocation of funds were also given greater emphasis in this plan. The plan target of growth of GDP was 5.4 per cent per annum. However, the important objectives of the TFYP were defined as follows:

(i) to reduce population growth;

(ii) to expand productive and gainful employment;

(iii) to improve technological base for structural change in production of rural industries and especially of small and cottage industries;

(iv) to raise economic growth;

(v) to ensure provisions of basic needs and services;

(vi) to promote self-reliance through mobilization of domestic resources;

(vii) to achieve self-sufficiency in foodgrain and;

(viii) to increase the human resource development and universal primary education.

It is interesting to note that the objectives stated in the TFYP do not differ much from the earlier plans but rather there were many common objectives, such as poverty alleviation, reduction of population growth, increase in economic growth, achievement of self-sufficient in food, employment generation, promotion of self-reliance etc. which were also stated in the earlier plans. But the Third Five Year Plan puts particular emphasis on the development of rural industries and specially small and cottage industry. The purpose is to create rural employment, generate higher labour incomes and poverty alleviation.

Fourth Five Year Plan

Considering poverty alleviation in rural areas as the prime aim, the Fourth Five Year Plan laid greater emphasis on three broad objectives, namely, acceleration of economic growth, rural development and promotion of self-reliance. In order to achieve these broad objectives, the plan enunciated other specific development objectives. These were

(i) to promote human resource, remove illiteracy, provide basic health care facilities and to take population control measures;

(ii) to promote and expand employment opportunity for the poor through appropriate rural institutional development;

(iii) to strengthen rural economy through development of agriculture sector;

(iv) to improve employment opportunities in agriculture and rural industry by adopting appropriate technology in these sectors;

(v) to generate interactive dynamic of growth through inter-sectoral linkage;

(vi) to decentralize macro-level planning and to ensure their integration with built-in accountability;

(vii) to strengthen national conservation policy and programmes, and ;

(viii) to promote private sectors for making them efficient in an open competitive environment and to create export initiative.

It can be seen from the stated objectives that social sectors development which are essential for poverty alleviation received greater emphasis in the fourth FYP compared to the earlier plans. Like other plans, the objectives of higher economic growth, employment generation, human resource development including universal primary education were also given importance in this plan.

Fifth Five Year Plan

After completion of fourth FYP, there was no development plan during 1995-97. But the development activities were continued on the basis of the annual Development programmes during that periods after which the Fifth Five Year Plan (1997-2002) was formulated and started since 1 July 1997. Poverty alleviation and promotion of employment opportunities in rural areas have been given greater importance in the list of the stated objectives of the Fifth Five Year Plan accompanied by larger allocation of funds for poverty alleviation. However, the operational terms of objectives for poverty alleviation along with others are

(i) to reduce poverty through accelerated economic growth of 7% per annum during the

plan period and through ensuring the increased access of the poor to resources;

(ii) to generate substantial employment opportunities and to increase productivity through labour intensive technologies;

(iii) to attain food production beyond the self-sufficiency level in the shortest possible time;

(iv) to develop human resources with emphasis on compulsory primary education, vocational training etc.;

(v) to promote diversified high valued export goods;

(vi) to develop infrastructure and other services needed to promote growth particularly in private sector;

(vii) to reduce population growth rate to the tune of 1.32% by the terminal year of the plan;

(viii) to develop of hitherto neglected and poverty stricken areas such as the north-west region, Chittagong Hill Tracts and costal areas;

(ix) to reduce the gender gap through different women's development programme, particularly on education, training, income generating employment etc., and

(x) to establish better social justice through an even distribution of income, resources and opportunities and creation of effective safety nets for the poor.

It is thus observed that the inter-related objectives of employment opportunities, equitable distribution of income and alleviation of poverty have always been included in all the plans along with other objectives. However, rehabilitation of war ravaged infrastructure was the major concern of the First Five Year Plan and Two Year Plans. As a result, alleviation of poverty could not be taken as a primary objective of the First Five Year and Two Year Plans since the implementation of these plans were seriously hampered by the scarcity of domestic resources and unfavourable conditions of developments at home and abroad. The second and third plans also could not attach high priority to poverty alleviation because of a dilemma that arose out of the conflict between growth and distribution. Moreover, the shortfall in the performance in the SFYP and TFYP periods can be attributed to a number of economic and non-economic factors such as resource shortfall, natural calamities, weak institutional framework, lack of skilled manpower and management problems. But the fourth and fifth plans asserted ideas of poverty alleviation in different sections of plan documents, but in the absence of priority rating of objectives, it is very difficult to judge intense priority of those objectives related to poverty alleviation. The list of stated objectives in all plans referred to poverty alleviation within the framework of a trickle down theory which means that economic growth alone in the long run may benefit the relatively less privileged classes of the society and also improve the lot of the poorer group. But it is important to recognize that growth alone may not be sufficient to ensure reduction of poverty, provision of basic needs and overall socio-economic development. To sum up, the focus of the First Five Year Plan for poverty alleviation was on economic growth and redistribution through public sector interventions. The second Five Year Plan was concerned for poverty alleviation through participation of the rural poor within an expanded programme with adequate supply of basic needs, and sharing benefits of development. Poverty alleviation through employment and income generations were the major theme of the Third Five Year Plan. The Fourth Five Year Plan stressed on poverty alleviation through linking of growth with employment and income generations, human resources development and greater participation of women in the development processes [country Paper Bangladesh P23]. A significant change in framing objectives was made with the advent of the Fifth Five Year Plan. The emphasis on poverty alleviation has been continued even in the present plan. The fifth Five Year Plan is concerned more with poverty alleviation through accelerated economic growth, improvement of employment opportunities, increased production, equitable distribution of income and ensuring access of the poor to resources.

It appears from the analysis of plan objectives that planners have always been concerned with the trade-off between economic growth and poverty alleviation. Between these two, greater emphasis has been given on economic growth in almost all the plans. Furthermore, the inter-related objectives of employment generation, even distribution of income, reduction of gender disparities in primary and secondary education, reduction of infant, child and maternal mortality rates, increase in literacy rate, poverty alleviation etc. have always been talked about in all Five Year Plans. But we must now admit that most of these objectives have not been significantly realized. Thus, the planning process has achieved very limited success in economic growth, redistribution of assets, employment generation and poverty alleviation. On the contrary, the poor, by and large remained untouched by the development process. As a result, nearly half of the total population are still living in poverty.

4

The Plan Outlay for Poverty Alleviation

Introduction

The Planning as well as budgetary system in Bangladesh is highly centralized and there is no scope for participatory decision-making. The budgetary process is very complex and difficult to understand for outsiders or common people. The whole economy of the country is divided into several sectors and sub-sectors and financial allocations to them are made on the basis of proposals from the planning commission both in plans and in the Annual Development Programmes (ADP). The ADP is the key to the implementation of the plans, as it contains the budgetary allocation for projects and other development activities. The total cost of a particular project includes cost for different components such as physical infrastructure development, institutional overhead, consultancy etc. As a result, it becomes difficult to estimate the share of budget actually allocated or spent for the main component for which the project was designed, such as, employment generation, poverty alleviation, skill formation, generation of higher labour income etc.

As most of the policies for poverty alleviation are a part of several macro-economic development policies, the allocation made exclusively for poverty alleviation is, therefore, hard to differentiate, and remains obscure.

Monitoring of public expenditure on poverty alleviation is also very difficult. Moreover, the documents do not provide any information on the amounts to be spent for the benefit of the poor, and for the development of backward areas which have a large concentration of poor such as Kurigram, Nilphamari, Gaibandha etc.

As to the revenue component of the budget, about eighty per cent of the public income is obtained from tax revenue. There are two types of taxes - one is direct and the other indirect. The major share of tax revenue comes from indirect taxes which are found to be regressive in nature and therefore, affect the poor first and most. There is no clear and simple system in tax structure for redistribution of income to the poor and poverty alleviation. The budgetary process is thus inconsistent in expenditure classification, complex in nature, conventional and insensitive to the needs of the poor [Proshika (2000)].

The Plan Outlay by Public and Private Sectors: An Overview

The plan outlay or size is determined on the basis of objectives, strategies, availability of resources and development management potentials. The national desire and aspirations to achieve sustainable growth is largely dependent upon the size of the plan. But the plan is crucially constrained by the availability of resources, both domestic and external, and management ability. However, the sectoral breakdown of total development outlay at respective base year price of successive plans by public and private sectors is shown in Table 4.1.

It is evident from Table 4.1 that since independence, the public sector has come to play a dominant role in the economy of Bangladesh, while the private sector was

Table 4.1: Plan Outlay by Public and Private Sectors

(in millionTaka)

Plans	*At respective base year price*		
	Plan size	*Public sector*	*Private sector*
First Five Year Plan (1973-78)	44,550 (100.00)	39,320 (88.71)	6,030 (11.29)
Two Year Plan (1978-80)	38,610 (100.00)	32,610 (84.46)	6,000 (15.54)
Second Five Year Plan (1980-85)	172,000 (100.00)	111,000 (64.53)	61,000 (35.47)
Third Five Year Plan (1985-90)	386,00 (100.00)	250,000 (64.77)	136,000 (35.23)
Fourth Five Year Plan (1990-95)	620,000 (100.00)	347,000 (55.97)	273,000 (44.03)
Two Years Plan Holiday* (1995-97)	508,760 (100.00)	217,160 (42.68)	291,600 (57.32)
Fifth Five Year Plan (1997-2002) proposed	1959,521 (100.00)	858,939 (43.83)	100,582 (56.17)

Source: The Fifth Five Year Plan (1997-2002), Planning Commission, Ministry of Planning, Table 3.1, p. 111-1

Notes: (i) Plan size and Shares of Public and Private sectors at respective base year prices

(ii) Figures in the parentheses are sectoral shares in per centages.

*ADPs at current prices against plan size at base year price

assigned a relatively smaller role in the First Five Year Plan with an allocation of Tk.6,030 million or only 11 per cent of the total financial allocation of Tk.44,550 million. The private sector was expected to supplement rather than compete with the public sector. However, in recognition of the importance of private sector, there has been substantial change in the policy and the private sector has come forward with higher investment in the development process. The private sector was also dependent on the support from the public sector. The share of private sector in the Two Year Plan was raised to 16 per cent in the total plan size of Tk.38,610 million and then to 35 per cent in the Second and Third Five Year Plans. It increased further to 44 per cent in the Fourth Five Year Plan. The Fifth Five Year Plan envisages a greater share of the plan for the private sector and it has envisaged a much higher share (56%) of the plan outlay from the private sector as against 44 per cent from public sector. However, based on plan development objectives, strategies and average annual GDP growth rate of 7 per cent, the total financial outlay of Tk.1959,521 million has been accepted for the Fifth Five Year Plan with 44 per cent in the public sector, (Tk. 858,939 million) and 56 per cent in the private sector (Tk.100,582 million).

Sectoral Plan Outlay by Public and Private

Sectoral allocations have been made on the basis of the objectives and strategies of the plan. Highest priority has been given to sectors that make significant contributions to poverty alleviation by providing for the basic needs and employment generating opportunities. Emphasis is also given on those sectors which have important bearing upon consumption targets that include essential consumer goods (food, edible, cloth etc.) as well as social consumption (mass literacy, basic health care, etc.), import substitution possibilities and export potentials. The structure of the Fifth Five Year Plan is set out in Table 4.2 by Public and Private sectors outlays.

It appears from Table 4.2 that after trade and other services, the highest priority has been accorded to

Table 4.2: Sectoral Distribution of Plan Outlay at 1996/97 Prices

(in million Taka)

Sector	*Public Sector**	*Private Sector*	*Total*
Agriculture	202674.68 (23.60)	119864.31 (10.89)	322538.99 (16.46)
Industry	11739.70 (1.37)	298776.16 (27.15)	310569.86 (15.85)
Housing and construction	49816.00 (5.80)	180017.61 (16.35)	229833.61 (11.73)
Power and Gas	114400.6 (13.32)	37726.07 (3.43)	152126.67 (7.76)
Transport and communications	145540.11 (16.94)	118876.80 (10.80)	264416.91 (13.50)
Trade and other services	334713.91 (38.97)	345321.15 (31.38)	680035.06 (34.70)
Total	858939.00 (100.00)	1100582.10 (100.00)	1959521.10 (100.00)

*Includes non-investment expenditures.

Source: The Fifth Five Year Plan 1997-2002, Table 3.9, P.63.

agriculture and related activities including forestry, fisheries, livestock and input and support services. This sector has been offered almost one-fourth of the public sector outlay or 16.46 per cent of the total financial outlay of the plan, which is closely followed by industry sector (15.85 per cent) and transport and communication (13.5 per cent). The share of public outlay in industry sector is only 1.4 per cent as against 27.15 per cent of private outlay. The plan also pays due attention to transport and communications and the share of this sector in the total public outlay is about 17 per cent. In the Fifth Plan, total outlay in trade and other sectors has been almost evenly splited between the public and the private sectors. However, the relative share of the public and private sectors in the plan outlay is observed to vary among different sectors of the economy. From this broad based sectoral allocation of plan outlay, it is difficult to estimate distributional impact of public expenditure on poverty alleviation. Estimation is made more difficult because the basic data are not available or provided by the government. For example, how can one divide the expenditure on agriculture or industry between the poor and non-poor. Despite this difficulty, it is easy to understand that bulk of the public outlay on agriculture or industry for technology development generally benefits the larger farmers and industrialists. The subsidy on food, fertilizer, transport etc. will be of more benefit to the urban people or rural rich. Moreover, in government's agricultural related incentive programmes, the benefits are largely associated with landholding size and access to irrigation and thus big land owners reap most of the benefits of such programmes [WB (1993)].

Public Expenditure: A Stagnant Share of GNP

Public expenditure, which comprises total revenue and development expenditure has progressively increased from Tk.125800 million in 1990/91 to Tk.267000 million in 1997/98, that is, by over 112 per cent (Table 4.3). Although public expenditure, has been increasing over the years, it was nearly 15 per cent of the GNP in FY 90/91, FY 91/92 and FY 92/93 and then it was estimated to rise by 17 per cent in FY 93/94 and FY 94/95. The share then fell by 1 per cent point and from FY 94/95 onwards, it was around 16 per cent. Thus the public expenditure as per centage of GNP was virtually stagnated from 1995/96 to 1997/98. The revenue and development expenditures as per centage of GNP were also found to remain at more or less the same level during that period (Figure 4.1).

Figure 4.1: Total Expenditure as % of GNP

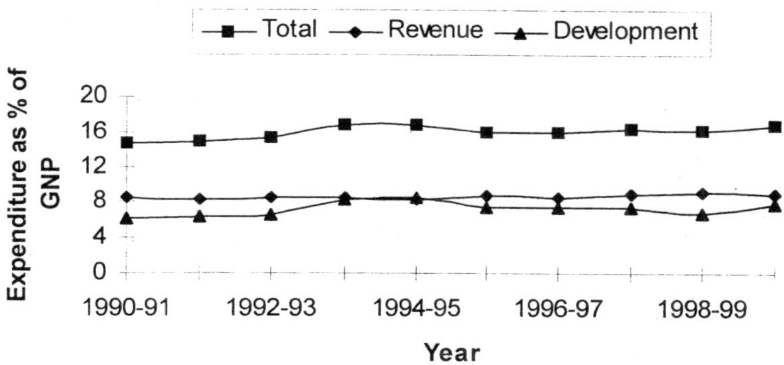

Table 4.3: Total Public Expenditure

(in million Taka)

Year	*Expenditure*			*GNP at current price*	*Expenditure as % of GNP*		
	Revenue	*Development*	*Total*		*Total*	*Revenue*	*Development*
1990-91	73100	52700	125800	860905	14.61	8.49	6.12
1991-92	79000	60240	139240	940353	14.81	8.40	6.41
1992-93	85100	65500	150600	988863	15.23	8.61	6.62
1993-94	91500	89830	181330	1079002	16.81	8.48	8.33
1994-95	103000	103030	206030	1225932	16.81	8.40	8.41
1995-96	118140	100160	218300	1361632	16.03	8.68	7.35
1996-97	125350	110400	235750	1468016	16.06	8.54	7.52
1997-98	145000	122000	267000	1632428	16.36	8.88	7.40
1998-99	167650	12090	292740	1813000	16.15	9.24	6.90
1999-00	178000	155000	333000	1983000	16.79	8.98	7.82

Sources: (*i*) Bangladesh Economic Review, 1998, P.2, and 2000, p.27.
(*ii*) Bangladesh Bureau of Statistics (BBS), Final Estimate of 1998-99, National Accounting Wing, April 2000.

Plan Outlay in the Social Sectors

Social sector development promotes well being of all mankind and it is the cornerstone of all development efforts. Poverty alleviation and higher level of living of the common masses can be achieved through social sector development and equitable distribution of benefits of the development. The World Summit on Social Development which took place in Copenhagen in March 1995, also advocated the need for social development. It identified three areas of concern which are vital for social development, namely, poverty, unemployment and social integration[1] [country Paper, Bangladesh (1995), P.1]. But social development is not confined within these three broad social factors; it is comprehensive as well as complex. It encompasses many non economic factors such as education, health, sanitation, housing conditions, production and distribution relation, rights and obligations to individuals' security, etc. The poor often lack adequate shelter, education and health, sanitation etc. and they face vulnerability of ill health and consequently income erosion. The development of these factors directly and indirectly determines the level of quality of life. The earlier plans except the fourth one, did not pay much attention to social development but rather put more emphasis on economic development only. In the recent past there has been a decisive shift in the development priorities. In pursuance of its constitutional obligations and commitments particularly in respect of education and health in the International forums on population and development held in 1994 [FFYP, p.447], the Government has committed to ensure education and Health For All. And Bangladesh was a signatory to the declaration at the World Summit on

Education For All, held in March 1990 [Ed. For All, P.12]. As education and health have been identified as a vehicle for the development of human resources and as a result of international commitment, the social sectors have received a significant priority in the Fourth and Fifth Five Year Plans and development outlay shows an increasing trend over the periods. Table 4.4 presents the development outlay for the Social Sectors.

The allocation in social sector-plan outlay ratio showed an irregular trend. It varied from the lowest of 16 per cent in the Second Five Year Plan to the highest of 22 per cent in the Fourth Five Year Plan. The proposed share in allocation in the Fifth Five Year Plan is about 39 per cent. The same figure for the years 1995-96 and 1996-97 was 25 per cent and 26 per cent respectively. It appears from the above figures of allocation that emphasis has been put by the Government on the importance of social sectors development. Social sectors development provides two types of benefits to the common masses. First, it increases the scope of human development (education, health etc.), empowerment, family welfare etc. Secondly, it creates employment opportunities for the poor, raises their income earning capabilities, reduces income erosion and thus leading to poverty alleviation. But the plan documents do not provide any information relating to allocation of funds for social development of rural areas and backward areas which have a higher concentration of poor.

ADP Allocation to Social Sectors.

In view of the urgency of accelerated socio-economic development and poverty alleviation, the ADP allocation

Table 4.4: Allocation to the Social Sectors Under Different Development Plans

(in crore Taka)

Sector	*1st Five YePlan (1973-ar 78)*	*Two Year Plan (1978-80)*	*2nd Five Year Plan (1980-85)*	*3rd Five Year Plan (1985-90)*	*4th Five Year Plan (1990-95)*	*5th Five Year Plan (1997-2002)*
Education & Religious Affairs	272	147	480	1220	2058	12868
Raral Dev. & Institution	163	148	482	1960	1650	8700
Health	200	118	288	550	1060	6227
Family Welfare	70	100	310	870	1598	2859
Social welfare, women's Affair & Youth Dev.	20	16	82	142	235	1429
Sports and culture	15	22	43	115	146	574
Public administration	26	11	38	65	201	968
Labour and Manpower	28	16	61	93	85	139
Total (Social Sector)	794	578	1784	5015	7633	33764
Total size of the plan	3952	3261	11100	25000	34700	85894
Social sector as % of total plan outlay	20.09	17.74	16.07	20.06	22.00	39.30

Sources: *(i)* First, Two Year, Second, Third, Fourth and draft Fifth Five Year Plans of Bangladesh.
(ii) Annexure 1, Follow up of the World Social Summit in Bangladesh: Agenda and Actions by the Year 2000, p.63.

Fig.4.2: Trend in share of social sectors as % of ADP

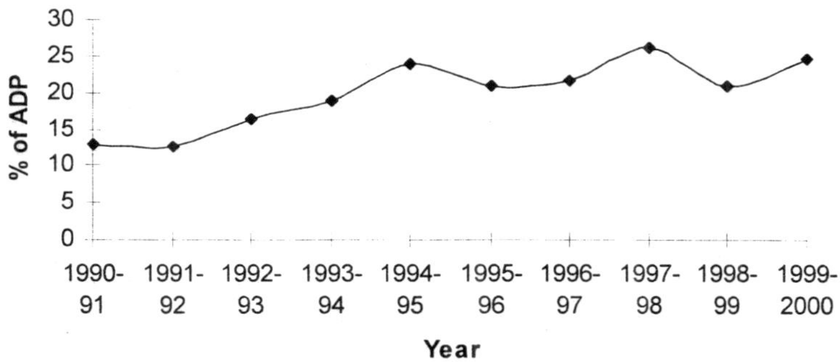

continues to be on the social sectors as well as on the social and physical infrastructures. The social sectors allocation as per centage of total ADP allocation increased from 13.0 per cent in 1990-91 to 25.0 per cent in 1999-2000. The per capita expenditure in this sector also showed a consistently increasing trend over the periods but with slight decline in 1995-96 as compared to 1994-95. Per capita ADP expenditure in social sectors in 1984-85 constant prices also showed a similar trend (Table 4.5). The trend in share of social sectors as per centage of ADP may be observed in Figure 4.2.

This significant increase in the ADP allocation to social sectors, however, does not imply that the expenditure for poverty alleviation has increased significantly. This is because the development budget includes a number of components of revenue expenditure which are spent for activities not related to poverty alleviation. Sector-wise allocation of public expenditure shows that the education sector has gained momentum with significant increase in expenditure from 3.28 per cent of the total ADP in 1990-91 to 13.00 per cent in

Table 4.5: Allocation for the Social Sectors in the Revised ADPs

(Taka in million)

Sector	*1990-1991*	*1991-1992*	*1992-1993*	*1993-1994*	*1994-1995*	*1995-1996*	*1996-1997*	*1997-1998*	*1998-1999*	*1999-2000*
1	*2*	*3*	*4*	*5*	*6*	*7*	*8*	*9*	*10*	*11*
Education & Religious Affairs	1730	2990	5280	9200	14650	13050	14470	14940	16930	19590
Sports & Culture	280	160	260	440	610	280	530	660	460	720
Health and Family Welfare	4760	5580	6300	7720	9460	8960	10790	11660	12560	15290
Social Welfare, Women Affairs & Youth Development	310	290	310	430	1000	950	1470	1560	1660	2230
Total expenditure in social sector	6830	7520	10740	16960	24680	2106	23930	28820	29660	37830
Total ADP	52700	60240	65500	89830	103030	100160	110410	110370	140000	155000

(Table Contd...)

Table 4.5: Contd...

1	*2*	*3*	*4*	*5*	*6*	*7*	*8*	*9*	*10*	*11*
Social sectors as % of ADP	12.96	12.48	16.39	18.88	23.93	21.02	21.67	26.11	21.00	24.80
Per capita development expenditure in social sector (in Tk.)	62.32	66.37	92.99	144.10	205.84	172.48	192.36	227.82	231.36	290.55
Per capita development expenditure in social sector at 1984-85 constant price (in Tk.)	38.42	39.26	54.96	81.65	87.61	85.13	93.24	105.76	100.68	122.70
Population (in million)	109.0	113.3	115.5	117.7	119.9	122.1	124.4	126.6	128.2	130.22
Implicit GDP deflator (base 1984-85)	162.19	169.06	169.20	176.48	191.91	202.60	206.30	215.40	229.80	236.80

Sources: *(i)* I.M.E.D., Ministry of Planning, 2000.
(ii) Bangladesh Economic Review, 1998; p. 94.
(iii) BBS, National Accounts Statistics of Bangladesh (Revised Estimates, 1989-90 to 1994-95) p. 57.

Note: According to budget allocation.

1999-2000. But it is more important to assess whether the public expenditure on social sectors resulted in redistribution towards the poor or the non-poor. The social welfare measures included free primary school text books, food for education, free primary education, secondary female stipend programme etc. These benefits were made available to all regardless of income and social class. Food for education programme was for the poor households with school children. The benefits of this programme constituted a significant transfer of income to the poor. It appears from the enrolment ratio in primary and secondary schools that expenditure on food for education, secondary female stipend programme and overall expenditure on primary and secondary schools have resulted in the most positive redistribution to the poor. Spending on social welfare, rural development, women and youth development, and family welfare also appears to have a positive bearing on redistribution to the poor. However, the public spending on hospitals and secondary and higher levels of education is less effective in benefiting the poor. The poor have limited access to Sports and Culture, Public Administration and tertiary education programmes. Although a direct linkage between alleviation of poverty and social sectors development is yet to be established, the linkage between social sectors development and economic development facilitated poverty reduction to a great extent. Improvements in the social sectors, particularly education, health and family planning have had positive impacts on productivity and entrepreneurial skill that are essential to the building up of a dynamic economy for the country. The educated people are more productive and contributive to a country's economic growth. The human development index (HDI) and per capita GNP are found to be highly and positively correlated and the correlation coefficient is estimated at 0.632, while it is negatively correlated with incidence of poverty (r = -0.852). A study of 88 countries showed that increase in literacy from 20 to 30 per cent was associated with an increase in real GDP between 8 to 16 per cent. Another study on 37 middle-income and 29 low-income countries also showed that a one per cent increase in primary enrolment was associated with 0.35 per cent increase in per capita economic growth [UNFPA (1992)]. The GOB has made several efforts to (i) improve educational attainment of females, (ii) increase primary school enrolment and (iii) reduce repetition rates. But the effort for increasing employment is only a part of the answer. It is also necessary to address the quality of education, cultural and economic factors, which act as disincentives in parents' decisions about whether to send their children to school or to the labour market. Like education, health is also a crucial part of human life that determines their well-being. Good health is necessary to increase working capability and to reduce the wastage of human and physical resources as well as income erosion due to worker's illness. Improved health status contributes to economic growth by increasing the efficiency of human capital among the poor and thus enhance living standard. A Health Survey Report prepared by the Bangladesh Bureau of Statistics (BBS) indicated that on the average about 18 work days in rural areas and 14 days in urban areas were lost due to sickness [BBS (1995)]. Another survey on outdoor patients conducted by Shamunnay indicated that the average income erosion due to sickness was TK. 245.15 for the patient of Thana Health Complex (THC) and Tk. 766.67 due to pregnancy related problems for the patients of Union Health and Family Welfare Centre (UHFWC). The income erosion for outdoor patient in urban areas is lower than that in rural areas due to better health facilities as well as services. The number of days and income lost due to sickness varies with the variation in the nature of disease. For instance, highest number of work days and income were lost due to tuberculosis as disease, followed by breathing trouble and pregnancy related problems. Therefore, social sectors development, particularly education and health services, is essential for increasing the income of the poor and raising their standard of living. Although the poor constitute about 50 per cent of the total population, the plan outlay under social sectors get less than their proportionate share. Thus, any effort aimed at increasing social sectors development requires a significant increase in ADP allocation for this sector.

Public Expenditure on Education Sector

It is observed from an initial equivalent intervention analysis made by expert group of CIRDAP on eleven production sectors that education sector has the highest poverty alleviation effects followed by health sector. The effective distributional effects are found to be the largest for the social sector of which education and health are the main components. Service sector and agriculture sector in this respect rank second and third. Poverty alleviation effects are, however, approach to be relatively small in the remaining sectors [CIRDAP, Dec. 1997].

As development of education and health have positive bearing on poverty alleviation, let us examine the public expenditure on education and health and population sectors to illustrate the expenditure pattern of the government for social development. Table 4.6 shows that the public expenditure on education sector amounted to Tk.14944 million in 1990-91 and Tk.46,339 million in 1998-99 showing an annual increase of 26 per cent. The share of education sector as per centage of total public expenditure constituted about 12 per cent in 1990-91 and 16 per cent in 1998-99 indicating about 4 per cent point increase over the period. Education sector as per centage of GNP accounted for only 1.59 per cent in 1990-91 and 2.56 per cent in 1998-99. Primary and mass education sub-sector as per centage of total public expenditure shows a divergent trend. After registering a rise during 1990-91 to 1992-93, the share shows a gradual decline from 1994-95 to 1997-98. The share of primary and mass education to total public expenditure was estimated at about 6 per cent in 1990-91, 8 per cent in 1994-95 and then again reduced to 7 per cent in 1998-99 reflecting a stagnant situation in respect of resource allocation in primary and mass education level.

Table 4.7 shows the trends in public expenditure in primary and mass education sub-sector from 1990-91 to 1997-98. The level of public expenditure in this sub-sector increased from Tk.7327 million in 1990-91 to Tk.20,169 million in 1998-99 registering an annual increase of 22 per cent. The share of primary and mass education as per centage of GNP was marked by stagnation and it was only 1 per cent over the period. The public expenditure in real term (at 1984-85 prices) per primary school aged children (6-10 years) was calculated at Tk.263.93 in 1990-91 and Tk.458.64 in 1998-99. Figure 4.3 shows the trend in public expenditure on education sector and primary and mass education as per centage of GNP.

Table 4.6: Public Expenditure for Education Sector

(Tk. in million)

Year	*Total Public expenditure*	*Expenditure on education sector*	*Expenditure on primary & mass education sub-sector*	*Education sector as % of total expenditure*	*Primary & mass education as % total expenditure*	*Education sector as % of GNP*
1990/91	125800	14944	7372	11.88	5.86	1.59
1991-92	139240	19088	10319	13.71	6.47	1.80
1992-93	150600	22674	11649	15.06	7.73	2.24
1993-94	181330	27608	14958	15.23	8.24	2.49
1994-95	206030	35263	17587	17.12	8.54	2.85
1995-96	218300	35226	17718	16.14	8.12	2.55
1996-97	235750	38473	18642	16.32	7.91	2.55
1997-98	267000	41788	19313	15.65	6.81	2.48
1998-99	292740	46339	20988	15.83	7.17	2.56

Sources: *(i)* Bangladesh Economic Revenue, 2000, p.25.
(ii) Draft Report For All (The Year 2000 Assessment), PMED, March 1999, p.39.

Table 4.7: Public Expenditure for Primary Education

Year	*Public expenditure in primary education (in million Tk.)*	*Primary school aged population (6-10 years) (in million)*	*Public expenditure in primary education as % of GNP*	*Per children real expenditure (at 1984-85 prices)*
1990-91	07324.1	17.11	0.85	263.93
1991-92	10149.8	17.28	1.08	299.59
1992-93	11579.4	17.43	1.17	404.46
1993-94	14764.7	17.69	1.37	472.94
1994-95	17237.5	17.94	1.41	500.67
1995-96	17399.5	18.24	1.18	470.83
1996-97	18048.8	18.47	1.23	453.47
1997-98	18296.3	18.39	1.12	428.28
1998-99	20168.6	18.93	1.11	458.64

Source: *(i)* Primary Education in Bangladesh (Education for All), PDE, July, 1998.
(ii) Bangladesh Bureau of Educational Information and Statistics (BANBEIS), Education for All (The Year 2000 Assessment, PMED, March 1999
(iii) Preliminary Report on GDP Estimation, BBS, April 2000.

Figure 4.3: Trend in Public Expenditure on Education As % of GNP

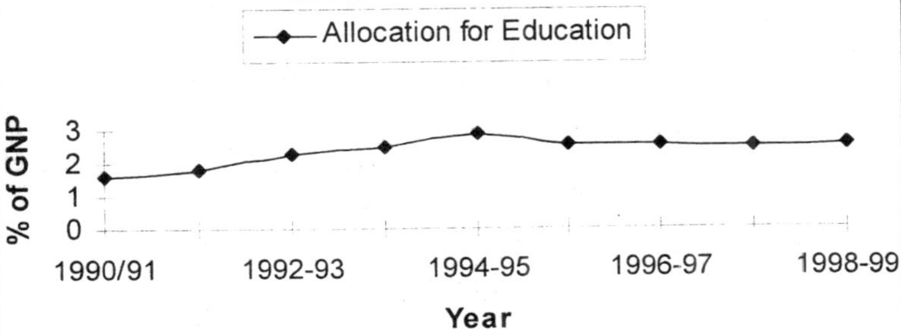

Public Expenditure on Education and Distribution of Benefits:

Greater priority has been set by the government to education sector to increase literacy rate, develop human resources, improve well-being of the people and to make a significant contribution to poverty alleviation. The public expenditure on education per person increased from Tk.137.0 in 1990-91 to Tk.361.0 in 1998-99 showing about 20 per cent increase per annum over the period. But the main issue of concern is whether and to what extent such increased expenditure reaches the poor. If we examine the distribution of share of benefit accrued from public expenditure to three levels of public education (primary, secondary and higher) it is observed that the inequality in distribution of benefits increases with the increase of level of education. Table 4.8 shows that bottom 10 per cent of the households enjoys nearly 7 per cent of the total benefit of expenditure in 1994, while the top 10 per cent enjoy about 15 per cent indicating an uneven distribution of benefits. The distribution of share of benefit of public expenditure in primary level education is, however, not found to be skewed, but in secondary and higher levels of education, it is highly skewed and the richer group derives more benefit than the poorer one. At the secondary level the bottom 10 per cent enjoys only about 3 per cent of the total benefits, whereas the top 10 per cent enjoys nearly 18 per cent indicating a high inequality in distribution of benefits of public expenditure in secondary level. Further inequality in distribution of benefits from public expenditure in the higher level of education is observed. It is only 0.76 per cent for bottom 10 per cent as against 29 per cent for top 10 per cent which explains a sharp inequality in distribution of benefits and the emerging pattern of distribution of benefits is generally not pro-poor. This is because the bottom 10 per cent of the households (corresponding to the extreme poor) has extremely limited access to the benefits. Thus, focus is needed for ensuring the access of the poor to secondary and higher education, otherwise increase in public spending in education sector will not benefit the poor for poverty alleviation.

Table 4.8: Distribution of Gross Benefits from Public Spending on Education: 1994

Per capita income decile	*Per cent of income*	*Per cent of benefits from*			
		Primary education	*Secondary education*	*Higher education*	*Total*
1	1.94	9.53	3.04	0.78	6.87
2	3.25	9.89	3.04	0.76	7.00
3	4.11	9.35	5.12	3.03	7.74
4	5.64	9.89	7.02	3.03	8.71
5	6.05	9.53	7.97	6.81	8.49
6	6.91	10.06	10.06	4.54	8.18
7	9.50	10.43	13.09	13.64	11.31
8	12.63	10.43	15.75	18.94	12.27
9	17.38	10.62	17.08	19.70	13.41
10	32.27	10.27	17.83	28.79	15.42
Total	100.00	100.00	100.00	100.00	100.00

Note: Public spending on education refers to current expenditure.
Source: MAP Focus Study, News Letter, No. 4, CIRDAP, December 1997.

Public Expenditure on Health and Population

Public Spending on Health and Distribution of Benefits

The national desire and aspirations are to provide adequate basic health care especially to those of children, women and the poor and providing medical care is the constitutional obligation of the government. In view of these, the public expenditure on health and population sector has been increasing reflecting priority of the government. In order to increase social services, increasingly more resources have been allocated to health sector. Public expenditure on health sector provide opportunities to improve health conditions and capabilities to earn higher incomes. Table 4.9 shows public expenditure on health sector from 1990-91 to 1998-1999.

Table 4.9 presents the trends in public expenditure on health and population sector. Expenditure on this sector increased from Tk.8393 million in 1990-91 to Tk.19090 million in 1998-99 indicating about 25 per cent increase per annum. Although about 7 per cent of total public expenditure was spent in this sector in each year over the period, only one per cent of GNP was allocated for health and population sector. The per capita expenditure in real term (at 1984-85 prices), was found to be Tk.46.25 in 1990-91, Tk.58.50 in 1995-96 and then to Tk.64.80 in 1998-99. The situation with respect to per capita expenditure in real terms not seem to have undergone some change over the years. Moreover, there is no conclusive empirical evidence to support the hypothesis that the benefits of expenditure on health sector are being equally shared by the poor people. Although the total public expenditure on education and health sectors appears to be a big amount, it absorbed a significant portion of the government recurrent expenditure. Inspite of considerable rhetoric about importance of health and education for poverty

Table 4.9: Public Expenditure for Health and Population

Year	*Total public expenditure on health and population (in million Tk)*	*Total development expenditure on health and population (in million Tk)*	*Total expenditure as % GNP*	*Development expenditure as % GNP*	*Per Capital real expenditure (at 1984-95 prices)*
1990-91	8393	4520	1.00	0.16	46.25
1991-92	8393	4080	1.05	0.16	43.82
1992-93	11090	5920	1.16	0.21	56.77
1993-94	12920	6850	1.28	0.26	62.20
1994-95	15290	8440	1.33	0.30	66.45
1995-96	14470	6870	1.19	0.20	58.50
1996-97	15630	7640	1.26	0.24	60.90
1997-98	19030	11260	1.17	0.36	69.78
1998-99	19090	10220	1.05	0.56	64.80

Source: Bangladesh Economic Review, 1998, MOF.

alleviation, the government efforts in these areas as measured by the share of budgets (1% of GNP) appear to be far from reflecting any sense of great priority. Figure 4.4 shows the share of total and development expenditure on health and population sector as per centage of GNP.

Figure 4.4 Total development Expenditure as percentage of GNP

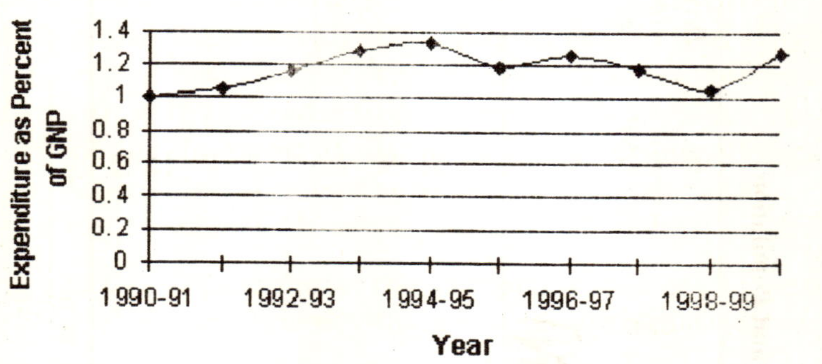

Table 4.10 shows the distribution of benefits of public health spending by income decile group in 1994. The results indicate that bottom 10 per cent of the households (who constitute extreme poor enjoys 13 per cent of the total benefits compared 14 per cent of the top 10 per cent. The lower 50 per cent of the household receive about 55 per cent of the total benefits, while the higher 50 receive 45 per cent. Thus the pattern of public health expenditure is more or less even and the pattern of distribution of benefit is not skewed. Thus, the emerging distribution of benefits of health spending is assumed to be pro-poor [CIRDAP, (1997)].

Table 4.10: Distribution of Benefits from Public Health Spending 1994

Per capita income decile	*Per cent of rural income*	*Per cent of benefits from public spending on rural health*
1	1.94	12.88
2	3.25	8.88
3	4.11	12.22
4	5.64	3.67
5	6.05	17.84
6	6.91	8.13
7	9.50	8.62
8	12.63	6.87
9	17.38	7.27
10	32.59	13.64
Total	100.00	100.00

Note: Public spending on health includes current expenditure only.
Source: MAP Focus Study, News Letter No.4, CIRDAP, December 1997.

Reference

1. Integration of women, children, disabled people, minority group, disadvantaged groups and areas [CPB, P. 67].

5

Socio-Economic Performance and Poverty Reduction

Introduction

The central concern of macroeconomic policies and development objectives is to improve the well-being of the poor. Sound macroeconomic framework to boost sustainable economic growth is a prerequisite for poverty alleviation in Bangladesh. But the development efforts of the government are adversely affected by the scarcity of domestic as well as public resources. On the other hand efforts are being strained by political unrest, lack of efficient institutions and skills, natural disasters like, floods, droughts, and economic disaster. From the perspective of poverty, the main concern is efficient economic management in (i) promoting economic growth with social justice that ensures employment generation and effective use of labour, and (ii) enabling the poor to respond to opportunities created from economic growth for their socio-economic development. Economic growth, employment generation and equitable distribution of income have been the principal development objectives of the successive plans. Reduction of poverty by linking economic growth with productive employment generation, creation of income opportunities and redistribution to the poor is the central theme of the country's planning process. This is because sustainable economic growth will react positively on other dimension of poverty and will do the most to reduce poverty. But in spite of considerable rhetoric concerning importance of economic development and its growth there has been no significant reduction in poverty as measured by head count-ratio particularly in rural areas, and nearly half of the population still lives in moderate poverty and one-fourth lives in extreme poverty. This section examines the trend and the recent record of GDP growth, employment generation, inequality in income distribution and other dimensions of poverty.

Economic Growth and Structure

Although the overall macroeconomic performance in 1990s was claimed to have been better in terms of economic growth and inflation, the GDP growth achieved in the last two decades appeared insignificant and far below the targeted growth. But in order to face the big challenge of poverty reduction, faster economic growth is required than that experienced in the last decade. Table 5.1 presents the targets and achievements in average annual growth rate of GDP in different plan periods.

Table 5.1 Targets and Actual Achievements in GDP Growth Rate (%)

Plan	*Target (%)*	*Achievement (%)*	*Short fall (%)*
First Five Year Plan	5.5	4.0	1.5
Two Year Plan	5.6	3.5	2.1
Second Five Year Plan	5.4	3.8	1.6
Third Five Year Plan	5.0	4.8	0.2
Fourth Five Year Plan	5.0	4.2	0.8
Fifth Five Year Plan	7.0	-	-

Source: First, Two year, Second, Third, Fourth and draft Fifth Five Year Plans of Bangladesh.

In terms of GDP growth, the experience of the last 25 years of the plan was disappointing. It is worth noting that none of the planned targets regarding average annual GDP growth rate set in different Five Year Plans was achieved and a significant-shortfall was seen in attaining the growth target. The average growth rate of GDP was 4.0 per cent against the first plan target of 5.5 per cent, while the achievement was only 3.5 per cent against 5.6 per cent during Two Year Plan period. During the Second Plan Period the average growth rate of 3.8 was realised against its targeted figure of 5.4 per cent. The Third and Fourth Plans targeted an average growth rate of 5 per cent but the actual growth rates achieved were 4.8 per cent and 4.2 per cent respectively. The fifth plan envisages a higher target of 7.0 per cent per annum but the GDP growth rate of 5.4 per cent in 1996-97, 5.3 per cent in 1997-98, 4.9 per cent in 1998-99 and 5.5 per cent in 1999-2000 was achieved [BBS (2000)]. The Fifth Five Year Plan target was not very optimistic but unfortunately under the present circumstances it appears to be unrealistic. The plan target of 7.0 per cent annual growth of the GDP, is largely dependent-inter alia-on a sustained growth in the industries sector and other related factors. However, the planned effort for poverty alleviation through higher GDP growth has not been able to free the economy from the clutches of the low economic growth. The shortfall in the GDP growth can be attributed to a number of economic and non-economic factors such as inadequate domestic and external resources, natural calamities, inflation and recession, inadequate institutional support and inefficient management. The key factor responsible for the poor performance of GDP is the inadequate utilisation of the country's productive potential. The structure and development of the economy of Bangladesh for some selected years are summarized in Table 5.2.

It is clear from the Table 5.2 that there have not been any significant changes in the structure of the economy during the last five years. The share of agriculture sector is, however, decreased from 41.77 per cent in 1984-85 to 25.47 per cent in 1999-2000. The industry sector went up from 10 per cent to 26 per cent, and social services sectors occupied around 50 per cent of the total GDP. In spite of the downward shift in the share of agriculture sector, the economy continued to be dominated by this sector.

Per Capita Real Income and Growth

The GDP growth shown in Table 5.2 provides a clear understanding of performance of the national economy, but it does not depict the state or condition of the people, especially the poor. However, discussions of policy for lifting poor from poverty usually depend on the trade off between growth of per capita income and poverty. In Bangladesh, the per capita income is very low and its growth is also not significantly high. Whereas rapid economic growth contributes to increase demand for labour and improve the situation of the labour market in which over supply and unemployment are prevalent. In this regard, appropriate sectoral policies in the manufacturing, agriculture and service sectors are needed to maintain rapid rates of economic growth to absorb labour force and reduce poverty. Table 5.3 presents the real per capita income and its annual growth.

The average per capita real income at 1995-96 market price was estimated at Tk.14558 in 1996-97 and

Table 5.2: Sectoral Composition of GDP at Constant Prices, FY1997-FY2000 (Base 1995-96)

	Industry Sector	*1996-1997*	*1997-19978*	*1998-1999*	*1999-2000**
	1	*2*	*3*	*4*	*5*
I.	Agriculture:	25.87	25.34	25.28	25.47
	1. Agriculture and Forestry	20.39	19.67	19.35	19.32
	(i) Crops & Horticulture	15.21	14.59	14.33	14.40
	(ii) Animal Farming	3.27	3.19	3.12	3.04
	(iii) Forest and related services	1.91	1.89	1.90	1.89
	2. Fishing	5.48	5.67	5.93	6.15
II.	Industry:	25.01	25.72	25.70	25.68
	3. Mining & Qurrying	1.03	1.03	1.00	1.00
	4. Manufacturing	15.41	15.88	15.60	15.40
	(i) Large & medium scale	10.88	11.29	11.20	11.06
	(ii) Small scale	4.53	4.59	4.41	4.34
	5. Power, Gas, Water	1.46	1.41	1.42	1.43
	6. Construction	7.12	7.39	7.67	7.84

(Table Contd...)

Table 5.2: Contd...

1	*2*	*3*	*4*	*5*
III. Service:	49.12	48.94	49.02	48.85
7. Wholesale and Retail Trade	12.94	13.02	13.21	13.38
8. Hotel and Restaurants	0.61	0.62	0.63	0.63
9. Transport Storage & Comm.	9.10	9.13	9.21	9.24
10. Financial intermediation	1.58	1.57	1.58	1.58
11. Real estate, Renting and Business activities	9.31	9.18	9.07	8.91
12. Public Adm. & Defence	2.52	2.54	2.55	2.56
13. Education	2.06	2.12	2.17	2.17
14. Health and Social Works	2.25	2.23	2.23	2.21
15. Community, Social and Personal Services	8.75	8.54	8.37	8.17
Per Capita GNI (Tk.)	14558	15053	15608	16217
Per Capita GNI (US$)	351	359	369	386
GDP growth rate(%)	5.39	5.26	4.88	5.47

Source: Preliminary Estimates of GDP, 1999-2000, National Accounting Wing, BBS, p.10.
*Provisional

Table 5.3: Revised Per Capita Real Income 1996-97 to 1999-2000

Year	*Per capita income (in Taka)*	*Annual growth rate (%)*	*Per capita income (in US$)*
1996-1997	14558	-	351
1997-1998	15053	3.40	359
1998-1999	15608	3.68	369
1999-2000	16217	3.90	386

Note: Real income at constant market price.
Source: BBS, National Accounts Statistics of Bangladesh (Revised Provisional estimates), 1998, p.490.

Tk.16217 in 1999-2000. The average annual growth rate of real per capita income during the same period was found to be 3.66 per cent. Sustainable economic growth is an important prerequisite for poverty alleviation. Benefits of economic growth may accrue only slowly to certain groups of the poor or to certain disadvantaged areas, and thus programmes focused on poverty reduction are essential, along with macroeconomic policies aimed at high economic growth. By following Kanbur's (1987) approach and using some results of 1994 survey carried out in the Analysis of Poverty Trends Project (ATP) of BIDS, and by considering certain assumptions on poverty line and income distribution Sen and Rahman (1998) have attempted to calculate roughly the cross over time of a poor person for different per capita income growth. According to their estimate it takes about 30 years for someone amongst the extremely poor to be pulled out of poverty if the per capita income growth rate is 3 per cent (our average growth between 1990-91 to 1995-96) per annum. The corresponding number of years for a moderately poor person is 17 years. The estimated cross over time for alternative growth rates is shown in Table 5.4.

Table 5.4: Cross over Time to Move out of Poverty Under Different Growth Rates by Type of Poor

Growth rate of per capita income (%)	*Cross over time (in years) for*	
	Moderate poor	*Extreme poor*
1	51	89
2	25	45
3	17	30
4	13	23

Note: The poverty line corresponds to Tk. 524 per person per month and the mean per capita monthly income of the moderate poor and extreme poor has been estimated at Tk. 317 and Tk. 215 respectively.

Source: Sen, B. and Rahman, A (1998). Bangladesh Poverty Monitor: An Overview (Based on the Report South Asia Poverty Monitor: The Bangladesh Chapter)

It appears from foregoing analysis that the growth of per capita income achieved in 1990s was very low and much higher growth than experienced in 1990s is required to lift the poor out of poverty within a reasonable period. Thus given the size of the problem, as indicated by the number of people below poverty line as well as the growing population of the poor, if the present growth rate of per capita income continues it may take several decades to eliminate poverty from the country.

Employment Generation: An Important Development Objective for Poverty Alleviation

Reliable statistics on employment situation in Bangladesh are extremely inadequate because among other possible shortcomings, they usually fail to capture seasonal character of employment in an agrarian economy, informal sectors and non-monetized labour relation. Data collected in different Labour Force Surveys also suffer from the same type of problems as evidenced by their low unemployment rates of 2.7 per cent for male and 2.3 per cent for female in Bangladesh [LFS (1995-96)]. Although, alleviation of poverty through employment generation continues to be the major development objective of all successive plans, the economic development in the last two decades has failed to make a significant contribution to employment generation for the vast majority of the labour force. Lack of employment opportunities is the core problem which must be addressed for poverty alleviation. Backwardness of industry sectors, inadequate non-farm activities and non-existence of diversification of economic structure resulted in a vast reservoir of unemployed persons. In view of this, the Fourth Plan put greater emphasis on employment generation through human resources development and created employment of 5.05 million man-years. During the Third Plan period only 3.93 million man-years of employment opportunities were created against the target of 5.09 million man-years which indicated a large short-fall in employment opportunities. Incidence of poverty is aggravated by the short-fall of employment opportunities for the existing vast labour force in the country. This is because the new entrants into labour force either work in low paid jobs or remain unemployed. Table 5.5 shows the employment situation in Bangladesh during different plan periods.

It appears from Table 5.5 that the labour force has increased by two fold since 1972-73 and it is growing faster than the population which resulted in a large gap between the supply and demand for labour force in the labour market. At the beginning of the First plan

Table 5.5: Labour Force, Employment and Unemployment During 1972 to 1997

(million person-year)

Year	*Labour Force*	*Employment*			*Unemployment*	*Unemployment Rate (%)*
		Domestic	*Foreign*	*Total*		
1972-73	21.38	13.09	-	13.09	8.29	38.78
1977-78	24.10	16304	0.05	16.09	8.01	33.24
1979-80	25.29	16.09	0.05	16.14	9.15	36.18
1984-85	29.50	18.97	0.32	193.29	10.21	34.61
1989-90	34.80	22.82	0.43	23.25	11.55	33.19
1994-95	40.47	26.88	0.95	27.83	12.64	31.23
1995-96	41.70	28.18	1.14	29.32	12.38	29.69
1996-97	42.97	29.62	1.34	30.96	12.01	27.95

Source: Fifth Five Year Plan 1997-2002, Table 1.10, P.9.

Notes:
(*i*) Unemployment counted on the basis of duration of work
(*ii*) LFS's usual definition used
(*iii*) Estimation of labour force for 1972-73 and 1977-78 based on 1974 and census 1981 population growth respectively and for 1979-80 manpower survey of 1980 adjusted; similarly, for 1987-90 LFS 1989 adjusted.
(*iv*) The rates of unemployment are computed on the basis of person year.
(*v*) Foreign employment figure shows cumulative net employment.

(1972-73) the labour force was estimated at 21.38 million of which only 13.09 million persons were employed and thus the unemployment rate stood at about 39 per cent. This rate, however, fell to 33 per cent in the terminal year of the First Plan (1977-78). The employment generation was significantly low at the end of the Two Year Plan which resulted in a higher unemployment rate of 36 per cent. Although an increasing trend in the availability of employment opportunities was seen since the beginning of the second plan, yet about one-third of the total labour force remains unemployed. The achievement of the different plans in such important social aspect-employment generation fell far short of the targets. The Fourth plan generated additional employment for 4.6 million against the planned target of 5.5 million. During the period, 5.7 million persons were added to the total labour force [FFYP]. The relatively rapid expansion of labour force, failure of desired investment, and simultaneous low growth rate of GDP exacerbated the poor performance of the economy in generating employment opportunities. The large scale unemployment can adversely increase incidence of poverty, affect the younger generation and create unrest in the society.

Employment in Vocational and Technical Areas

Vocational and technical education is an essential building block in any development effort. These types of education are important for increasing productive capacity of individuals as well as for shifting from traditional agriculture to modern manufacturing industry and services. As for example, in India on-the-job training has increased the productivity of a worker by 7 per cent and in Pakistan the productivity of vocationally trained workers in the industrial sector in

1985-86 was found to be 3 times higher in terms of value-added per worker than their counterpart in agricultural sector [Haq and Haq (1998), P.96]. It is also a good ladder for better and prompt employment. But evidence regarding employment opportunities in vocational and technical areas is discouraging in Bangladesh. What is happening in Bangladesh is that, despite increasing skills in terms of vocational and technical education, demand for them in the labour market is decreasing. Table 5.6 shows employment in vocational and technical areas.

Table 5.6: Per centage of Workers Employed in Vocational and Technical Areas

Year(s)	*Employment in areas of vocational and technical education(%)*
1978-82	75
1983	60
1984	69
1985	47
1986	43
1990	30

Source: *(i)* ADB, 1996; World Bank 1990
(ii) Haq, M. and Haq. K (1998). Human Development in South Asia, UPL, Table 7.1, P. 96

Table 5.6 reveals that there has been a much faster decline in proportion of employment in vocational and technical areas between 1978 and 1990. In 1978-82, 75 per cent of technically trained people were employed, while in the following year this figure was 60 per cent. In 1990, it came down to only 30 per cent indicating a depressing situation for employment of vocationally and technically trained personnel, who are assumed to be more productive and essential for economic development. Figure 5.1 shows the trend of employment rate of vocational and technical educated personnel. The technical education is more expensive than the general education and if many technically trained people remain unemployed, it leads to wastage of public money and thus the social rate of return for technical education is lower than that for general education.

Figure 5.1: Per centage of Workers Employed in Vocational and Technical Areas

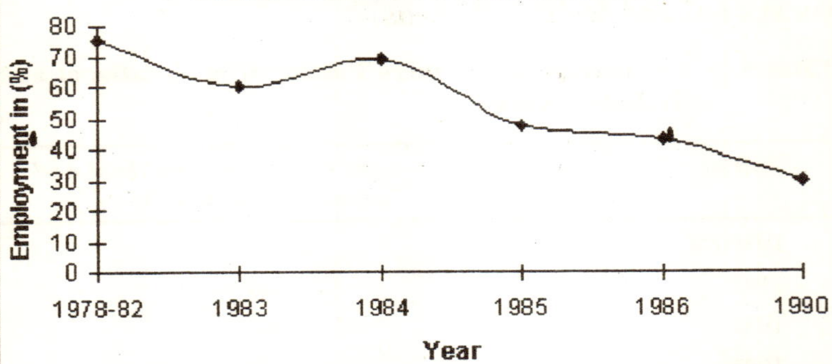

Table 5.7 shows the resource allocation in revised ADP for technical education (Technical Directorate) and

Table 5.7: Resource Allocation in Revised ADP for Technical Education.

Year	*ADP allocation (in million Tk.)*	*% of total ADP in Education Sector*	*% of GDP*
1996-1997	162.6	1.76	0.09
1997-1998	241.7	2.19	0.12
1998-1999	543.6	4.98	0.24
1999-2000	726.9	5.43	0.30

Source: Revised ADP figures from respective ADP

it indicates that only 4-5% of the total resource allocation for education sector as a whole is allocated for technical education.

It reveals from the above table that the resource allocation for technical education is very small. The share of GDP spent for technical education is also very small and it varies from 0.09 per cent in 1996-1997 to 0.30 per cent in 1999-2000. With this small amount of budgetary allocation, it is very difficult to meet the daunting challenges of skill formation in the country.

Inequality in Income Distribution

An important social objective of the development plans is to achieve an equitable distribution of benefits of development and reduction of poverty. Equitable distribution of income is a precondition for ensuring improvement of standard of living and hence poverty alleviation. It is one of the important development objectives of all the plans. But due to uneven distribution of wealth, unequal access to resources, institutional limitation and resource constraint this objective could not be fulfilled. Rather there has been a further deterioration in income inequality as measured by Gini index[1]. High degree of inequality is the main descriptive feature of income distribution in Bangladesh. This becomes evident when the frequency distribution of households is found to be clustered around the lower end of the income range. To examine the degree of inequality and pattern of change in income share over the time period, the sample households have been classified in decile income group and presented in Table 5.8.

It transpires from Table 5.8 that the income share of the poorest 10 per cent households has been gradually

Table 5.8: Per centage Share of Income by Given Quantile Group for Some Selected Years

Decile group	*% Share of total income of households*						
	1973-1974	*1983-1984*	*1985-1986*	*1988-1989*	*1991-1992*	*1995-1996*	*1999*
Bottom 50%	26.4	26.33	25.15	24.48	24.49	21.89	19.70
Decile 1	2.40	2.89	2.81	2.64	2.58	2.24	1.20
Decile 2	4.80	4.31	4.18	4.00	3.94	3.47	3.00
Decile 3	5.60	5.39	5.13	4.96	4.95	4.46	4.60
Decile 4	6.50	6.36	6.05	5.93	5.94	5.37	4.90
Decile 5	7.10	7.38	6.98	6.95	7.08	6.35	6.00
Decile 6	8.00	8.56	8.09	8.10	8.45	7.53	7.30
Decile 7	9.80	9.99	9.48	9.61	10.09	9.15	8.90
Decile 8	13.50	11.74	11.25	11.62	12.10	11.35	11.40
Decile 9	16.10	15.08	14.58	15.20	15.64	15.40	15.90
Decile 10	26.40	28.30	31.46	31.00	29.23	34.68	37.40
Top 50%	73.60	73.67	74.85	75.82	75.60	78.11	8.30
Gini index	0.35	0.36	0.37	0.38	0.39	0.43	0.39

Source: (*i*) Report of the Household Expenditure Surveys, 1973-74 and 1995-96, BBS.
(*ii*) Report of the Poverty Monitoring Survey, 1999, BBS.

decreasing since 1983-84. It was 2.89 per cent in 1983-84, 2.64 per cent in 1988-89, 2.24 per cent 1995-96 and then further declined to 1.20 per cent in 1999. However, the worsening situation in distribution of income was not confined to this group only. The share of income of first through eighth decile groups clearly declined while that of the richest 10 per cent households showed some improvement. Though there was some decline (29.23%) in the share of this group in 1991-92, it rose again to 34.68 per cent in 1995-96 and then further to 37.40 per cent in 1999. The most noteworthy feature of income distribution is that the share of bottom 50 per cent households is much lower than that of top 10 per cent households. It is evident from the pattern of distributional change that the position of the upper income group has strengthened in the process at the cost of declining share of lower income group. The trend in income distribution is consistent with that of Gini index. It was 0.35 in 1973-74, 0.37 in 1985-86, 0.39 in 1991-92 and rose to 0.43 in 1995-96 and then decline to 0.39 in 1999. The trend in income share of decile group has been illustrated in Figure 5.2.

Figure 5.2: Percentage Share of Income by Given Quantile Group for Selected Years

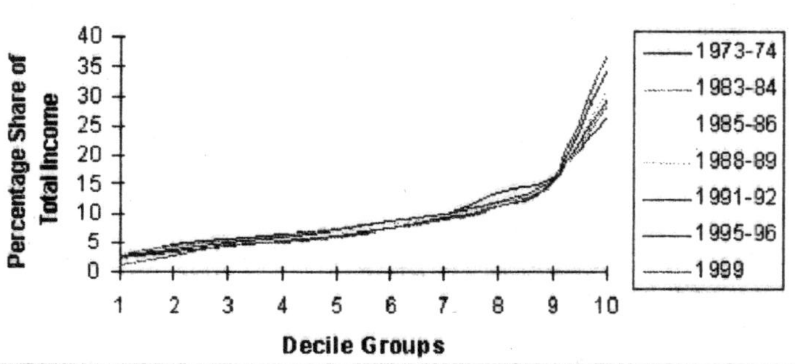

The distribution of income has deteriorated mainly because of the fact that access to new resources such as inputs subsidy, credit and public resources is largely dependent upon the existing distribution of wealth and the poor have little or no access to them. So inequality continued to accentuate due to concentration of wealth in a few hands. Thus the development process has failed to address the problems of inequality in income distribution.

Performance of Social Indicators

Poverty has many dimensions among which inadequate income is a core one, but many other social dimensions of it are important for poverty reduction. Among these, human resource development, adult literacy, life expectancy, participation of children in primary and secondary schools, infant and maternal mortality rates, etc. are notable. All these indicators are important directly or indirectly for poverty reduction. Development policies and budgetary provisions are made to improve these social indicators, and some progress has been noticed during the 1980s and 1990s (Table 5.9). Slow progress in per capita GNP was observed during the first half of the 1980s, while its progress was modest during the second half of the 1980s and faster during the 1990s.

The gross primary school participation rate for boys in 1980s was moderately high but for girls it was very low. The gross secondary school participation rate was almost one-fourth of the total school aged population, while the situation in case of girls was much discouraging and 9-13 per cent of the total girls participated in secondary schools during 1980-95. However significant change occurred in the second half of the 1990s. The adult literacy rate was 59 per cent for

Table 5.9: Performance of Socio-Economic Indicators

Indicators	*1980*	*1985*	*1990*	*1995*	*Latest year*
1. Per Capita GNP (in US$)	130	150	210	240	380 (2000)
2. Gross Participation Rates in Primary School (%):					
Male	75	72	77	84[a]	
Female	46	54	66	73[a]	94.5 (1990)
3. Gross Participation Rate in Secondary School (%):					
Male	26	26	25	25[a]	41[d] (1999)
Female	9	11	13	13[a]	40[d] (1999)
4. Adult Literacy Rate[b] (%):					
Male	41	40	47	50	59 (1998)
Female	17	18	23	26	43 (1998)
5. Life Expectancy at Birth (Years):					
Male	49	56[c]	56	58	59 (1998)
Female	48	55	55	58	59 (1998)
6. Infant Mortality Rate (below 1 year, per 1000 live births)	136	123	105	79	73 (1998)
7. Maternal Mortality Rate (Per hundred thousand life births)	-	-	850	-	449 (1997)
8. Total Fertility Rate (birth per woman)	-	4.7	4.3	-	3 (1998)
9. Human Development Index	-	0.369	0.400	-	0.461(1998)

Notes:
[a] Refers to period 1990-95.
[b] Adult literacy rate refers to population of 15 years old and over.
[c] Refers to the period 1980-85.
[d] Based on National Education Survey, BANBRIS, 1999.

Sources:
1. ADB Key Indicators of Developing Asia and Pacific Countries, Vols. XXXI, XXXVIII, XXXVI, XXX
2. UNDP, Human Development Report (1999)
3. WDR, 2000-2001, Word Bank.

males and 43 per cent for females in 1998; but these figures in 1980s were only 41 per cent and 17 per cent respectively. It is highly satisfying to note that the long-term trend (1980-1998) in life expectancy shows a clear and marked improvement. Significant decrease in infant, maternal and total fertility rates are observed between 1980s and 1990s. Indeed, the situation has improved because of increase in health care services, sanitation, availability of safe drinking water and expansion of immunization programmes in the country. The overall improvement of all indicators over the entire 18-year period appears extremely significant although their values are still too high compared to developed and many developing nations. However, improvement of these social factors will contribute to poverty reduction either by helping to accelerate other development interventions or by focussing on poverty directly.

The poor households have frequently larger household size, lower level of education, lower occupational status and inadequate productive assets. Smaller household size, higher occupational status, higher educational level and assets reduce poverty. They should be viewed together because they are mutually reinforcing. Higher educational level reduces household size and increases occupational status and productive assets. Better occupational status again increases wealth and reduces poverty. There are large differences in incidence of poverty by education, occupational status, land ownership, and demographics such as household size, female-headed households, and sex-ratio

Poverty Profile

Educational Status of Head of Household and Poverty

Education is an essential element for improving

knowledge, skill, human resources and for raising awareness of the masses. Lack of education, on the other hand, poses as an obstacle to find good job as illiterate people are unskilled and have limited mobility with respect to income generating opportunities. Thus poverty status is expected to be negatively associated with the level of education, and this indeed has been observed in Table 5.10. The proportion of poor is the highest (57% at the national, 69% in urban and 56% in rural areas) among the households whose heads are in never read category and this group comprises almost half of all households. The per centage of poor is the lowest among the households whose heads have graduate/Post-graduate level of education. But the households of this category comprises only about 3 per cent of all households at the national level. Incidence of poverty decreases with the increase of education level. Thus lack of education, among others, is the main factor in trapping households in poverty.

Table 5.10: Incidence of Poverty by Level of Education, May 99

Household Head Education	*Head count Measure (%)*		
	National	*Urban*	*Rural*
Never read	56.8	69.1	56.0
Class I-V	43.1	54.4	41.8
Class VI-IX	32.5	38.1	31.3
SSC/HSC or equipment	18.0	20.5	17.1
Technical education	15.9	9.2	25.4
Graduate/post-graduate (general)	5.9	6.6	5.3
Graduate/post-graduate (technical)	7.5	2.2	14.2
Total	44.7	43.3	44.9

Source: Poverty Profile of Bangladesh (Selected Socio-economic Indicators), BBS and CIRDAP, May. 2000.

Household Size and Poverty

The demographic characteristics such as age of head of households, sex-ratio, child dependency ratio, family size are important factors particularly in the rural areas where employment opportunity is low. However, among these factors, household size is an important element in determining the level of incidence of poverty. Given the household income, an increase in household size depresses the real consumption level and hence increases poverty level income. The issues of household size have been examined and the evidences are summarized in Table 5.11. The table shows that the proportion of poor for household of size 1-2 was quite small (about 23% for 1 member and 21% for two members at the national level) but this size comprises about 31 per cent of all

Table 5.11: Incidence of Poverty by Number of Members in the Households, May 99

Number of Members	*Head count Measure (%)*		
	National	*Urban*	*Rural*
1	0.230	0.164	0.238
2	0.205	0.180	0.209
3	0.348	0.325	0.359
4	0.418	0.404	0.421
5	0.466	0.411	0.474
6	0.493	0.476	0.496
7	0.500	0.518	0.498
8	0.494	0.456	0.488
9	0.482	0.559	0.473
10+	0.416	0.425	0.414

Source: Poverty Profile of Bangladesh (Selected Socio-economic Indicators), BBS and CIRDAP, May. 2000.

the households at the national level. The highest incidence of poverty was observed among the household size of seven members (about 50% at the national, 52% in urban and 50% in rural areas). This group of household comprised about 5 per cent of all households. But in urban area, the highest incidence of poverty (56 per cent) was observed for 9 member household.

Occupational Status and Poverty

Welfare as well as social status of a household depends upon the occupational status and the nature of work done by the members of the family. Among the various factors, nature of employment is important in determining the intensity of poverty. An individual without good job finds difficult to lead a better life unless he or she has access to inherited assets. For instance, a person without education, skill and land assets or with too little of them cannot find enough and good job throughout the year and thus cannot lead a better life, since employment is the main source of income for the vast majority of the people. The nature of poverty can, therefore, be more properly understood by identifying poor in terms of occupational status. In the present context, the work force has been divided into two broad categories, namely, agriculture and non-agriculture. Agriculture is again sub-divided into nine groups and non-agriculture is sub-divided into seventeen groups (Table 5.12). In agricultural category, the incidence of poverty among the landless labour households (71% at the national, 85% in urban and 71% in rural areas), was the highest, while in non-agricultural category the proportion of poor was found to be the highest among the labour households (67% at the national, 78% in urban and 64% in rural areas), which is followed by

Table 5.12: Incidence of Poverty by Occupational Status of Head of Households

Main Occupation	*Head count Poverty Measure (%)*		
	National	*Urban*	*Rural*
(a) Agriculture:			
Owner farmer	0.287	0.498	0.282
Owner-cum-tenant farmer	0.413	0.718	0.404
Tenant farmer	0.505	0.716	0.499
Labour (landowning)	0.615	0.685	0.614
Labour (landless)	0.711	0.853	0.708
Fishery	0.585	0.821	0.566
Livestock	0.713	0.601	0.740
Poultry	0.229	0.576	0.213
Other (agriculture)	0.444	0.565	0.433
(b) Non-agriculture:			
Officers (executive/administrative service)	0.051	0.079	0.009
Office staff	0.302	0.269	0.320
Teaching	0.175	0.171	0.176
Business	0.363	0.304	0.383
Production labour	0.608	0.607	0.609
Garment worker	0.584	0.600	0.550
Construction labour	0.543	0.622	0.519
Transport labour	0.456	0.535	0.415
Other labour	0.672	0.784	0.635
Driver (rickshaw/van/push cart)	0.636	0.753	0.607
Black smith/gold smith	0.364	0.526	0.328
Pottery	0.653	1.000	0.596
Wearing	0.486	0.738	0.459
Carpentry	0.490	0.597	0.479
Professionals (lawyer/doctor/engineer)	0.095	0.122	0.079
Tailor, laundry, barber	0.482	0.575	0.467
Others	0.452	0.447	0.453

Source: Poverty Profile of Bangladesh (Selected Socio-economic Indicators), BBS and CIRDAP, May. 2000.

rickshaw/van/push cart puller. The lowest incidence of poverty is observed among owner farmers in rural areas and executive/administrative officers in urban areas.

Land Ownership Size and Poverty

Ownership of land assets is possibly the most important factor in determining the economic status of rural households than any other factors. A wide socio-economic disparity is observed when the rural

Table 5.13: Incidence of Poverty by Land Ownership Size

Land Ownership Class	*Head count Poverty Measure (%)*		
	National	*Urban*	*Rural*
Landless	0.600	0.501	0.666
small	0.487	0.435	0.496
medium	0.259	0.360	0.263
large	0.176	0.161	0.175
	Urban		
	April 98	April 97	April 96
Landless	0.612	0.519	0.514
small	0.436	0.441	0.473
medium	0.179	0.064	0.078
large	0.064	0.136	0.118
	Rural		
	April 98	April 97	April 96
Landless	0.814	0.727	0.704
small	0.538	0.533	0.550
medium	0.298	0.272	0.287
large	0.178	0.181	0.134

Source: Poverty Profile of Bangladesh (Selected Socio-economic Indicators), BBS and CICDAP, May. 2000.

households are classified according to land ownership size. The indicators like monthly income, human resource development, education, infant mortality, maternal mortality, etc. show a direct relationship with land ownership size. The incidence of poverty also varies with the variation of landholding size. The proportion of poor is the highest (67%) among the landless households, while it is the lowest among the households owning land more than 7.50 acres (Table 5.13). Thus, an inverse relationship is noticed between incidence of poverty and land ownership size.

The proportion of poor in May 99 of landless households in rural areas was 3.8 times higher than that of large farm households. This figure in 1998, 1997 and 1996 was 4.6, 4.02 and 5.25 times respectively.

Pace of Poverty Reduction

Government planning for poverty alleviation through employment generation, economic growth and equitable distribution of income was laid down in all of the country's Five Year Plans. The poverty alleviation programs have also been gradually receiving greater attention in budgetary allocations. By looking at trends in development in those aspects, we can evaluate their impact on poverty situation over the years.

The incidence of poverty, as measured by the head count ratio has registered some progress but this has been only marginal and slow. Moreover, the extent of poverty reduction has varied considerably between urban and rural areas. Tables 5.14 and 5.15 show the head count index for urban and rural areas respectively. The head-count index[2] in urban area decreased from 40.9 per cent in 1983-84 to 26.3 per cent in 1995-96 showing about 14.6 per cent point decrease over the years, while in rural areas it decreased from 53.8 per cent to 51.1 per cent, indicating only 2.7 per cent point decline over the same period. When the direct calorie intake (DCI) method is taken into consideration, very little change in head-count index is observed. The depth of poverty as measured by the poverty gap index (P_1) and the severity of poverty as measured by the squared poverty gap index (P_2) are also found to be lower in urban areas than the rural areas.

Table 5.14: Income Poverty Measures in Urban Areas 1983-84 to1995-96

Year	*Head count index(%)*	*Poverty-Gap index(%)*	*Squared Poverty-gap index(%)*
1983-84	40.9	11.4	4.4
1985-86	30.8	7.3	2.5
1988-89	35.9	8.7	2.8
1991-92	33.6	8.4	2.8
1995-96	26.3	6.0	1.9

Table 5.15: Income Poverty Measures in Rural Areas 1983-84 to 1995-96

Year	*Head count index(%)*	*Poverty-Gap index(%)*	*Squared Poverty-gap index(%)*
1983-84	53.8	15.0	5.9
1985-86	45.9	10.9	3.6
1988-89	49.7	13.1	4.8
1991-92	52.9	14.6	5.6
1995-96	51.1	14.1	5.5

Source: Sen, B and Rahman, A. (1998). Bangladesh Poverty Monitor: An Overview (Summary Tables) Hand out 2.

According to Poverty Monitoring Surveys (PMS) reports published by the Bangladesh Bureau of Statistics [BBS (1999)] indicated a significant improvement in incidence poverty in both urban and rural areas (Table 5.16). The estimated head count ratio based on Food and Energy Intake (FEI) method in rural areas reduced from 46.8 per cent in December 1995 to 44.9 per cent in May 1999 showing only 0.5 per cent decline per year, while in urban areas no such improvement was observed. Slight improvement was, however, observed in respect of poverty gap ratio but squared poverty gap remains more or less at the same level over the period (Table 5.16).

Table 5.16: Incidences of Poverty Based on Food and Energy Intake Method

Year	*Head count ratio*		*Poverty gap* (p_1)		*Squared Poverty gap* (p_2)	
	Urban	*Rural*	*Urban*	*Rural*	*Urban*	*Rural*
May 1999	0.433	0.449	0.112	0.111	0.042	0.040
April 1998	0.443	0.476	0.136	0.123	0.057	0.046
April 1997	0.434	0.468	0.135	0.112	0.058	0.039
April 1996	0.444	0.479	0.142	0.120	0.061	0.044
December 1995	0.433	0.468	0.145	0.116	0.061	0.042

Public investment is the most important means for the government to influence the direction of socio-economic development and poverty alleviation. Although poverty alleviation and improvement of social factors such as education, healthcare etc. have been given greater emphasis in all successive plans and larger allocations of funds in social sectors have been made, insignificant reduction in incidence of poverty is observed in the second half of 1990s. This implies that the development policies and strategies undertaken for socio-economic development failed to reduce rural poverty significantly and the different programmes were able to reach out to only a small fraction of the rural poor. But the pace of poverty reduction needs to be further accelerated.

Conclusions

Satisfactory progress in human capital related indicators, such as formal and functional literacy of the household head and the head's spouse, and in other socio-demographic indicators have resulted in an improved human poverty index. The incidence of human poverty has declined over the years from 61.3 per cent in 1981-83 to 47.2 per cent in 1983-84 and then to 40.1 per cent in 1995-96 [Sen, B. (2000)]. Yet, despite these improvements and increased public expenditure in the social sector, incidence of income poverty remains pervasive particularly in rural areas. The incidence of income poverty at the national level declined from 52.3 per cent in 1983-84 to 46.6 per cent in 1995-96 indicating a very slow decline per year over the period. This small reduction in income poverty indicates that improvements, which occurred in various social indicators, probably failed to create sufficient impact on other factors such as employment opportunities, higher wages etc. that might reduce poverty. For instance, a higher literacy rate is expected to result in greater employment and consequently higher income and faster alleviation of poverty. Yet, the minor reductions in income poverty indicate that this is far from being the case. The indicators that have been used to measure our socioeconomic development are nation-wide indicators, which reflect the situation in Bangladesh as a whole. However, they tell us nothing about the level of development among the poor and non-poor households making it difficult to assess whether conditions are really improving among the poor. Thus, the nation-wide indicators could be misleading because improvements in their values may be the result of large improvements made by the rich and urban households and not due to improving conditions among the rural poor households. In this case, separate estimates for the poor and non-poor households and urban and rural households might provide better insights as to why the overall reduction in income poverty in Bangladesh remains low. Alternatively, it is possible that whatever improvements had occurred were not large enough to bring about notable reductions in income poverty. Another possible explanation is that the potential decline in income poverty may have been negated by inequality in income distribution and unequal development between urban and rural areas or disproportionate progress in different aspects between males and females. Thus, several constraints need to be overcome in the process of alleviating poverty. Steps need to be taken to strengthen and sustain targeted interventions over longer periods of time; otherwise, it will take an unacceptably long time to bring about significant reductions in income poverty. Other important measures for fast poverty reduction include narrpwing the gender gap, priority for women's education, provisions for skilled training, and employment generation.

References

1. The Gini index is the ratio of the difference between the line of absolute equality (the diagonal) and the Lorenz curve to the triangular region underneath the diagonal.
2. It is simply the per centage of the population living in households with a consumption below the poverty line.

6

Public Policies and Expenditure for Poverty Alleviation

A Brief Review of Policies for Poverty Alleviation

For several years, the government has been giving efforts in the direction of poverty alleviation and there is a general agreement among the policy makers that (a) a market oriented and growth-inducing development, (b) social sector development, (c) targeted financial services and (d) social safety nets are the key policies for poverty alleviation in rural Bangladesh. The main concern of these polices is to promote labour intensive growth that expand opportunities for production and remunerative employment among the landless poor labourers and enables them to respond to opportunities to improve their standard of living. The development of agriculture, industry and service sectors are important for higher economic growth. The social sector development policies which include policies towards education, health, nutrition, family planning, women development, youth development etc. affect, the human resources development and socio-economic conditions of the poor and have positive impact on poverty alleviation. Policies for easy access to financial service in the form of microcredit particularly in rural areas are also critical for increasing empowerment, access to resources, self-employment opportunities of the poor and their living standard [WB (1990)]. The policies for safety net which include food stamp, subsidised food distribution, nutrition programme etc. are also crucially important for the poor and the disadvantaged. Alleviation of poverty is one of the prime objectives of each of these factors of development policies. The policy actions which include general and targeted are aimed at combating poverty. The policy stream for poverty alleviation is illustrated through Figure 6.1.

Figure 6.1 Development Policy Stream for Poverty Alleviation

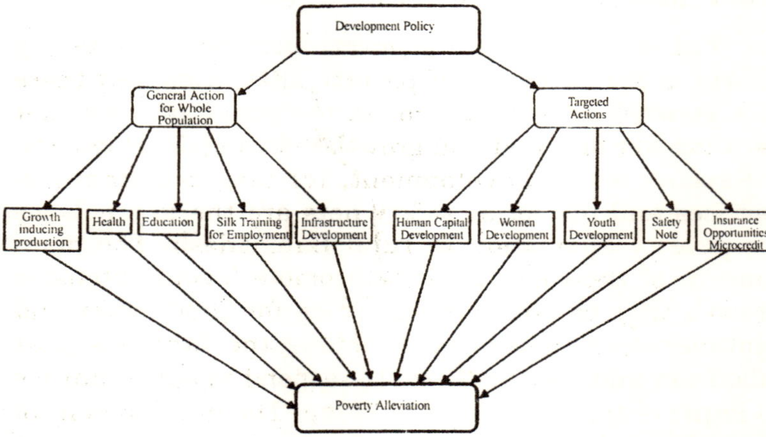

Policies for poverty alleviation can broadly be classified into two categories, viz. (i) Indirect policies, and (ii) Direct policies. The indirect macroeconomic policies are designed for achieving objectives other than poverty alleviation, but nevertheless they may come to the benefits of the poor indirectly. These policies include long-term as well as short-term development policies. The long-term policies include agriculture, industry, education, health etc., while the short-term policies include fiscal, monetary, price, wage, exchange rate etc. The macroeconomic polices benefit all groups of the population along with poorer groups through the trickle-down process. For instance, high economic growth may benefit the poor through increasing employment opportunities, social services, infrastructure development etc. Increased demand for labour, the only income generating asset of the poor, will enhance the wage rates at all levels and hence will increase their standard of living. Credit to crop, fishery and livestock sub-sectors has an indirect impact on important macroeconomic issues such as food security, employment generation, sustainability and poverty alleviation. Development in education increases awareness and social mobility, income and employment opportunities of people. Health and nutrition are important basic elements for increasing working capabilities and income of the poor. These factors help in reducing income erosion, wastage of human resources and productivity losses due to worker's illness and thus improves the quality of life of the poor. Among the Asian countries, China, South-Korea, Singapore, Indonesia, Malaysia and Thailand have experienced the benefits of high economic growth. Their growth strategy was relatively labour intensive which induced demand for the factors of production owned by the poor. Public spending in social sectors (education, health, family planning etc.) in these countries has reduced poverty to a significant level.. There are, however, some limitations of indirect policies for poverty alleviation. In the absence of policies for promoting social justices, high economic growth alone may not alleviate poverty completely. This is because the growth process sometimes bypasses some groups of the population in the absence of equitable distribution of income and assets. It is, therefore, imperative to frame policies for equitable distribution of income and to make provision for social services to disadvantaged groups along with high economic growth.

The direct microeconomic policies are specifically designed for poverty alleviation. Some of these policies are not targeted and some others are target group oriented. The target group-oriented policies on the other hand have specific objectives that benefit the poor directly. Policies for social services, women's development, youth development, rural Development etc. fall under the preview of direct or target-group-oriented policies. There are several programmes and projects for their development. Apart from target group-oriented policies and programmes, there are several interventions under safety net programmes in Bangladesh for direct income supplements to vulnerable people. The largest of these programmes are Food for Work (FFW), Vulnerable Group Development (VGD), Rural Maintenance Program (RMP) and Food for Education (FFE). These programmes extend benefit directly to the target-groups. Although these programmes extend immediate help to the poor, they have certain limitations and in the absence of well designed strategies they may not be effective for poverty alleviation. Moreover, these programmes are more dependent on foreign aid and external funds. However, both GOB and NGOs have been playing important roles in poverty alleviation through direct and indirect policies and programmes. The major component of policies designed for poverty alleviation is creating income through employment generation, reducing seasonal unemployment, generating income through wage employment options, improving productivity in existing self-employment and generating new sources for self-employment.

Public Expenditure for Poverty Alleviation

Policies for poverty alleviation are a part of several macro-economic development policies and as such the budget allocations under the head of poverty alleviation are not well documented and transparent. Thus the complicated budgetary system makes it difficult to work out the precise estimate of public resources allocated for poverty alleviation through different programmes and projects. Moreover, there are components in development expenditure which are essentially revenue expenditures. As a result, segregation of public expenditure into revenue and development is very difficult. These phenomena create serious obstacles in arriving at the actual budget for poverty alleviation. However, ADP allocation (revised) for sectors/sub-sectors, which are directly related to poverty alleviation programmes is shown in Table 6.1.

Table 6.1: Actual ADP Allocation to Poverty Alleviation Related Sectors[a]

Year	*(Taka in million)*	*% of ADP*	*% of GDP[b]*
1990-91	12100	22.96	1.09
1991-92	14930	24.78	1.25
1992-93	18142	27.70	1.45
1993-94	26933	2998	1.99
1994-95	36838	35.75	2.42
1995-96	32378	32.33	1.95
1996-97	38725	35.07	2.14
1997-98	42395	38.41	2.12
1998-99	46422	33.16	2.11
1999-00	48511	31.30	2.45

Notes: *(a)* Crop, Fisheries, Livestock, Rural Development and Institutions, Primary Education, Non-formal Education, Health, Population control and Family Welfare, Social Services, Women Affair and Youth Development.

(b) GDP at current price.

Source: Estimated from Bangladesh Economic Review, 2000, p.27.

It appears from Table 6.1 that ADP allocation for poverty alleviation related sectors/sub-sectors registered an increase in nominal terms over the period. The allocation as per centage of total ADP increased from 23.0 per cent in 1990-91 to 38.0 per cent in 1997-1998 and then registered some decline in 1998-1999 and 1999-2000. This figure as per centage of GDP is small and varies from 1.09 per cent in 1990-91 to 2.45 per cent in 1999-2000. Some portion of this allocated resource is expected to be spent on wage and other components of revenue expenditure. The position is, therefore, unsatisfactory with respect to allocation of funds for poverty alleviation and there has been an extremely limited allocation of funds for each of several programmes. The average allocation per person per annum was only Tk.109.0 in 1990-91 and Tk.373.0 in 1999-2000 in the nominal term which is much lower in real term. These amounts were meager by any standard to make a significant dent in the colossal problem of mass poverty.

Targeted Public Policies for Poverty Alleviation

Besides those general approaches to poverty alleviation through investment in poverty alleviation related sectors, the government of Bangladesh has sought to alleviate poverty through investment in a number of target-group oriented programmes such as provision of social services, women development, youth development, rural development etc. These programmes are undertaken by the Ministry of Women Affairs, Ministry of Youth and Sports, Ministry of Labour and Manpower, Bangladesh Rural Development Board (BRDB), Local Government Engineering Department

(LGED) etc. The main focus of these programmes is to increase income opportunities for the poor through:

(i) Skill development;

(ii) Pro-poor socio-economic development;

(iii) Easy access to resources and services;

(iv) Credit facilities etc.

The programmes undertaken by the selected ministries of the GOB along with targeted public expenditure are highlighted in the following sections.

Social Services Department in Poverty Alleviation

In view of the objectives for poverty alleviation, many programmes and projects have been implemented in social services sub-sector. The main projects are (i) Sarkari Shishu Paribar for providing shelter, education and food to the helpless orphans, (ii) Shanti Nibash for providing shelter and health services to helpless poor elderly people, (iii) Development and expansion of Training and Rehabilitation Centre for the distressed and vagrants home, (iv) Training and Rehabilitation Centre for Socially Handicapped Women, (v) Community Based Rehabilitaiton programmes for the distressed etc. The main aim of these projects is to improve the socio-economic condition of distressed poor through improvement of skill and to rehabilitate the orphans, the disabled and elderly people. Under these projects, the poor, assetless, unemployed and landless families are provided with credit to help them become self-reliant. Besides, more attention is given to rehabilitation and development of physically disabled, mentally retarded, visually impaired persons and socially disadvantaged women [ADP (1999-2000), p.245].

Ministry of Women's Affairs in Poverty Alleviation

Women, in Bangladesh, comprise almost half of the country's total population. A growing number of women from landless poor families are now joining the labour force outside agriculture. Women have become increasingly involved in earth cutting, brick breaking and construction, sewing, embroidering and in making handicrafts. Thus, without integration of women in the mainstream of the development process, balanced socio-economic development is not possible. Customs, traditions and social milieu have resulted in unequal opportunities to them in respect of education, skill development, employment and access to social services. As a result, participation of women in labour market and other economic activities is also poor. Moreover, the macroeconomic growth and gender-neutral development policies have failed to equitably benefit the poor women and children and the policies have been seriously questioned in respect of poverty alleviation particularly for women in poor households. The vicious circle of poverty could be broken effectively if the poor and disadvantaged women could be provided with opportunities to learn, acquire knowledge and skill and to become productive members of the society. Besides these, the rationale for women focus in the poverty alleviation policy arises from observed gender differentials in literacy rate, health status, malnutrition, employment opportunities in labour market, and access to resources.

Realizing the importance of women's development, the Government of Bangladesh (GOB) has formulated some development policies which aim to bring them into the development process in order to ensure their education, employment and empowerment. Keeping the poverty alleviation aspect in view, the Ministry of Women's Affairs has identified and implemented certain programmes through the Department of Women's Affairs. The important programmes among others are:

(i) Skill Development Training Programme;

(ii) Development of Women Entrepreneurship;

(iii) Women's Credit Programme;

(iv) Strengthening of Policy Leadership;

(v) Poverty Alleviation Programme for Women;

(vi) Assetless Women Development Programme and Advocacy for Gender Equity;

(vii) Support Services (Accommodation facilities, Day Care Services. Legal Aid, Employment, Information, Marketing outlet etc.);

(viii) Special Women's program etc.

Besides these programmes, about 20 development projects were undertaken since 1984 out of which 12 were related to poverty alleviation and 8 had the specific objective of improving the socio-economic condition of women. Thus almost all the projects are claimed to have had a direct or indirect impacts on poverty alleviation [GOB in Poverty Alleviation, P.63]. The title of the eight projects for women development are:

(i) Community Based Programme for Women and Children through NGOs.

(ii) Rural Women Development Programme;

(iii) Self-Reliance Program for Rural women;

(iv) Women's Vocational Training for Population Activities;

(v) Day care Service for the Children for Working Women;

(vi) Technologies for Rural Employment with Special Reference to Women;

(vii) Rural Women Employment Creation Project;

(viii) Integrated Program for Women's Participation in Income Generation Activities and to Give Legal Assistance.

The Ministry of Women's Affairs has also prepared a plan of action for women's development in line with Nairobi Forward Looking Strategies and Jakarta Declaration [UNDP (1992)]. The main aims of the plan of action are to:

(i) Eliminate all forms of discrimination against women;

(ii) Alleviate Poverty among women;

(iii) Increase women's participation as beneficiaries and agent in education, health, agriculture, industries and other sectors of development;

(iv) Provide skill training and credit for self-employment;

(v) Increase female literacy rate from 23 to 50 by the year 2000;

(vi) Ensure health for all women by the year 2000.

Between 1994 to 1998, a total of 3050 women were trained by the Department of Women Development. There are, however, several projects at the district and thana levels under which different vocational training are imparted to women. Under the poverty alleviation programme, a total of 1,90,000 women have been trained in different trades and a total of Tk. 406.50 million has been disbursed as loan to 1,50,000 beneficiaries up to June 1998. The average size of loan stands at Tk. 2710.0 which is not likely to be a significant amount for any gainful investment for poverty alleviation.

Plan Outlay and Public Expenditure for Women's Development

The First Five Year Plan did not visualize the need for women's development separately and as such there was no separate allocation for this purpose. But there was a program entitled "Rehabilitation of War Affected Destitute Women and Children" to help the poor and destitute women and children. In later development plans high priority was laid on the role of women in development process and different measures were taken to improve the status of women. In fact, women's status largely depends on their legal rights, education, health, position in the households and family decision-making power etc. These in turn have an impact on their role and participation in the development process. Accordingly several efforts are being made by the government and budgetary allocations have been made in all successive plans for women's development which may be seen in Table 6.2.

It is observed from the table that the successive plans have made increasingly higher allocations in absolute terms. It increased from Tk.105.60 million

Table 6.2: Allocation to Ministry of Women's Affairs in Various Plan Periods

Plan Period	*Allocation (in million Taka)*	*% of total plan outlay*
Two Year Plan	105.60	0.2735
Second Five Year Plan	310.00	0.1802
Third Five Year Plan	500.00	0.1295
Fourth Five Year Plan	880.00	0.1419
Fifth Five Year Plan	3358.00*	0.1714

Source: Country Paper, Bangladesh, World Summit for Social Development, Denmark 1995.

Note: *Including 598.0 million for VGD programme.

during the Two Year Plan period to Tk.880.00 million during Fourth Five Year Plan period. This significant increase in allocation, however, does not necessarily mean that the development expenditure on women's development for poverty alleviation has increased significantly as this allocation includes a number of components of revenue expenditure which are used to support the development projects. For instance, in Fourth Five Year Plan out of the total allocation of Tk.880.0 million, only Tk.200 million was spent for poverty alleviation programmes. Allocation for women's development is, however, not confined to the Ministry of Women's Affairs only but a sizeable investment on this issue is also made by other line Ministries/Division such as Ministry of Youth and Sports, Ministry of Social Welfare, Ministry Labour and Manpower, Ministry of Fisheries and Livestock, Bangladesh Rural Development Board etc. to coordinate women's development programmes. The ADP allocation for Women's Affairs during 1990-91 to 1999-2000, is set out in Table 6.3.

Table 6.3: ADP Allocation for Women's Affairs

(Fig. in million Tk.)

Year	*ADP Allocation*	*% of total ADP*	*% of GDP*
1990-1991	138.98	0.29	0.02
1991-1992	140.60	0.26	0.02
1992-1993	116.77	0.20	0.01
1993-1994	180.29	0.24	0.02
1994-1995	275.38	0.31	0.03
1995-1996	240.00	0.24	0.03
1996-1997	347.00	0.28	0.03
1997-1998	357.80	0.34	0.02
1998-1999	373.10	0.29	0.02
1999-2000	387.00	0.25	0.02

*GNP at current price

Source: Annual Development Program, 1990-91-1999-2000s, Planning,Commission, Government of Bangladesh.

Although the ADP allocation for Women's Affairs increased from Tk. 138.38 million in 1990-91 to Tk.387.00 million in 1999-2000, the share of this sub-sector to total ADP remains almost at the same level and the share to GDP is very small and varies from 0.01 per cent in 1992-93 to 0.03 per cent in 1996-97. These figures are quite low and revealing. The share of plan outlay and ADP allocation devoted primarily to the development of women, who constituted almost half of the total national population (49.41) is substantially lower, inadequate and inequitable by any standard. The allocated fund is thus not sufficient to cover all the poor women in the country and a vast majority of them will be out of the preview of the women development programmes. The impacts of the programmes on the poorest women are therefore, likely to be insignificant for their socio-economic development and improvement of their socio-economic status.

Ministry of Youth and Sports in Poverty Alleviation

Youth is an important and productive segment of the population within the age group of 15-30 years. This group constitutes more than one-fourth of the total population in Bangladesh and about 36 per cent of the total labour force [BBS (1999]. In order to bring economic prosperity to the country, there is a need for specific policy to mobilize them. The youth could play a vital role in poverty alleviation if they could be provided with proper guidance and training for skill development and acquiring knowledge. The Department of Youth Development (DYD) has been assigned the responsibility of organizing the unemployed youth into organized, disciplined, skilled and productive forces. Youth as a special group has, therefore, been targeted by the DYD for their socio-economic development through motivation, skill development, credit support etc. The following programmes have been undertaken by the DYD with a view to engaging the youth in the mainstream of the country's development process

(i) Skill development training programmes for the youth;

(ii) Self-employment programme for the unemployed youth

(iii) Poverty alleviation programme;

(iv) Youth leadership and human relations development programme;

(v) Programme for involvement of youth organisations in community development activities;

(vi) Involvement of youth in population control and welfare activities;

(vii) Participation of youth in population control and welfare activities;

(viii) Participation of youth in national social service programme;

(ix) Youth training and self-employment;

(x) Entrepreneurship Development for Educated unemployed Youth;

(xi)· Supply of Equipment to trained youth for self-employment.

For skill development and self-employment of the young men and women several projects have been undertaken among which (i) Thana Training and Self-employment, (ii) Thana Resource Development and Employment, (iii) Technical Training for unemployed youth, (iv) Establishment of Youth Training Centres, (v) Youth training and self-employment (vi) Enterprenureship Development for Educated unemployed Youth and (vii) Supply of Equipment to trained youth for self-employment are important. The main components of these projects among others are given in Table 6.4 along with their target groups.

The main aim of the youth training and self employment project is to train unemployed youth in various skill development trades and to help them establish self-employment activities, while the objective of the technical training project for unemployed youth is to provide training to unemployed educated youth on computer use, repair of radio, TV, VCP, Electrical and

Table 6.4: List of Project Components Alongwith Their Target Groups

	Project	*Target group*
(i)	Skill Development Project	School and college dropouts and unemployed youth
(ii)	Livestock and Poultry Training	Rural youth who drops out from school after eighth grade
(iii)	Secretariat Service Training	Youth having HSC and above degree
(iv)	Typing Training	Youth having SSC and above degree
(v)	Dress Making Training	Female youth having at least eighth grade education & housewife
(vi)	Block and Batik Printing	School dropouts having at list eighth grade level education
(vii)	Vocational Training	Unemployed youth
(viii)	Fisheries Training	Youth having minimum educational qualification upto eighth grade
(ix)	Computer Course Training	Unemployed youth having minimum qualification of HSC level
(x)	Wool-kniting Training	School dropouts having minimum qualification of eighth grade.

House-wiring, refrigeration etc. The main objective of youth training centres is to train the youth in livestock, poultry and pisciculture for engaging them in self-employment. The "Thana Resource Development and Employment" project (THARDEP) aims at alleviating poverty of the rural poor by providing training and credit to the young men and women. Family based approach is followed by this project. The training and credit are offered to family groups in different trades based on local needs. The main components of this project cover literacy, family planning and tree plantation. Integrated community development is another important aim of this project. The number of working villages of THARDEP now stands at 2130 with 7123 centres having 50971 groups. A total of 2,54,859 group members have received loan of which 1,45,269 are male and 109590 are female members [DYD (1999)].

There are 299 training centres of DYD to train unemployed youth in various skill development trades. According to DYD, a total of 9,68,845 youth have been trained for self-employment in different trades up to June 1998 under the on-going and suspended projects. Out of those, 5,87,308 youth have been trained under the Thana Resource and Employment Projects. Under the credit scheme an amount of Tk.1403.18 million was sanctioned as loan to 3,46,842 beneficiaries from the inception of DYD. In 1997-98, a total of Tk.796.18 million was sanctioned to 1,10,798 beneficiaries. The average size of loan was Tk.7,186. The target and achievement of these projects in respect of training in different plan periods is shown in Table 6.5. It appears from the table that there is no regular trend in self-employment and 2 per cent of total number of youth who received training was self-employed in Second Five Year Plan while this figure increased to 41.31 per cent in Third Five Year Plan and then reduced to 20 per cent in Fourth Five Year Plan.

Plan Outlay and Public Expenditure for Youth Development

As mentioned above, the government programmes and strategies for youth development and creation of self-employment opportunities were laid down in the country since 1979. Special emphasis was given in Second [1980-85] and Third [1985-90] plans for creation

Table 6.5: Number of Unemployed Youth Received Training in Successive Plan

Period	*No. of youth targeted for training*	*No. of youth received training*	*No. of youth self-employed*	*Youth self employed as % of youth received training*
Two Year Plan	42,255	36,200	–	–
Second Five Year Plan	–	1,63,070	3,000	1.84
Third Five Year Plan	43,935	42,937	17,739	41.31
Fourth Five Year Plan	–	2,54,074	50,808	29.0

Source: The Fifth Five Year Plan, 1997-2002, pp. 36-37.

of employment opportunities for them as a vehicle of poverty alleviation. Subsequently, the Fourth Plan [1990-95] envisaged several programmes for the unemployed youth. The budgetary allocation for youth development in different plan periods is shown in Table 6.6.

Table 6.6: Allocation for Youth Development in Different Plans

Plan Period	*Allocation in million Tk.*	*% of total plan outlay*
Two Year Plan	70.10	0.1816
Second Five Year Plan	255.00	0.1483
Third Five Year Plan	930.00	0.2409
Fourth Five Year Plan	-	-
Fifth Five Year Plan	6280.00	0.3205

Source: The Fifth Five Year Plan, 1997-2002, pp. 36-37.

As revealed by Table 6.6, there has been a substantial increase in absolute term in allocation for youth development. A particularly sharp increase is observed in the current plan period. But the allocation as per centage of total plan outlay is not encouraging. The share of plan outlay for youth development, who constituted about 27 per cent of the total population, is substantially low compared to its demand. Thus the allocated fund is not sufficient to cover the vast poor youth population in the country.

During 1990-91 to 1999-2000, the ADP allocation for youth development increased from Tk.105.12 million in 1990-91 to Tk.872.51 million in 1994-95 and Tk.605.0 million in 1999-2000. Although, the ADP allocations increased, their shares as per centage of total ADP and GDP were very small as shown in Table 6.7.

Table 6.7: ADP Allocation for Youth Development 1990-91 to 1999-2000

Year	*ADP Allocation (Tk. in million)*	*% of ADP*	*% of GDP*
1990-91	105.12	0.22	0.0126
1991-92	62.23	0.11	0.0069
1992-93	95.28	0.16	0.0100
1993-94	330.24	0.44	0.0321
1994-95	548.10	0.53	0.0369
1995-96	439.50	0.42	0.0338
1996-97	406.80	0.64	0.0289
1997-98	594.00	0.54	0.0384
1998-99	585.70	0.46	0.0337
1999-00	650.00	0.42	0.0328

Source: *(i)* Budget Estimation, Ministry of Finance, Various Issues, GOB

(ii) Annual Development Programme, 1996-97.

As shown by Table 6.7, the per centage share of ADP allocation for youth development to total ADP and GDP is very small between 1990-91 and 1999-2000

The average allocation per youth in 1999-2000 was only Tk.19.0 which was a meager amount by any standard. With this small amount of allocation, the youth development programme was able to reach out to only a small fraction of the youth population (total number of youth being about 34 million). The share of the youth development in total ADP was substantially lower than their share in total population and thus the share is grossly inadequate and inequitable. The strategy adopted by the plan documents does not seems to be consistent with the objectives dealing with youth development for poverty alleviation. Even the Fifth Plan which laid greater emphasis on poverty alleviation failed to provide a substantially higher share in plan outlays for the youth development.

Ministry of Local Government and Rural Development in Poverty Alleviation

Poverty Alleviation through rural development is one of the prime objectives of the LGRD Ministry. It has several sectors/sub-sectors among which Rural Development and Institution, Bangladesh Rural Development Board (BARD), Local Government Engineering Department (LGED), Bangladesh Academy for Rural Development (BRDB), Comilla and Rural Development Academy (RDA), Bogra are important. Several programmes have been designed for employment generation, rural physical infrastructure development and poverty alleviation. Besides these, a programme has been made for rehabilitation of the landless and rootless families through providing housing facilities and necessary helps for self-employment opportunities. However, programmes relating to poverty alleviation of some of the important sub-sectors along with resource allocation in revised ADP is briefly described below:

Bangladesh Rural Development Board

The Bangladesh Rural Development Board (BRDB) is a statutory body under the Ministry of Local Government and Rural Development (LGRD) and Co-Operatives. It is the major Government agency involved in rural development of the country since independence. The BRDB inherits the activities of former Integrated Rural Development Programme (IRDP) which was started in 1971 to promote two tier cooperatives to increase food production through farmers' organization [Amin, M.N. (1998)]. The Integrated Rural Development Programme (IRDP) was transformed into BRDB in 1982 by an ordinance of the Government. The BRDB has been directly involved in rural development activities for socio-economic development and poverty alleviation by organizing them into cooperative institutions. It basically aims at organizing the farmers, the assetless men and women into an institution for increased production and income. The institutional structure is of two-tier cooperatives in nature and practice. The initial focus of two-tier cooperatives is on the formation of primary Krishak Samabaya Somity (KSS) at the village level federated into the Thana Central Co-operative Association (TCCA). In addition to these, there are other co-operatives such as Bittahin Somabaya Samity (BSS) and Mohila Bittahin Samabaya Samity (MBSS), Mahila Somabaya Samity (MSS) and other informal groups. Of the total, female cooperatives or groups constitute about

60 per cent and regarding membership, the one-family – one member principle is followed. However, the progress of organization of cooperatives/groups in terms of members and amount of credit disbursed upto September 1999 is shown in Table 6.8.

Table 6.8: Coverage of Different Cooperatives Upto June 1999

Type of Society	*Cumulative number of Society*	*Cumulative No. of members*	*Cumulative amount of credit disbursed (in million Taka)*
Krishak Samabaya Samities (KSS)	62447	225637	78189.70
Bittahin Samabaya Samities(BSS), Male	13837	394117	21656.58
Mahila Bittahin Samabaya Samities(MBSS)	21486	629499	84484.66
Mahila Samabaya Samities (MSS)	7039	247093	12929.08
Informal Group	16225	332268	35513.48
Total	121034	3859814	232773.36

Source: Annual Report, 1998-99, BARD, pp. 79-81.

It appears from the above table that upto June 1999, a total of 121034 co-operative societies of different types were formed and organized with the number of members being 38,59814 so that there are about 32 members per society. According to the May 1999 Household Expenditure Survey (HES), about 55.3 million people were poor and thus only 7.0 per cent of the poor people of the country were covered by the co-operatives of BRDB. By the end of June 1999, an amount of Taka

232773.36 million was disbursed among eligible members of the society and on the average Tk.6030.0 was distributed to each co-operative member. It is worth noting that the number of societies and their members showed an absolute decline in 1990-99 period except for MBSS. The number of KSS, BSS and MBSS upto June 1990 was 67653, 14735 and 9091 respectively and the corresponding enrolled members were 245135, 415033 and 223632. But over the same period, the amount of loan disbursed increased from Tk.6879.53 million to Tk.23277.36 million showing about 238.36 per cent increase over the period.

Keeping in view of the problems of rural poverty, the BRDB has taken up a number of poverty alleviation projects. The list of projects with their coverage and broad objectives is shown in Table 6.9.

The coverage of the three major poverty alleviation projects and credit operations upto June 1999 under BRDB is shown in Table 6.10.

The above listed projects have focussed on poverty alleviation and have provided credit, skill development training, organizational help and other human resource development inputs to the poor. These projects have both employment and income effect. A survey report conducted in June 1997 on RD-5 indicated that a borrower engaged in fish cultivation earns Tk.144.0 on the average per day, in shopkeeping earns Tk.115.0, and in small trading Tk.101.0 per day etc [Annual Report 1996-97, P.63]. Another survey on 535 men and 465 women borrowers from RD-12 project indicated that, on the average, annual net income of Tk.3089 was generated from the investment of Tk.2126 by a male borrower, while a female borrower generated on the

Table 6.9: List of Existing BRDB Projects, Coverage and Their Broad Objectives

Name of Project	*Coverage*	*Broad Objectives*
1	*2*	*3*
1. Rural Development-5 (RD-5) Project	Faridpur, Madaripur and Kurigram districts	Socio-economic development, employment generation, increase employment etc.
2. Rural Development-9 (RD-9) Project	20 thanas of Rangpur, Nilphamari, Gaibandha and Lalmonirhat	Increase income through self-employment generation and Small and Marginal farmers, Landless and assetless people
3. Rural Development-12 (RD-12) Project (Phase II)	139 thanas of Panchagarh, Thakurgoan, Dinajpur, Bogra, Joypurhat, Jamalpur, Sherpur, Khulna, Shatkhira, Bagerhat, Barisal, Jhalokati, Bhola, Pirojpur, Mymensingh, Kishoregonj, Netrokona	Poverty alleviation of rural assetless people through group formation, skill development training, provision of credits etc.

(Table Contd...)

Table 6.9: Contd...

1	*2*	*3*
4. Rural Livelihood Project (RLP)	152 thanas in 33 districts three regions – Rajshahi, Dhaka and Chittagong	Increase socio-economic conditions of assetless poor men and women through bringing then into development processes
5. Rural Poverty Alleviation Programme (Phase-II)	145 thanas in Bangladesh	Improve standard of living of rootless people, through employment generation and increase in income opportunities
6. Greater Noakhali Rural Poor Co-operative Support Project	16 thanas of Feni, Noakhali and Laksmipur districts	Human resource development, social development, skill training etc.
7. Kurigram Poverty Alleviation Project	9 thanas of Kurigram district	Generation of employment opportunities & income generation of disadvantaged women

(Table Contd...)

Table 6.9: Contd...

	1	*2*	*3*
8.	Sharishabari Rural Development Project	25 villages in Sharishabari thana	Socio-economic development of marginal farmers and assetless women
9.	Primary Health Care Project	3 thanas of Bagerhat, Bakergonj and Chittagong districts	Healthcare service development for rural poor
10.	People's Participatory Capacity Building in Project Formulation Implementation for Poverty Alleviation	2 thanas of Sylhet and Sunamgonj	Improve Standard of Living, Create Social awareness, develop human resources, generate employment of the poor etc.
11.	Bangabandhu Poverty Alleviation Training Complex	Kotalipara thana of Gopalgonj	Self-employment generation for assetless men and women, human resources development, poverty alleviation

(Table Contd...)

Table 6.9: Contd...

1	*2*	*3*
12. Social Empowerment Project (Phase-II)	Rajshahi district	Increase income through use of local resources and participation of people at the grass root level planning
13. Self-employment Project for Poor Women	21 thanas of Jessore, Jhinaidah, Magura and Narail	Socio-economic empowerment of poor and distressed women, poverty alleviation and increase standard of living
14. Integrated Rural Women Development Project	120 thanas	Poverty alleviation, skill development training, increase awareness regarding health, nutrition, family planning, generate working capital

(Table Contd...)

Table 6.9: Contd...

1	*2*	*3*
15. Family Welfare Education, Motivation and Provision for Family Planning Services	299 thanas in Bangladesh	Motivate co-operative members regarding reproductive health, increase CPR to 65% and reduce TFR to 2.75% etc.
16. Model Rural Development Project	2 thanas of Comilla districts	Increase agricultural productivity through Krishi Co-operatives, import skill development training marketing of agril and non-agricultural products etc.
17. Extension and Strengthen of agriculture and Irrigation activities through Tangail Zila Co-operatives	11 thanas of Tangail district	Achieve Self-sufficiency in agricultural production; create employment opportunity in agriculture sector, poverty alleviation etc.
18. BRDB Institutional Support Project	Bangladesh	Provide support services for socio-economic development of the rural poor, strengthen and coordinate the BRDB to implement poverty alleviation projects

Table 6.10: Coverage of the Poverty Alleviation Projects Upto June 1999

Name of the project	*No. of Thana covered*	*No. of Group Member*			*No. of Members received credit*			*Amount of an Disbursed (in Million Tk)*		
		1994	*1999*	*% change over 1994*	*1994*	*1999*	*% change over 1994*	*1994*	*1999*	*% change over 1994*
RD-5	32	66,415	110970	67.09	22,220	151142	-	86.41	752.81	771.21
RD-9	20	32,135	37,337*	16.19	14,323	-	-	26.72	98.77	269.65
RD-12	139	46,857	4,59,534	800.72	81,002	451352	457.21	702.67	4443.0	411.11

Source: Annual Report, 1994-95 and 1996-97 and 1998-99, BRDB.
* For 1997.

average Tk.4721 annually from the average investment of Tk.2242. The baseline survey for RD-12 also indicated that household income of borrowers was found to be 48 per cent higher than the income of a non-borrower counterpart. The above findings on RD-5 and RD-12 demonstrate the positive impact of the BRDB programmes on the target groups. However, the evaluation reports did not mention about the delivery cost, transformatory effect on rural areas and sustainability of the beneficiaries.

The BRDB is also concerned with women's development for poverty alleviation. The main strategies adopted through its women's development programme are to organize women into a cooperative and provide training for skill formation, family welfare services such as health, education, population control etc. During the Fourth Five Year Plan period, about 0.78 million members were enrolled in co-operatives of different types of which about 60 per cent were women. Most of the co-operative members were expected to be self-employed and a total of Tk. 3,019.0 million were disbursed to various formal and informal groups under BRDB [5th FYP, P. 277]. In 1999 about 58.1 million people were found to be poor but upto June 1999 about 3.97 million poor were given microcredit which comprises only 6.7 per cent of the total poor. Thus the BRDB programmes are inadequate to cover all the families below poverty line. In other words, a vast majority (54.13 million) of the poor will still be left out of the preview of BRDB programmes. Thus, the present allocation would at best make a small dent in the vast problem of poverty.

Local Government Engineering Department (LGED)

Besides BRDB, the LGED under the Ministry of LGRD and cooperatives is also entrusted with poverty alleviation through infrastructure development and minor irrigation development programmes. Under the infrastructure development programme of LGED, 3709 kms of roads were constructed and 42000 metres of bridges and culverts were constructed or rehabilitated. In addition to these, 277 growth centres were developed through construction of sheds, internal roads, trading areas etc. during Fourth Five Year Plan period. Under the infrastructure development programme more than 112 million person-days of seasonal employment opportunities were created against the target of 133.1 million person-days during the same period [5 FYP, P. 278]. However, the targets and achievement of various programmes during Fourth Five Year Plan is shown in Table 6.11. It appears from the table that the achievement in most of the components of production and employment programme (PEP) is much higher than the set target except that in the irrigated agriculture and management programmes and other minor programmes. During the period under reporting, 0.78 million persons-days were self-employed under PEP programme against the target of 0.53 million person-days.

It is now recognised that economic growth, widespread access to social services such as health, education, family welfare, and targeted income transfer schemes such as food stamps, subsidised food distribution, food for education etc. are vital in any comprehensive policy for poverty alleviation. Likewise, there is no disagreement among the policy makers that infrastructure development is also an important development policy for poverty alleviation particularly in rural areas where majority of people have no access to even the most basic infrastructure facilities. In order

Table 6.11: Targets and Achievements of Major Programmes for Rural Development and Institutions During Fourth Five Year Plan (1990-95)

A. Production and Employment Programme (PEP)			
Programme	*Units*	*Targets*	*Achievements*
Formation of primary societies/group	number	23,581	16,882
Enrolment of members	number	529,621	777,660
Skill training	number	166,695	616,800
Shares/savings	million taka	159.6	449.33
Credit	million taka	330.3	3,019.00
Realization of credit	million taka	-	2,559.15
Small Farmers Development Programme (SEDP)			
Formation of groups	number	1,982	5,625
Enrolment of members	number	12,145	35,597
Share/savings	million taka	7.3	30.4
Disbursement of credit	million taka	60.7	166.4

Table 6.11: Contd...

B. Development of Physical Infrastructure			
Development of Growth Centres	number	316	277
Development of Feeder Road Type – B	km	2,399	3,709
Construction of Bridges and culverts	metre	15,039	41,987
Rehabilitation of flood/cyclone damaged bridges and culverts	metre	15,057	
Rehabilitation of flood/cyclone damaged pucca roads	km	2,929	2,574
C. Irrigated Agriculture and Irrigation Management Programme (IMP)			
IMP coverage (DTW)	number	1,556	1,499
(LLP)	number	207	156
IMP training	persons	8,555	6,215
D. Other Minor Programmes			
Settlement of families in Adarsha Gram	number	35,140	17,315
E. Employment Generation			
Infrastructure Programme	million person days	133.1	112.0
Self-employment under PEP	million persons-days	0.53	0.78

Source: Fifth Five Year Plan 1997-2002, p. 278.

to improve poor people's productive capacity and quality of life, it is essential to develop both production-oriented and welfare-oriented infrastructure. For instance, providing services such as irrigation, power, road communication, transport in rural areas would create new opportunities for diversifying income and employment of the poor. It may also be pointed out that even if the infrastructure project such as irrigation benefits the larger farmers more, the demand for the landless labourerer will still rise [WP (1990)]. This phenomenon will lead to an increase in agriculture wage rates and distribution of project benefits among the poor as well. Similarly, better school buildings and hospitals would help improve the quality of education and life and make poor children upwardly mobile [Gunatilaka, R. (1999)]. Keeping the problems of rural poverty in view, the LGED had taken up several infrastructure development projects which are listed in Annexure 6.1.

ADP Allocation for Rural Development and Institution

More than one hundred programmes/projects with local and foreign assistance have been designed and implemented under this sector to develop rural road communication to facilitate easy access to agricultural inputs, to strengthen the rural economy, promote production and generate rural employment opportunities. These programmes may help significantly in reducing rural poverty.

The Rural Development and Institution sector's allocation aims at the poor so that they can engage themselves in self-employed activities. In the revised ADPs an amount of Tk.516.1 million or 4.2 per cent was allocated for BRDB, Tk.10427.3 million or 84.84 per cent for LGED and Tk.203.0 million or 1.65 per cent for cooperatives [ADP, 1999-2000). The allocation and share of RDI in ADP is shown in Table 6.12.

Table 6.12: ADP Allocation for Rural Development and Institution[1]

Year	*ADP Allocation (in million Tk.)*	*% of total ADP*
1990-91	2220	4.2
1991-92	3190	5.3
1992-93	3660	5.6
1993-94	4800	5.3
1994-95	6840	5.69
1995-96	7270	·6.96
1996-97	9750	7.80
1997-98	8167	7.40
1998-99	12291	9.10
1999-00	15595	9.86

Sources: *(i)* Bangladesh Economic Review, 1996, Table 4.6, p. 28.
(ii) For 1996-97, Annual Development Programme, 1996-97.
(iii) Bangladesh Economic Review, 2000, p. 27.
(iv) ADP, 1999-2000, p. 62.

The share in ADP of RDI sector increased from 4.2 per cent in 1990-91 to 9.86 per cent in 1999-2000 showing about 5.48 per cent point increase over the period. Again within the RDI sector, the allocation to LGED is the highest while allocation for BRDB and cooperatives ranks second and third respectively. The share of BARD/RDA is only 0.58 per cent of the total [ADP, 1999-2000, p.54].

Grameen Bank in Poverty Alleviation

Organisation, Policies and Actions

The Grameen Bank (GB), a target group oriented

project, was first started in Jobra a village adjacent to the Chittagong University Campus in December, 1976. The main objectives of the project were to (i) extend collateral free banking loan to the poor men and women, (ii) eliminate exploitation of the money lenders, (iii) create self-employment opportunity for the poor, (iv) organise disadvantaged people and transform them into a workforce etc. Until the transformation of the GB project into an independent bank with its own branches in September 1983, the GBP operated in collaboration with participating bank such as Bangladesh Bank, Sonali Bank and Janata Bank. It received its legal framework from the Government through an ordinance first in 1983 amended later in 1990. A major change in the amendment was that the number of directors appointed by the Government was reduced and the number of representatives of the GB share- holders was increased. There are 9 out of 12 directors from the share-holders group. Thus GB is, theoretically, owned by the share-holders and the Government has a small share in the total capital [Asaduzzaman, M. (1999)]. This is how the GB differs from the nationalized and other schedule banks. From the operational side the GB is more like an NGO, but in character it is a formal sector microfinance institution (MFI).

The GB has initiated intervention programmes in various areas having certain interfaces with poverty. The clients of GB are generally poor women who are unable to provide any collateral and this is the essential feature that distinguishes GB from traditional banking practice. This bank works on the principle that if some capital money is made available to the poor without collateral, under reasonable terms and conditions they can create self-employment opportunities for themselves, earn income and thereby alleviate poverty. The target group of GB for credit operations consists of the rural poor owning less than 0.50 acres of land, or owning other assets worth less than the market value of one acre of land. Priority is given to poor women falling in this category. At the initial stage, loans are provided on an individual basis only, but in the recent past the bank has started providing credit to the group of 3-5 persons without any collateral. A group of people who constitute a loan group are neighbours from the same village and they are likely to be known to each other. The group of 3-5 persons make up a centre of 6-10 groups for collective enterprises such as joint share cropping, ownership and management of power pump, leasing of market, rice milling, fish pond cultivation, weaving etc. The poor men and women are organised into small informal groups through which services are rendered to members under the supervision of institutions of people at the grass-root level. Apart from the credit operation for income generating activities, the bank has also gradually introduced social development activities which include improvement of personal hygiene, literacy and children's education, skill development training etc. The group based development aims to promote joint responsibility among the group members for other social goals such as education, health care, family planning etc. Group pressure also ensures a high loan recovery. It is, therefore, increasingly recognised that such types of institutions are essential to organise the disadvantaged and to transform them into a workforce for capacity building or empowerment. The GB is now the largest Micro Finance Institution (MFI) with 2.36 million members and the cumulative amount of credit disbursement upto December 1999 was Tk.12,035.0 million [BER, 2000, p.178].

Areas of Investment of Loans

Loans are used by recipients in some productive economic activities approved by the group and bank workers. However, the following broad categories of activities have been considered important for poverty alleviation and loans are provided for the following activities:

- *(i)* Processing and manufacturing;
- *(ii)* Agriculture and forestry;
- *(iii)* Livestock and Fisheries;
- *(iv)* Service;
- *(v)* Trading;
- *(vi)* Peddling;
- *(vii)* Shopkeeping;
- *(viii)* Collective enterprises etc.

Poverty Alleviation and Microcredit Programmes

The Grameen Bank is the largest microcredit provider in Bangladesh. It has disbursed between Tk.104.0 million to 2.36 million poor upto February 1999. Under its microcredit programmes, poor and disadvantaged women are organised, trained and credit facilities are provided to them for collective or individual income generating activities. As shown in Table 6.13. livestock and fisheries were important activities for rural women. More than 33 per cent of the women loanees were engaged in these activities. The next important activity for them is agriculture and forestry. The important activities for male loanees were trading (30.46%), which is followed by agriculture and forestry (21%) and processing and manufacturing (17%). As the rearing of livestocks and fisheries is one of the important sources of income for rural women and providing them with continuous income, a major share of loan is disbursed to women for these activities. The loan portfolio in Table 6.13 on account of livestock and fisheries appears to be 31 per cent in 1996. Rural women are also traditionally involved in agriculture and forestry for their livelihood and thus 29 per cent of the total loan was disbursed for these activities to them. On the average, Tk. 3390.0 has been disbursed to each loanee as general and collective loans upto December, 1996. This amount, however, includes repeat loan to the same person.

Coverage

The coverage, in terms of number and size, of the GB's credit operation upto the end of December, 1999 is shown in Table 6.14. The GB operated in 39,706 villages covering more than 58.39 per cent of the 68000 villages of Bangladesh under 490 thanas in 64 districts. It had 24345 (6%) men and 459446 (94%) female groups with a total of 117850 (5%) men and 2239150 (95%) female members. More than Tk.124035 million was disbursed to its members for improving their earnings and self-employment opportunities. Among the loanees about 95 per cent were poor women. Thus, the poor women constitute the majority among the GB clients of the loans disbursed by the Bank. The per centage of housing loans given to women was also about 92 per cent of the total (Table 6.14).

Table 6.13: Disbursement of Loans Since Inception to 31 December, 1996 by Category of Activities and Sex

(Amount in million Tk.)

Activity	*Landless male*		*Landless female*		*Total*	
	No. of loans	*Amount of loans*	*No. of loans*	*Amount of loans*	*No. of loans*	*Amount of loans*
Processing & Manufacturing	256409 (17.34)	953.11 (19.68)	3665335 (20.53)	10624.58 (17.51)	3921744 (20.29)	11577.79 (17.63)
Agriculture & Forestry	311745 (21.08)	972.26 (20.08)	4834563 (27.09)	17559.72 (28.94)	5146308 (26.63)	1853.98 (28.29)
Livestock & Fisheries	305242 (20.64)	746.67 (15.42)	5930455 (33.23)	19613.39 (32.33)	6235697 (32.26)	20360.06 (31.08)
Services	52376 (3.54)	258.23 (5.33)	145836 (0.82)	682.87 (1.13)	198212 (1.03)	941.10 (1.44)
Trading	450396 (30.46)	1463.06 (30.22)	2349561 (13.16)	8471.20 (13.96)	2799957 (14.49)	9934.26 (15.16)
Peddling	26831 (1.82)	81.47 (1.68)	174165 (0.98)	616.14 (1.02)	200996 (1.04)	697.61 (1.06)
Shopkeeping	73123 (4.95)	303.37 (6.27)	740344 (4.15)	2979.93 (4.91)	81346 (4.21)	3283.30 (5.01)
Collective Enterprises	2519 (0.17)	63.68 (1.32)	8118 (0.05)	120.00 (0.20)	10637 (0.06)	183.68 (0.28)
Total	1478641	4841.85	17848377	60667.83	19327018	65509.78

Source: Annual Report, 1996, GB, Table 1, p.40.

Table 6.14: Coverage of GB Activities, Upto December 1999

Year (upto)	*No.of group (5 per cent group)*	*Membership coverage (No. of members)*		*Geographical coverage*		*General loan disbursed (in million Tk.)*	*Housing loan disbursed (in million Tk).*	*Total loan disbursed (in million Tk.)*
		Male	*Female*	*No.of village*	*No. of district*			
1993	363,984	107,361	1707,555	33,667	95	25,056	3,333	28,389
1994	402,626	120,843	1892,287	34,913	57	39,969	64,671	44,640
1995	413,133	123,297	1942,364	35,533	58	53,632	5,384	59,016
1996	433,791	122,162	1937,348	36,420	58	66,510	5,553	72,063
1997	465,384	123,659	2148,844	37,937	60	81,780	6,241	88,021
1998	486,870	124,621	2243,726	39,045	60	100,900	7,215	108,115
1999	-	117850	2239150	39706	-	-	-	124035

Source: (i) Mortuza, M. (1999). Microcredit Operation in Bangladesh: The Case of Grameen Bank, p. 17.
(ii) Grameen Bank.

Impacts of Programmes

According to all evaluations made so far by different organisations or experts, the GB is a success story in banking business in terms of loan recovery and in target group oriented development particularly in rural areas. The loan recovery rate is very high ranging between 96 to 100 per cent. This signifies that loanees are utilizing the loan for productive purposes and are capable of repaying their loans out of the profits they make. The loan provision has been associated with productive self-employment opportunities particularly for poor women who were either unemployed or underemployed earlier and thus it has a positive effect on employment generation.

As majority of loanees is women, it is very difficult to estimate the exact income effect on household income or it is difficult to separate the income of GB members from their household income. However, the total cumulative amount of savings in the group fund of all the GB members was calculated at Tk.9675.8 million by the end of December, 1999 (CDF 1999). This fact indicates a significant positive income effect of GB's loan.

Different impact surveys show higher income, savings, employment opportunities and higher social empowerment for GB members as compared to non-members but most of the surveys failed to provide any information with regard to the number of poor that have successfully moved out of the poverty line. However, Mahbub Hossain (1988) in his survey report indicated that the proportion of the population living in moderate poverty was 84 per cent for non-participants in a project village, while this figure was 80 per cent for the target-group in a control village. The proportion of GB members living in moderate poverty was 61 per cent in the target village. There was a large variation in proportion of people living in extreme poverty between members (48%) and non-members (78%). These findings indicate that GB is capable of reducing poverty for its members.

Palli Karma Sahayak Foundation (PKSF) in Poverty Alleviation

The PKSF was set up by the government in May 1990 as a non-profit organisation. It functions as an apex financial organisation. The main objective of this organisation is to undertake nationwide programmes for providing microcredit funding to the potential institutions to undertake poverty alleviation programmes for the poor, landless and assetless people. The Foundation channels its fund for the poverty alleviation programme through the NGOs which are termed as Parter Organisations (POs) [Khan, M.H. 1998]. Besides providing loanable funds to POs the Foundation has many other objectives among which the following are important

- *(i)* to help build and strengthen the institutional capacity of the POs;
- *(ii)* to initiate and undertake research activities for poverty alleviation and employment generation for the poor;
- *(iii)* to set up an effective Management Information System (MIS) for proper monitoring and evaluation of the activities of POs;
- *(iv)* to establish and maintain contact and collaboration with POs as well as other national and international organisations;

(v) to arrange training for its own staff as well as field staff of POs, etc.

Main Feature of Credit Programme

The following are the main features of the PKSF's credit programmes:

(i) the Foundation collects 3-5% service charges from POs depending on the amount of loan taken, while POs collect interest from the beneficiaries at the rate of 15% on the average per annum;

(ii) loans received by the POs from the Foundation are repayable within a period of 3 years, while the repayment period for those who take loans from POs is one year and loans are repaid in weekly installments;

(iii) the administrative and other related expenses of POs are met from the margin of service charge received from credit beneficiaries;

(iv) the main non-farm activities for which credits are provided by the Foundation through POs are rice husking, nursery, cane work, beef fattening, poultry, duckery, milch cow, rickshaw/van pulling and various type of small enterprises;

(v) experience, expertise and potentialities to operate micro-credit programmes for self-employment and income generation of landless and assetless people are the main criteria of selecting POs for providing loanable funds by the Foundation. More

specifically, quality and nature of organisation, organiser, management, human resources, working area and field activities, past performance, management information system and accounting system are the main criteria of selecting POs [Khan, M.H. (1998)].

Coverage

As of December 1999, the Foundation has funded 172 POs and a total of 1.79 (0.19 million male and 1.60 million female) million individual members have received credit from the microcredit programme of the Foundation. The cumulative amount of loan disbursed by the Foundation upto June 1999 was Tk.6024.8 million [BER (2000), p.118].

Credit Disbursed by the Administrative Division of the Government

Besides, Grameen Bank and the PKSF, different Ministries and Administrative Divisions of the government have also been providing microcredit to the poor. Table 6.15 shows the amount of microcredit disbursed by them upto December 1999.

As shown in Table 6.15, the Rural Development and Cooperative Division is at the top in respect of volume of microcredit disbursed which is followed by Ministry of Youth and Sports and Ministry of Women and Children Affairs. As of June 1996, the cumulative amount of microcredit disbursed was Tk.8396.3 million, while this amount rose to Tk.23675.0 million in December 1999 showing about 181.97 per cent increase over the period. The above trend of increased amount of microcredit by the government was accompanied by favourable shifts of public spending towards the poor for

Table 6.15: Amount of Credit Disbursement by the Administrative Divisions of the Government Under Microcredit Programmes

(Fig. in million Tk.)

Ministry / Division	*Organisation*	*Cumulative amount of credit disbursed upto June 1996*	*1996-97*	*1997-98*	*1998-99*	*1999-2000 December 1999*	*Cumulative amount of credit disbursed upto June 1998*
1	*2*	*3*	*4*	*5*	*6*	*7*	*8*
Ministry of Finance	Banking wing	53.3	91.1	128.0	165.0	89.6	527.6
Rural Development and Co-operative Division	BRDB	5051.7	2314.2	2937.8	2780.6	1577.5	14661.8
	BRDA	254.1	86.1	75.9	89.4	550.1	44.6
	RDA	3.6	6.1	7.7	10.5	38.2	10.3
Ministry of Women and Children Affairs	Department of Women Affairs	326.8	191.1	301.1	389.0	124.4	1332.5
	National Women Organisation	10.0	9.8	4.5	8.4	0.9	23.5
Ministry of Social Welfare	Department of Social Welfare	1075.2	74.8	57.6	159.9	72.4	1439.6

Table 6.15: Contd...

1	2	3	4	5	6	7	8
Ministry of Labour and Manpower	BEMT	107.2	49.2	39.6	21.5	0.0	196.0
Cabinet Division	-	6.0	5.0	7.9	2.7	3.4	3.4
Ministry of Fisheries and Livestock	Department of Fisheries	15.4	6.6	24.5	31.8	2.8	82.7
	department of Livestock	109.4	23.8	45.4	152.1	210.0	388.6
Ministry of Industries	BSIC	238.7	120.0	138.5	157.2	63.5	718.0
	Cotton Development	14.0	3.4	3.9	2.7	3.5	27.5
Ministry of Agriculture	Based Agril Extension Division	108.7	13.2	34.6	76.8	46.2	275.5
Ministry of Land	-	126.9	12.6	-	-	0.0	139.5
Local Government Division	Local Government Division	38.0	2.1	15.0	10.0	5.0	60.1
Ministry of Youth & Sports	Department of Youth Development	857.4	598.6	564.7	781.0	350.2	3151.8
Ministry of Textile & Handloom Board	-	-	-	-	23.5	9.3	32.8
Total	-	8396.3	3607.6	4386.6	4862.8	2613.7	23675.0

poverty alleviation. In the absence of any idea about the rate of return of microcredit, it is difficult to assess how effective microcredits have been in poverty alleviation. Moreover the poverty, particularly in rural Bangladesh, has persisted despite many poverty alleviation programmes undertaken by the government. The existing major projects exclusively for rural poverty alleviation in the government sector is shown in Annexure 6.1.

ANNEXURE 6.1

Existing Major Projects Exclusively for Poverty Alleviation in Government Sectors

Sector/Agency	*Name of the Project*	*Total Project Cost (in lakh taka)*	*Source of Aid*
1	*2*	*3*	*4*
A. Agriculture:			
Department of Agricultural Extension (DAE)	Netrokona Integrated Agricultural Production & Water Management:	5027.00	IFAD
	(a)DAE Part	2098.00	
	(b) LGED Part	2188.00	
Department of Agricultural Extension (DAE)	Crop Diversification and intensification Project	14517.00	IFAD
	(a) DAE Part	6764.00	
	(b) LGED Part	7753.00	
Forest Department	Rehabilitation of Unemployment Freedom Fighters through Raising /forest Nursery	440.00	
Department of Fisheries	Poverty Alleviation Programme through Integrated Fish Cultivation (Phase-II)	2932.18	

Annexure 6.1 Contd...

1	*2*	*3*	*4*
Directorate of Livestock Services (DLS)	ADB Assisted Participatory Livestock Development Project	13196.00	DANIDA, ADB
B. Industry:			
Bangladesh Small & Cottage Industries Corporation (BSCIC)	Poverty Alleviation through Income Generating Activities	2500.50	
Bangladesh Small & Cottage Industries Corporation (BSCIC)	Women Entrepreneurship Development Programme	4700.00	
Bangladesh Small & Cottage Industries Corporation (BSCIC)	Establishment of Skill Development Centre of Gopalgonj	233.00	
Bangladesh Handloom Board	Banarashi Palli (Revised)	2446.00	
Bangladesh Handloom Board	Micro credit Programme for the weavers	5000.00	
Bangladesh Sericulture Board (BSB)	Rehabilitation Credit Programme of 1998 Flood Affected Small Silk Farmer, Silk Fabrics and Silk Cloth Products	625.00	
C. Rural Development and Institution:			
Bangladesh Rural Development Board (BRDB)	Rural Development Project-5, Productive Employment Project in Five Districts of Greater Faridpur (Phase-III)	3871.00	SIDA
Bangladesh Rural Development Board (BRDB)	Rural Development Project-9	6809.00	EC
Bangladesh Rural Development Board (BRDB)	Rural Development Project-12 (Phase-II) for Assetless, RD-12	11850.00	
Bangladesh Rural Development Board (BRDB)	Rural Livelihood Project	34500.00	ADB

(Appendix 6.1 Contd...)

Annexure 6.1 Contd...

1	2	3	4
Bangladesh Rural Development Board (BRDB)	Rural Poverty Alleviation Programme in 145 Thanas of Bangladesh (Phase-II)	12507.00	
Bangladesh Rural Development Board (BRDB)	Greater Noakhali Rural Poor Co-operative Support Project	2500.00	
Bangladesh Rural Development Board (BRDB)	Kurigram Poverty Alleviation Project	865.00	Norway
Bangladesh Rural Development Board (BRDB)	Sharishabari Rural Development Project	12.00	
Bangladesh Rural Development Board (BRDB)	Primary Health Care Project	20001.00	
Bangladesh Rural Development Board (BRDB)	People's Participatory Capacity Building in Project Formulation and Implementation for Poverty Alleviation	1949.00	UNDP
Bangladesh Rural Development Board (BRDB)	Bagabandhu Training Complex for Poverty Alleviation	1692.07	
Bangladesh Rural Development Board (BRDB)	Social Empowerment-2 (Poverty Alleviation Through Local People's Participation in Development Activities), Phase-2, Rajshahi	2677.49	UNDP
Bangladesh Rural Development Board (BRDB)	Self-employment Project for Poor Women in Greater Jessore	1000.00	
Bangladesh Rural Development Board (BRDB)	Integrated Rural Women Development Project	3552.12	
Bangladesh Rural Development Board (BRDB)	Family Welfare Education, Motivation and Family Planning Services Give Project Through Rural Cooperative		

Annexure 6.1 Contd...

1	*2*	*3*	*4*
Bangladesh Rural Development Board (BRDB)	Model Rural Development Project (BRDB Component)	1977.00	Japan
Bangladesh Academy for Rural Development (BARD), Comilla/ Rural Development Academy (RDA), Bogra	Community Empowerment for Rural Poverty Alleviation Through Participatory Planning Project (BARD)	2753.00	UNDP
Bangladesh Academy for Rural Development (BARD), Comilla/ Rural Development Academy (RDA), Bogra	Community Empowerment for Poverty Alleviation at the Grass-roots Level (RAD)	1998.00	UNDP
Bangladesh Academy for Rural Development (BARD), Comilla/ Rural Development Academy (RDA), Bogra	Comprehensive Village Development Programme (Extend Phase): (a) BARD, Comilla (b) RDA, Bogra	363.00 181.50 181.50	
Bangladesh Academy for Rural Development (BARD), Comilla/ Rural Development Academy (RDA), Bogra	Small Farmer and Landless Labour Development Programme	999.79	
Co-operative Department (DRGA)	Emergency Rehabilitation Project of Bangladesh National Fishermen's Co-operative Society Ltd. Affected by Cyclone and Tidal Surge	10977.00	Japan (DRGA)
Co-operative Department	Physical Infrastructural Development of Eight Co-operative Zonal Institutes	1595.00	
Local Government Engineering Department (LGED)	Rural Infrastructure Development Project-3: Infrastructure, for Greater Sylhet Division	19000.00	

(Appendix 6.1 Contd...)

Annexure 6.1 Contd...

1	*2*	*3*	*4*
Local Government Engineering Department (LGED)	Rural Development Project-18: Infrastructure, Greater Khulna, Jessore & Kushtia	47066.00	ADB
Local Government Engineering Department (LGED)	Rural Infrastructure Development Project (Important Roads & Hat Bazar Development)	21598.00	
Local Government Engineering Department (LGED)	Integrated Food Assisted Development Programme (IFADEP): Growth Centre Connecting Road (GCCR) – 3rd Revised	12487.00	EEC
Local Government Engineering Department (LGED)	Cyclone Rehabilitation Project: Entire Coastal Areas–3rd Revised	15650.00	OPEC
Local Government Engineering Department (LGED)	Rural Infrastructure Development Project (Important Roads & Hat Bazar Development): Part-II (Revised)	20348.00	
Local Government Engineering Department (LGED)	Rural Development Project: Infrastructure; Greater Rajshahi, Pabna, Bogra and Dhaka District (Rural Roads and Markets Improvement and Maintenance Project-2)	87782.00	SDC, IDA
Local Government Engineering Department (LGED)	Small Scale Water Resources Development Sector Project at Thana and Union Level	27146.00	ADB, Netherlands, IFAD
Local Government Engineering Department (LGED)	Rural Infrastructure Development Project (Important Roads & Hat Bazar Development): Part III (Revised)	25929.00	
Local Government Engineering Department (LGED)	Rural Development Project-14: Infrastructure Tangail District (Phase-II)	8787.00	Germany

Annexure 6.1 Contd...

1	*2*	*3*	*4*
Local Government Engineering Department (LGED)	Rural Infrastructure Development Project	12500.00	
Local Government Engineering Department (LGED)	Rural Development Project-19: Infrastructure, Greater Barisal District	16531.00	OPEC
Local Government Engineering Department (LGED)	Rural Development Project-20: Infrastructure, Greater Comilla District (2nd Revised)	13700.00	
Local Government Engineering Department (LGED)	Greater Khulna District integrated Rural Development Project (2nd Revised)	2600.00	IDB
Local Government Engineering Department (LGED)	Rural Infrastructure and Community Development Project	965.00	Germany
Local Government Engineering Department (LGED)	Rural Development Project-21: Infrastructure: Greater Rangpur, Dinajpur, Mymensingh and Jamalpur Districts (Revised)	83284.00	SID, OECF, ADB, IFAD
Local Government Engineering Department (LGED)	Development of Infrastructure in CHTs Region to Accelerate Economic Activities	52218.00	
Local Government Engineering Department (LGED)	Rural Development Project-22: Infrastructure: Noakhali District (Revised)	8707.00	SDC
Local Government Engineering Department (LGED)	Greater Faridpur Infrastructure Development (Important Road, Bridges, Culverts and Growth Centre) Project	20000.00	
Local Government Engineering Department (LGED)	Sylhet Division Rural Infrastructure Development Project	19000.00	

(Appendix 6.1 Contd...)

Annexure 6.1 Contd...

1	2	3	4
Local Government Engineering Department (LGED)	Greater Jessore District Infrastructure Development Project	15200.00	JICA
Local Government Engineering Department (LGED)	ADB Assisted 1998 Flood Damage Rural Infrastructure Rehabilitation Project	12319.00	ADB
Local Government Engineering Department (LGED)	Rehabilitation of 1998 Flood Damage Rural Infrastructure in the Completed RDO-7 Areas with KFW Assistance	1484.00	KFW
Local Government Engineering Department (LGED)	Rural Development Project-16: Infrastructure, Patuakhali and Barguna District (Phase-II)	10780.00	DANIDA
Local Government Development (LGD)	Rural Maintenance Project (3rd Phase)	47673.77	CIDA
Ministry of Land	Adarsha Gram (Phase-III)	27414.00	EC
Chittagong Hill Tracts Development Board (CHTDB)	Integrated Community Development Programme for Hill Tracts Area (Phase-II)	3484.00	UNICEF
Ministry of Agriculture (MOA)	Barind Village Road Development Project	12600.00	
Asrayon Prokalpa Bastobayan Sangstha (ABSH)/Prime Minister's Office	Asrayan Project for Shelter and Self-employment Programme for Landless People of Bangladesh	16400.00	
D. Social Welfare:			
Social Services Department	Conversion of Existing Sarkari Shishu Sadans into Shishu Paribars (Phase-II)	7670.00	
Social Services Department	Development and Expansion of Training and Rehabilitation Centre for the Distressed and Vagrants Home	1340.00	

Annexure 6.1 Contd...

1	2	3	4
Social Services Department	Training & Rehabilitation Centre for Socially Handicapped Women (Dhaka, Chittagong, Rajshahi, Khulna, Barisal and Sylhet	1350.00	
Social Services Department	Expanded Rural Social Services (Phase-V)	12150.00	
Social Services Department	Institute of Coreectional Service for Girl, Dhaka	663.00	
Social Services Department	Shekh Rasel Distressed Children Training and Rehabilitation Centre at Tungipara, Gopalgonj	721.00	
Social Services Department	Establishment of Sarkari Shishu Paribar in Mujibnagar Complex	311.00	
Social Welfare	Bangladesh Andhakallan Samity, Zinaidah	489.26	
E. Women Affairs:			
Directorate of Women's Affairs	Community Based Programme for Poor Women & Children (NGOs Phase-IV)	1216.94	WFP
Directorate of Women's Affairs	Assetless Women Development Programme	4613.00	EC
Directorate of Women's Affairs	Day Care Centre for Children of Working Women	550.00	
Directorate of Women's Affairs	Women Support Programme (Phase-II)	965.00	
Directorate of Women's Affairs	Advocacy Awareness and Strengthening of Information Base (Phase-III)	1629.00	UNICEF
Directorate of Women's Affairs	Urban Based Women Development Project (Phase-II)	999.50	
Directorate of Women's Affairs	Rural Women Development Project (Phase-II)	955.00	

(Appendix 6.1 Contd...)

Annexure 6.1 Contd...

1	2	3	4
Directorate of Women's Affairs	Development of Women Enterpreneureship	1903.00	UNDP
Directorate of Women's Affairs	Agriculture Training Institute for Women at Bagerhat	507.00	
Directorate of Women's Affairs	Rural Women Employment Creation Project (Phase-II)	300.00	
Directorate of Women's Affairs	Devevelopment of Food Securitiless Poor Women	13085.03	
F. Youth Department:			
Directorate of Youth Development	Youth Training & Self Employment Project	21137.00	
Directorate of Youth Development	Supply of Equipment to Trained Youth for Self-employment	615.00	
Directorate of Youth Development	Technical Training Project for Unemployed Youths (Phase-II)	1862.00	
Directorate of Youth Development	Advocasy on Reproductive Health and Gender Issue through Youth Club	186.00	UNFPA
Directorate of Youth Development	Pro-Active Involvement of Rural Youth in Participatory Development	890.00	UNDP
G. Health, Population and Family Welfare:			
Local Government Division	Urban Family Health Care Project	24950.00	ADB
Rural Development & Cooperative Division	Family Welfare and Motivation for Family Services through Rural Co-operative (Phase-III)	249.00	UNFPA
H. Education & Religious Affairs:			
Non-formal Education	Integrated Non-formal Education Phase-1	20527.00	World Bank, SDC, ADB

Annexure 6.1 Contd...

1	*2*	*3*	*4*
Non-formal Education	Integrated Non-formal Education Phase-2	28000.00	Norway
Non-formal Education	Integrated Non-formal Education Phase-3	7431.00	UNICEF
Non-formal Education	Integrated Non-formal Education Phase-4	68300.00	
Directorate of Secondary and Higher Education	Secondary Education Development Project	38178.00	ADB
Directorate of Secondary and Higher Education	Female Secondary School Assistance Project	35360.00	IDA
Directorate of Secondary and Higher Education	Award of Stipend for Girls of Secondary Schools (Class VI-X)	60916.00	
Directorate of Secondary and Higher Education	Award of Stipend at Secondary Level for Expansion of Female Education (Phase-II)	6000.00	Norway

Source: Annual Development Programme, 1999-2000 and 2000-2001, Planning Commission, GOB.

Reference

1. Rural Development and Institution has several components such as BRDB, BARD/RDA co-operatives, LGED, LGED, Directorate of Relief and Rehabilitation, Chittagong Hill Tract Development Board and some programes under Ministry of Agriculture.

7

Non-government Organisations (NGOs) in Poverty Alleviation

Introduction

Experience shows that despite budgetary provision for poverty alleviation programmes in successive Five Year Plans, the poor and disadvantaged groups do not have easy access to public services and the positive impacts of the budgetary provision sometimes bypass the interests of the poor. This situation arises due to the government budgetary complexities as well as complicated bureaucratic systems which are found to be insensitive to the needs of the poor. Other reasons behind this fact are inefficient management, weak programme design, inappropriate strategy and weak institutional framework. In view of these problems, various NGOs in many countries are working side by side with the government to help mitigate the sufferings of the poor and to reduce poverty. Many NGOs around the world have been successful in achieving their goals and objectives in respect of poverty alleviation. In Bangladesh too, a large number of NGOs are engaged in poverty alleviation activities. There are as many as 830 NGOs receiving foreign aid from international and bilateral agencies for poverty alleviation programmes (CPB, Denmark, 1995, P.28). But, the distinct activities of 533 NGOs in respect of poverty alleviation are observed and reported [CDF (1999)]. As of December

1999, these NGOs reported that they had 94,33,974 active members and disbursed Tk.92,436.20 million as micro-credit. The top 20 NGOs covered about 83 per cent of the total active members and 90 per cent of the total amount of micro credit disbursed (Table 7.1). Among the larger national NGOs, Bangladesh Rural Advancement Committee (BRAC), Proshika Manobik Unnayan Kendra (PROSHIKA), Association for Social Advancement (ASA) and Swanirvar (Self-Reliance) Bangladesh are most important in terms of their size, coverage and investment in poverty alleviation programmes. These four NGOs covered about 68 per cent of the total active members and 78 per cent of the total amount of micro credit disbursed. The Grameen Bank (Village Bank), a government apex body also plays a vital role in the country's poverty alleviation efforts. The NGOs and the GB follow a target group oriented approach while implementing their programmes for poverty alleviation.

Under the target group approach, the NGOs put particular emphasis on social mobilisation of the poor in small informal groups. These groups are supposed to have the ability to organise themselves, identify their own problems and make their own development decisions particularly in areas relating to their income generation and welfare. This approach is claimed to be successful under the NGOs' pro-poor programmes. These, programmes, however, may be classified into two broad categories – one is the direct poverty alleviation programme and the other is the indirect poverty alleviation programme. Among the direct programmes, credit for self-employment, income generating activities like handicrafts, poultry, cow and goat rearing, rearing of HYV of chicken, fish culture etc. are notable. The indirect

Table 7.1: List of Top 20 NGOs in Terms of Membership and Credit Disbursement

Serial	*Name of Organization*	*As of December 1999*	
		Active Member-ship (in 000)	*Disbursement (in million Tk.)*
1.	BRAC	3,057	40,791
2.	Proshika	1,453	18,306
3.	ASA	1,179	11,304
4.	Swanirvar Bangladesh	694	1,846
5.	Thengamara Mohila Sabuj Sangha (TMSS)	299	1,687
6.	CARITAS-Bangladesh	264	1,546
7.	RDRS-Bangladesh	232	1,088
8.	BURO, Tangail	67	963
9.	Bangladesh Extension Education Services (BEES)	66	784
10.	HEED Bangladesh	64	736
11.	Society for Social Service (SSS)	58	734
12.	BAWPA	57	520
13.	Shakti Foundation	50	490
14.	Prodipan	49	343
15.	VOSD	46	340
16.	SAMATA	42	331
17.	ARBAN	40	331
18.	CODEC	38	321
19.	Jagorani Chakra	37	272
20.	Manab Kalyan Parishad (MKP)	33	231
	Total	7,826	82,964
Total 20 As % of Reported (533) NGOs		83	90

Source: CDF Statistics, Vol. 9, December, 1999.

poverty alleviation programmes include, among others, skill development, health and family planning, education, nutrition, sanitation, plantation, infrastructure development, awareness and empowerment creation, raising of consciousness etc. But it is worth mentioning that the activities of NGOs and revolving loan fund (RLF) mainly depend on government, schedule banks, foreign aid and donations and the future development plan depends to a large extent on the donor's commitment and attitude if the NGOs are not self-sustainable. It appears from Table 7.2 that on the average about 25 per cent of the total RLF is received from the savings of members, 24 per cent from PKSF, 11 per cent from local banks, 19 per cent from international donors, 12 per cent from service charge and 4 per cent from other sources. It is interesting to note that only 4 per cent of the total RLF comes from the NGO's own fund.

Table 7.2: Sources of Revolving Loan Fund of 533 Reported NGOs

Source	*As % total RLF (As of December 1999)*
Members Savings	25.37
PKSF	23.81
Local Bank	11.33
International Donors	18.82
Service Charge	12.47
NGOs Own Fund	3.79
Others	4.41
Total	100.00

Source: CDF Statistics, Vol. 9, December, 1999, p. 87.

The Semi-Formal Sector Micro Finance Institution (MF-NGOs)

Along with formal sector institutions (commercial and specialised banks and cooperatives and the government agencies), the semi-formal sector institutions comprising mainly of NGOs also operate micro-finance programmes that target the poor. As micro-finance initiative is acclaimed as a new approach for bringing about development and thereby poverty alleviation, these NGOs are playing a very important role in financing micro-credit programmes/projects in Bangladesh. The main feature of micro-finance is that it is a collateral free micro credit and can be easily availed by the landless poor.

It transpires from Table 7.3 that 94 per cent of the total micro-credit was disbursed for the income and employment-oriented sub-sectors. The majority of which was disbursed for small business (42%), followed by livestock (20%) and agriculture (13%). These sub-sectors have large scope for both income and employment generating opportunities. It is to be pointed out that less than one per cent of the total micro-credit was disbursed for education and health sub-sectors which are essential for human resources development, skill formation, social mobility and thereby poverty alleviation. This means that the NGOs role in credit disbursement for welfare-oriented sub-sectors is insignificant. However, there are some NGOs which provide micro-credit for housing and other sub-sectors.

Most of the NGOs provide micro credit services to employment and production-oriented as well as welfare-oriented sub-sectors. The main production-oriented sub-sectors are agriculture, fisheries, livestock, cottage industries, food processing, transportation and small business while the welfare-oriented sub-sectors are housing, health, education and others. The credit disbursement on these sub-sectors is shown in Table 7.3. Most of the NGOs provide entirely micro-credit services, some others provide micro-credit plus social development or non-credit services such as skill training, creation of social awareness, education, health care etc. For

Table 7.3: Credit Disbursement by 445 MF-NGOs to Different Sub-Sector (As of December, 1999)

Sub-Sector		*Credit disbursement (in million Tk.)*	*% of Total*
A.	Income and employment oriented		
	Agriculture	9016.32	12.75
	Fisheries	3416.52	4.83
	Livestock	14154.62	20.01
	Cottage Industry	2107.40	2.98
	Small Business	29738.98	42.05
	Food Processing	5451.72	7.71
	Transportation	2319.52	3.28
	Total (A)	66205.08	93.61
B.	Social Welfare-Oriented		
	Education	8.94	0.01
	Health	365.18	0.52
	Housing	944.38	1.34
	Others	3203.25	4.53
	Total (B)	4521.75	6.39
	Grand Total (A+B)	70726.83*	100.00

Source: CDF Statistics, Vol. 9, December, 1999, p. 118.

*Total is based on 445 NGOs.

instance, ASA provides entirely microfinance services to the target group but BRAC and PROSHIKA provide microfinance services as well as social development services. Similarly the Grameen Bank - a formal specialized rural bank for the poor, provides only microcredit services to its target groups for microenterprises, mostly for non-farm activities. Although 533 NGOs are reported to have microcredit services, 4 MFIs (BRAC, PROSHIKA, Swanirvar, and ASA) dominate this sector. At the end of December 1999, there were about 6.38 million active members of which BRAC had 3.06 million or 47.96 per cent, PROSHIKA 1.45 million or 22.72 per cent, ASA 1.18 million or 18.50 per cent and Swanirvar Bangladesh had 0.69 million or 10.82 per cent. A cumulative total amount of Tk.72,247.00 million was disbursed by the four large semi-formal sector MFIs to the borrowers. Of the total amount of credit about 56.46 per cent was disbursed by BRAC, 15.65 per cent by PROSHIKA, 25.34 per cent by ASA and 2.56 per cent by Swanirvar Bangladesh.

However, the policies and activities for poverty alleviation of 4 major NGOs are briefly described below:

Bangladesh Rural Advancement Committee (BRAC)

Organisation, Policies and Actions

Established in 1976, BRAC is now one of the largest multi-functional national NGOs in the country. It pursues different development policies at micro level with the primary goal of improving socio-economic empowerment of the poor and poverty alleviation. In pursuance of these goals and objectives, it has undertaken nation-wide development programmes such as (i) Rural Development Programme (RDP), (ii) BRAC

Education Programme (BEP), (iii) Health, Nutrition and Population Programme (HNPP) and BRAC Urban Programme (BUP) for the poor in general and rural poor women in particular. Although BRAC has been in existence since 1976, it started its Rural Development Programme (RDP) 1986 and has completed two years of three phases of this programme and has initiated the fourth current programme of work (1996-2000). Most of the poor in Bangladesh live in rural areas. Therefore, the question of the impact of rural development policies on the rural poor is an important one. However, the RDP is the core programme of BRAC for socio-economic development and poverty alleviation. Under this programme, the rural poor are organised into a small group consisting of about 25 persons (male and female separately) and this group is termed as Village Organisation (VO). RDP also includes the Human Rights and Legal Education (HRLE) and Essential Health care services. The major components of RDP are Agriculture, Poultry, Livestock, Fisheries, Small business, Cottage Industries, Food processing, Transportation etc.

Besides these activities, BRAC runs health and education programmes mainly for VO members. The health programme includes training of women members to prepare salt and sugar solution for combating diarrhoea. It also provides essential health services to the villagers as and when deemed necessary. Under the educational programme, BRAC caters to the education needs of VO members and other poor children who do not have the opportunity to enter into formal schools or have dropped out due to poor economic conditions.

Thus, the RDP covers the following four major activities:

(i) Institution building;

(ii) Sectoral development;

(iii) Credit operation, and

(iv) Support services.

The main objectives of these activities are to

(a) Increase agricultural production;

(b) Increase poultry, livestock and fish production;

(c) Promote human resources of the poor;

(d) Improve the social empowerment of the rural poor;

(e) Increase income and employment opportunities of the rural poor;

(f) Poverty alleviation etc.

The distinguishing feature of RDP is that it adopts an integrated approach especially for poor women through skill development training, human resource development, logistic and technical supports, inputs supply, empowerment, awareness building, infrastructure development services etc.

Target Group

Households owning less than 0.50 acres of land and selling manual labour for survival are considered as BRAC's target group.

Microcredit Operation

Policies for providing microcredit to group members through BRAC's banking project is also an important component of RDP. Schemes for income generation for the VGD as well as for VO members are financed by BRAC's rural microcredit operation. The main sub-sectors for which credit are provided are agriculture, poultry, livestock, fisheries, rural petty trade, food processing, rural industries, health, housing etc. BRAC's microcredit program aims at ensuring financial sustainability of members as well as of the organisation. Over the last twenty years or so, BRAC has transformed into a large microfinance institution (MFI) with 3.35 million beneficiaries and credit disbursement of Tk. 40791.0 million by the end of 1999 [BER (2000)].

Table 7.4: BRAC's Micro-Credit Disbursement by Sub-Sector (As of December, 1999)

Sub-Sector	*Credit disbursement (in million Tk.)*	*% of Total*
A. Income and Employment Oridented		
Agriculture	3839.2	9.41
Fisheries	1943.7	4.77
Livestock	9497.1	23.28
Cottage Industry	503.4	1.23
Small Business	17448.6	42.78
Food Processing	4854.4	11.90
Transportation	929.1	2.28
Total (A)	39015.5	95.65
B. Social Welfare-Oriented		
Education	0	0
Health	86.3	0.20
Housing	561.2	1.38
Others	1128.0	2.77
Total (B)	1775.5	4.35
Grand Total (A+B)	40791.0	100.00

Source: CDF Statistics, Vol. 9, December, 1999, p. 95.

The average loan size was estimated at Tk. 4100 for current loanee, Tk. 2,255 for new loanee, Tk. 4,230 for loanee having length of membership of 12-47 months and Tk. 5,477 for loanee having length of membership of 48+ months [Haider R.S (1998)].

It appears from Table 7.4 that small business sub-sector was in first rank in respect of number of projects and amount of loan disbursed (43.0%) followed by livestock (23.0%), food processing (12.0%), agriculture (9.0%) and fisheries (5.0%). Cottage Industries as a sector of investment ranked the last. It is worth mentioning that slightly more than half (52%) of the current loan received was invested for the activities specified in the application form. This means that the loanee did not utilize their loans for the activities they applied for. Thus it is very difficult to assess the impact of credit and its actual achievement in terms of development of the respective sector.

Vulnerable Group Development (VGD) Programme

BRAC has also been supplementing the government's Vulnerable Group Development (VGD) programme since 1988. Under this programme, the Government and the World Food Programme provide a monthly stipend of 30 kg. of wheat, while BRAC imparts training to VGD members on income generating activities, Human Rights and Legal Education, Essential Health Care and Credit for the period they receive the free wheat ration. To make them sustainable, BRAC also extends credit facilities to purchase and rear poultry. The main idea behind this credit service is that when the ration is withdrawn after two years, the VGD members continue to earn income from poultry rearing equivalent to the value of free wheat ration [Choudhury R,M, P.183]. Moreover, there is a special programme known as "Income Generation for the Vulnerable Group Development (IGVGD). The IGVGD programme is designed to link the socially and economically disadvantaged group of women to the development processes and income generating activities for their socio-economic empowerment and poverty alleviation.

The average amount of microcredit disbursed per borrower under IGVGD programme was Tk.2708 during January 1998-June 1999 cycle. The repayment rate of poor borrowers was excellent and BRAC was able to recover almost 100 per cent of its loans. But the outstanding loan for IGVGD members during the period from January 1998 to June 1999 was Tk.209.26 million or 47 per cent of the total credit disbursed indicating a large number of defaulters in repayment of loan among VGD members. This large sum of outstanding loan may be the result of many factors such as borrowers not being capable of entrepreneurship and management, even with financial support and training, thus making them unsuccessful in investing credit in income generating activities and in repaying their credits. This clearly indicates that credit alone is not the answer to poverty alleviation. Other means such as education, skill development training and support services must be provided along with credits.

Under the IGVGD programmes, BRAC extended its role in 274 thanas covering more than 59 per cent of the total number of thana (496) and 193,378 received training in income generating activities during the last cycle (July-Dec 1999). It provided loans to the group members and an amount of Tk.445.56 million was disbursed to 164533 borrowers during Jan – June 1999. But the outstanding loan during the same period was Tk.209.26 million indicating a large number of defaulters in respect of repayment of loans. Some basic facts on coverage about IGVGD programmes are shown in Table 7.5.

Table 7.5: Some Basic Facts About the IGVGD Programme of BRAC

Particulars	*June 1992- June 94*	*July 1994- June 96*	*Jan-Dec. 1997*	*Jan-June 1999*
Thana covered	84	74	118	296
Trained cardholders	105504	185096	248129	284689
Loan disbursed (million taka)	161.18	524.86	225.65	445.56
Loan realized (million taka)	143.16	263.38	98.34	236.29
Loan outstanding(million taka)	18.04	267.38	127.31	209.26
Borrowers	79834	178933	134827	164533

Coverage of Programmes

As of December 1999, BRAC served more than 50,000 villages in 64 districts covering more than 58 per cent of the total number of villages (86000) in the country. Currently, more than 2.3 million rural households are covered by different programmes. There were 90,250 VOs with 3.3 million VO members of which 97 per cent were women. This points to the fact that women are the major beneficiaries of BRAC's programmes. The amount of loan disbursed upto December 1999 to the VO members was Tk.40,791 million and the amount of money saved by the poor VO members was Tk. 2,900 million. There were 34,481 non-formal primary schools with 1.1 million students of which 66 per cent were girls. The coverage of RDP along with other basic facts about BRAC may be seen in Table 7.6.

Table 7.6: Coverage of RDP and Other Basic Facts About BRAC

Particulars	*December '95*	*December '96*	*December '97*	*December '99*
No. of VO	44656	54238	63846	90250
No. of VO members (million)	1.51	1.84	2.23	3.30
Participants in RDP programme (in million)	1.51	1.84	2.23	3.30
Amount of loan disbursed to the poor (million taka)	9619	14724	21615	40791
Repayment rate (%)	98.9	98.7	99.6	98.0
Amount saved by the poor (million taka)	802	1181	1755	2900
Village with BRAC programmes	26940	32102	37740	50000
Total students enrolled	1137767	1112171	1103378	1100000
Total annual budget (million taka)	2808.7	3951.6	4310.1	6420.0
Number of districts covered	58		64	64

Source: Annual Reports, BRAC, 1995 to 1999.

Impact of the BRAC's Programmes

The impact study was undertaken during August – September 1996 and then again in February - March 1997 by Research and Evaluation Division (RED) to closely examine the impact of BRAC's rural development programmes on its member households. The impact analysis was based on the comparison of socio-economic indicators such as housing status, landholding and other assets, food stock, education level, health and sanitation, income level, employment opportunities, empowerment, incidence of poverty etc. between groups old and new, and between BRAC and non-BRAC households. The Second Impact Assessment Survey (IAS II) based on 322

BRAC member households and 223 non-BRAC member households indicated a positive impact of RDP on social factors for BRAC members. The per capita monthly expenditure and per capita calorie intake are found to be significantly different between BRAC and non-BRAC households. Programme participants are found to be better off than their non-participant counterpart. The IASII also showed that BRAC members have higher income, assets and employment opportunities than the non-member households. The average value of household assets and weekly expenditure by length of participation have been set out in Table 7.7.

It appears from Table 7.7 that the average value of household assets and household weekly expenditure are much higher in BRAC member households than the non-member households. The level of these indicators are closely and positively related to the length of involvement in the BRAC activities [Choudhury, M. R, P.187]. The longer the length, the higher is the achievement. In order to examine the differences in the magnitude of poverty between the groups, the study estimated proportion of households living below poverty line income, and the depth and severity of poverty. The IAS II results showed that about 52 per cent of BRAC member households and 69 per cent of non-BRAC member households were below the upper poverty line, while 27 per cent member and 37 per cent non-member households lived in extreme poverty. The poverty gap was estimated at 13 per cent among BRAC member households but it was 19 per cent among non-BRAC member households. The degree of severity of poverty, as measured by the FGD index, was also observed to be much lower among the BRAC member households than among the non-member counterpart [BRAC (1998), P.100]. These findings lead us to conclude that BRAC is

Table 7.7: Material Improvements of Member Households According to Length of Involvement with BRAC

Indicators	Length of involvement with BRAC in months				Comparison Group
	1-11 (n=434)	12-29 (n=262)	30-47 (n=389)	48+ (n=221)	
Average value of gross H/h assets (Tk.)	10.959	14.037	20.282	23.230	7.250
Average % (& value) of assets which are productive (revenue earning)	32.9 (3.6060)	39.1 (5.488)	31.6 (6.409)	31.0 (7.201)	-
Average H/h weekly expenditure (Tk.) including peak & slack seasonal data	419	455	560	528	382

Source: Mustafa et al. (1996).

reasonably successful in improving socio-economic empowerment and in reducing poverty of its member households. BRAC has also been able to promote participation of women in the development process. Breaking the ice of conservativeness, women are now running restaurants, treating patients, engaging themselves in small enterprises, petty trade's etc. BRAC has made significant contribution in respect of non-formal education particularly among the poor children and it has also been successful in developing the primary health care services for the poor particularly in preventive measures.

But the unsuccessful story of BRAC is that it failed to capture the poorest of the poor such as the landless, women-headed households having no land, homeless etc. and these section of people had no participation in many of BRAC's activities [Evans et al (1995)]. This may be substantiated by the fact that the impact of BRAC intervention is the highest for households owning 1-50 decimals of land and it is the lowest for the absolute landless households. The results also showed that members receiving more loans responded more positively in terms of BRAC's success in improving their material well-being. But the limitation of the impact study is that it failed to provide any insights regarding the time length required to achieve self-reliance, cross-over time of poverty line income, sustainability and vulnerability of the BRAC's beneficiaries.

Proshika

Organisation, Policies and Actions

Proshika was established in 1976 and it is now one of the largest national NGOs in Bangladesh. Its main aims and objectives are to promote sustainable rural development, improve socio-economic empowerment of the poor men and women, and to raise human and material capacity to reduce poverty. Proshika's development strategies are generally directed towards the target groups which include (i) landless labourers, (ii) small farmers who work on rented land for cultivation, (iii) occupational working people such as fishermen, weavers, artisans, slum dwellers, rickshaw-pullers, (iv) illiterate poor, (v) disadvantaged women etc. Proshika works through informal group formation and by imparting formal and non-formal training to these groups. These training programmes help improve various income generating skills, trade and create self-employment opportunities for the target groups. Up till June 1999, Proshika formed 51,713 women's and 35,947 men's primary groups with a total of 1.69 million women and 1.30 million men group members. Like other NGOs, Proshika has also initiated a system of "Revolving Loan Fund (RLF)" to provide loans to those groups who are capable of undertaking the development projects. Like BRAC, PROSHIKA has been following the strategy of providing microcredit plus social development or non-lending services such as skill training, social awareness, health, education, agriculture development etc. In addition to providing loans, it also provides necessary technical support to the projects. Under Proshika's sustainable development programmes, the following are important:

(i) Organization building among the poor;

(ii) Universal education;

(iii) Integrated Multi-Sectoral Women's development.

Employment and income generation activities

(iv) Agriculture development;

(v) Minor irrigation;

(vi) Sericulture development;

(vii) Fisheries development;

(viii) Social forestry;

(ix) Empowerment of women;

(x) Health and educational development;

(xi) Urban poor development;

(xii) Infrastructure development;

(xiii) Small business;

(xiv) Multipurpose production;

(xv) Plantation and nursery etc.

Socio-economic and cultural empowerment is a major area of Proshika's programme. Special emphasis is, however, given to women participation in all areas of its activities. By the end of June 1999, about 59 per cent of the primary groups were formed with women, 67 per cent of the human development trainees and 64 per cent of the skill development trainees were women. Fifty nine per cent of the RLF recipient were women and 64 per cent of the adult literacy centres were for women [Activity Report, 1998-99, Pp.12-18].

Educational Development Programme

Under the theme of educational development, Proshika has developed four different programmes for providing adult literacy skill to its group members and rendering educational facilities to their children, who have either dropped out of schools or have seldom attended any formal school. These programmes are (i) non-formal primary education [NFPE) (ii) post-literacy education activity, (iii) enrolment of children of the poor households in formal schools and (iv) adult literacy for non-literate group members. By June 1999, Proshika had 3,138 non-formal Primary Schools, with the total number of students exceeding 64 thousand. The children of 8-11 years age group are to complete their education in three academic years under the NFPE programme. The post-literacy programme was designed to encourage them to continue with their learning process through simple practice such as tutoring school-going children at homes, maintaining one's family account, keeping records of group meetings, maintaining group pass book, etc. The adult literacy programme is beneficial to the non-literate adult group members. For this component, a total of 25,430 literacy centres were opened from which more than 5.34 lakh members had graduated. Under the enrolment programme about 40 thousand poor children enrolled their names in formal schools among which about 53 per cent were girls. Focus of those programmes has been to change the values and attitude of the poor in addition to increasing their earnings and bargaining capabilities.

Besides these educational programmes, there are different human development training (HDT) programmes which enhance the participants' understanding regarding social processes and widen their knowledge, analytical skills, operational skill, management and attitude regarding different aspects and issues of development. By June 1999, 2332 centrally organized courses, and 33,875 village based courses were offered. Among the 694,055 human development trainees, about 67 per cent were women (Activity Report, 1998-99, P.12).

Employment and Income Generating (EIG) Programme for Poverty Alleviation

Proshika is keen to see poverty alleviation through a series of Employment and Income Generating Programmes (EIGP). The EIGP facilitates self-employment opportunities and enables the poor men and women to be economically self-reliant. It imparts appropriate training and mobilizes its group members for successful implementation of employment and income generating (EIG) projects so that they can achieve social and economic empowerment and go beyond the vicious circle of rural poverty through better income and higher employment opportunities. The EIG projects are undertaken by the trained group members either with their own savings or with credit assistance from the Revolving Loan Fund (RLF) of Proshika. The group members, however, choose those projects which are less capital-intensive, somewhat conventional and assumed to be more profitable, suitable for rural society, and easy to implement. In 1998-99, 44,453 RLF supported EIG projects were undertaken and a total of Tk.2872 million was disbursed among group members of which Tk.1163 million was disbursed among male group members and Tk.1709 million among the women's group members. The average amount of loan disbursed per men's group was Tk.94378 while this figure for women's group was Tk.82969. It is evident from Table 7.8 that small business (48%) as an EIG project occupies the first position in terms of its number, followed by agriculture (27%),

Table 7.8: List of RLF Supported EIG Activities for Poverty Alleviation, 1998-99

Name of Activities	*Total Group*			*Men's Group*			*Women's Group*		
	No.of Loans	*Amount (Tk.)*	*% of Activ**	*No.of Loans*	*Amount (Tk.)*	*% of Activ***	*No.of Loans*	*Amount (Tk.)*	*% of Activ***
1	*2*	*3*	*4*	*5*	*6*	*7*	*8*	*9*	*10*
Agriculture	8795	788152350	27.4	4037	384157350	49	4758	403995000	51
Redemption of Mortgaged Land	2	182000	0.0	1	110000	60	1	72000	40
Livestock Raising	3125	167577910	5.8	761	56016050	33	2365	111561860	67
Apiculture	53	746000	0.0	34	493000	66	19	253000	34
Rice Husking	271	24537500	0.9	19	1419000	6	252	23118500	94
Cottage Industry	43	3558000	0.1	14	1408000	40	28	2150000	60
Handicraft	297	29144500	1.0	48	5541000	19	249	23603500	81
Small Business	13360	1380354200	48.1	4459	506662900	37	8901	873691300	63
Fisheries	903	65649500	2.3	508	37100000	57	395	28549500	43
Seeds	24	814400	0.0	20	604400	74	4	210000	26
Sericulture	130	1785500	0.1	51	848000	47	79	937500	53
Transportation Homestead	51	5033000	0.2	36	4111000	82	15	922000	18

(*Table Contd...*)

Table 7.8: Contd...

1	2	3	4	5	6	7	8	9	10
Gardening Plantation and	508	22375000	0.8	150	7091000	32	358	15284000	68
Nursery	335	7947700	0.3	209	5300200	67	126	2647500	33
Irrigation	262	7624800	0.3	211	6284300	82	51	1340500	18
Sanitary Latrine Production	92	3820000	0.1	77	3190000	84	15	630000	16
Multipurpos^ Production Loan	4213	317970200	11.1	1355	109894300	35	2858	208075900	65
Treadle Pump	7	183100	0.0	5	181000	99	2	2100	1
Tube-Well Installation Loan	116	16824273	0.6	115	16574273	99	1	250000	1
Construction Loan	48	5251918	0.1	45	4156000	97	3	125000	3
Power Tiller	117	6366000	0.2	113	6156000	97	4	210000	3
Weaving	98	9474500	0.3	43	4332000	46	55	5142500	54
Net making	76	8097500	0.3	16	1800000	22	60	6297500	78
Total Achievement	32926	2872469851	100	12327	1163400691		20599	1709069160	
Total Target	44453	3903819000		18816	1660593000		25637	2243226000	
Achievement %	74%	74%		66%	70%		80%	76%	

* Indicates the percentage of activity-wise disbursement of total disbursement

** Indicates the percentage of activity-wise loan disbursement for mean's and women's group.

Source: Activity Report, July 1998-June 1999.

multipurpose production (11%) and livestock raising (6%). Small business as the EIG project is the highest among the men's and women's group which is followed by agriculture and multipurpose production activities. Rice husking is a very common activity among the women's group. In the absence of evaluation in respect of net return of investment in different activities, it is difficult to assess which activity is more effective in bringing about benefits to the poor and for their poverty alleviation.

Apart from these projects in rural areas, Proshika also helps the urban poor in identifying entrepreneurial opportunities and provides credit facilities to them. It also extends credit assistance to the slum dwellers, especially to women who are organized, trained and ready to undertake EIG projects.

Microcredit Operation

Microcredit is also provided by the PROSHIKA to different income and employment-oriented projects/ activities like agriculture, fisheries, livestock, cottage industries, small business, transportation etc. and social welfare-oriented projects such as health, education, housing, etc. Upto December 1999, a cumulative amount of Tk.11304.11 million was disbursed by PROSHIKA. Of the total credit about 93 per cent was disbursed for income and employment generating activities, while only 7 per cent was given to social welfare-oriented projects/ activities. Among the activities, small business ranks the first and about 53 per cent of the total credit was disbursed in these activities (Table 7.9).

Coverage

Since the inception of the Proshika, a total of 1.30 million households in 12,776 villages under 182 thanas

Table 7.9: PROSHIKA's Micro-Credit Disbursement by Sub-Sector (As of December, 1999)

Sub-Sector	*Credit disbursement (in million Tk.)*	*% of Total*
A. Income and Employment-Oriented		
Agriculture	2935.12	25.97
Fisheries	317.74	2.81
Livestock	1176.60	10.41
Cottage Industry	129.38	1.14
Small Business	5945.08	52.59
Food Processing	0	0
Transportation	52.72	0.47
Total (A)	10556.64	93.39
B. Social Welfare-Oriented		
Education	0	0
Health	95.59	0.85
Housing	156.05	1.38
Others	495.83	4.38
Total (B)	747.47	6.61
Grand Total (A+B)	11304.11	100.0

Source: CDF Statistics, Vol. 9, December, 1999, p. 109.

of 51 districts were covered upto June 1999. The total number of programme beneficiaries was 7.43 million. An amount of Tk.9646 million was disbursed so far as loan for the group's EIG activities and the number of loans provided to the groups for EIG activities was 1,66,623. A total of 30,504 houses, 23,277 hand tube-wells and 259,863 low-cost sanitary latrines were constructed and installed for the poor. Among primary group members, about 59 per cent of the total were for the women folk.

The number of adult literacy centres and non-formal primary schools established was 25,430 and 10,405 respectively and the number of persons who graduated from non-formal primary schools with functional literacy was estimated at 3,24,326.

Impacts of Programmes

Collateral-free credit provision, group formation and mobilization, and distribution of scarce resources for self-reliance have increased to a great extent over the period. Participatory efforts for income and self-employment generation and other conscientization efforts through non-formal education, adult-literacy, skill development training etc. that Proshika brings in at the grass-root level provide a new institutional context for socio-economic development of the poor. Proshika's development programmes begin with people's organization, succeeded by education and skill development training, and flourish with employment and income generating activities, followed by savings accumulation and investment ultimately resulting in socio-economic development and poverty alleviation. The impact assessment survey indicated that Proshika created significant positive impact on literacy, health care and family planning among its beneficiaries. These social indicators were observed to be higher in Proshika members than non-proshika members. Proshika members also demonstrated higher income (27% higher), higher savings (239%), and higher investment (40% higher) and have more assets (57% higher) than their non-Proshika counterpart. These facts indicate that Proshika's development programmes have been successful in promoting social and economic empowerments of the beneficiaries, but the impact assessment failed to throw any light on incidence of poverty among the Proshika members and non-members. Thus an important question that needs to be addressed is whether or not the socio-economic empowerment achieved through various development programmes is sustainable without further interventions or even after termination of the project and whether the attained empowerment is sufficient for poverty alleviation. We have not been able to make any comment regarding actual impact of Proshika's programmes on the poverty status of its programme beneficiaries. The available reports or studies have failed to provide any information regarding number of poor that have moved out of the poverty line. It should be mentioned that most of the impact studies stress on income generation, recovery rate, savings but do not examine whether a redistribution of credit fund has a redistributive impact on poverty alleviation of credit borrowers.

Association for Social Advancement (ASA)

Organisation and Policies

The Association for Social Advancement (ASA) was established in 1978 at a remote village in Manikgonj district as a non-government organisation to address the problems of rural poor. At the first phase of its emergence as NGO, it emphasized on conscientization for social actions, legal aid, awareness building, human development training, communication support etc. At the reformative phase, ASA focussed on various integrated approaches such as education for empowerment, credit for income generation, institution building etc. In 1993 it shifted to programme specialization of microcredit services and within a short period, ASA reached a sustainable status in this respect. Through a series of experiments, modifications and innovations, ASA has scaled-up its activities all over Bangladesh. It aims at providing sustainable cost-effective financial services to the poor in order to improve their livelihood. ASA has dramatically shifted its paradigm from social development programmes to a pure micro credit programme and is entirely involved in micro-credit operations. Thus it has become a pure micro-finance institution (MFI)..

A Unit which includes one unit manager (UM) and four community organisers (CO) is called the basic organisational cell of ASA. Each CO is responsible for 15-18 groups each with about 20 members. And each unit is considered as the development institution at the grass root level. The main components of its programme include group members' education, mini irrigation, women's development, health programme with different component, human skill development training and post-disaster management programme. The main objectives of the programmes are:

(i) To empower the landless poor through raising awareness and developing leadership;

(ii) To activate rural poor in various developmental activities;

(iii) To help the poor in undertaking different income generating activities;

(iv) To help the poor in marketing their products to ensure fair price for their products;

(v) To help the poor in selecting appropriate income generating activities for improving their socio-economic conditions;

(vi) To establish women rights at all levels of the society;

(vii) To ensure proper utilization of local resources;

(viii) To encourage grass root communities in the society to protect their cultural values through various activities etc.

ASA provides credits to group members with a 12.5 per cent service charge. Schemes for income generating activities (IGAs) are financed by this programme and it aims at ensuring financial sustainability of members as well as of the organisation. Upto December 1999, about Tk. 20689.04 million was disbursed to 1084318 borrowers as loan. The loan repayment rate was excellent, reaching almost 100 per cent. The small entrepreneurship development programme (SEDP) is also another microcredit programme of ASA. This programme is designed to benefit small traders who lack necessary capital for running their business smoothly and whose livelihood is dependent on the small trades. As of 31st December 1999, the number of SEDP members was 82,672, and a total amount of Tk. 2371.61 million was disbursed to 77,241 borrowers. Besides credit for group members and SEDP, ASA also provides loan to individual members. Both males and females eligible members of the individual credit programmes and the average ceiling of the individual credit is fixed at Tk. 20,000. Under this programme, a total of Tk. 21,788,950 was disbursed among 1.156 million individual members upto December 1997

Target Group

Any male or female between 18 to 50 years of age, having an income not exceeding Tk. 1200 per month, is considered to be an eligible group member of ASA. Only one adult member from one family can qualify as a member of a group and he or she must live in the same locality.

Coverage

As of December 1999, there were 58,972 groups with 1,178,987 group members spread over 61 districts. About 96 per cent of the total members and 96 per cent of the total borrowers were female. The majority of the ASA's programme beneficiaries are therefore females. A total of Tk. 20,689.05 million was disbursed to 1.08 million borrowers. Thus the average loan size was calculated at Tk. 19,156. This amount, however, includes repeat loans to the same person.

Impacts of Programme

In order to assess the impact of ASA's programmes, a total of 23,288 borrowers were surveyed in 1999. In the absence of baseline survey results, it is difficult to assess the changes in socio-economic development over time and even more difficult to identify the causes of these changes. It is also difficult to determine the part of ASA's condition of microcredit programmes to socio-economic development. However, cross-sectional comparisons on different aspects of development were made between old and new ASA members and between ASA and non-ASA member households.

The impact assessment study in 1996 showed that ASA's microcredit was more than proportionately invested in small trade and income generating activities (IGAs). In terms of occupations, about 34 per cent households are found to be in animal husbandry, 23 per cent in agriculture and 15 per cent in trade activities.

Another 15 per cent of all activities are labeled as services, which include labourers, rickshaw renting and pulling etc. The income impact assessment of ASA member households indicated an annual income growth of 5-7 per cent compared to the non-ASA member households. Assets are observed to be 60 per cent higher in the old and 30 per cent higher in the new groups compared to the control group. The main difference is found to be in agricultural land, animal, housing and productive assets. The use of credit has clearly increased the self-employment opportunity of female and male members of the households. Employment also increased through credit. The survey results indicated that 42 per cent of the old, 37 per cent of the new ASA members and 21 per cent of the non-ASA members employed hired labour in the last three years. The impact assessment study in 1999 indicated that about 90.42 per cent of the total borrowers were able to increase capital, 90.88 per cent income, 89.12 per cent food intake, 86.89 per cent literacy rate, 88.41 per cent better treatment, 38.93 per cent land, 59.66 per cent live stock, 30.32 per cent ornaments and 95.47 per cent savings. These results indicate two main issues for poverty alleviation. First, ASA's credits strengthen the economic power of the poor and small traders. Second, the credit helps generate employment opportunity for the poor. The IGAs programmes also raise the income of programme beneficiaries. The impact analysis mainly concentrates on the improvement of income. Thus questions can be raised on two aspects. First, whether the increase in income is sufficient to lift the Macrocredit borrowers above poverty line, and second, whether the increase in income takes place on a sustainable basis. But the available findings of the impact study failed to throw any light on these aspects. It provided no information on self-reliance of the ASA's beneficiaries, cross-over time to move out of poverty and sustainability of the members and organisations.

Swanirvar Bangladesh

Organisation and Policies

Swanirvar Bangladesh is a non-political, non-profit and non-government voluntary organisation. It was established in 1975 with the aim promoting self-reliance in economic and social life among the poor through mobilisation of the political leaders, bureaucrats, local leaders and the target groups. At the beginning, voluntary mass participation schemes, family planning programmes, and literacy programmes were undertaken to achieve these goals and objectives. It then gradually gained in organisational strength to undertake specific programmes in selected areas for the poor. The main thrust of the programme is motivation of people at the grass root level to increase their social awareness. This is done with the hope that if the poor can be organised into a group, they will identify their own problems and find solutions with their own initiatives. Group approach income, employment generation and thereby poverty alleviation are also important objectives of its development programme. Over time, Swanirvar Bangladesh has extended its credit facilities to the poor for undertaking income generating activities. However, this organisation has been carrying out the following programmes for poverty alleviation:

- *(i)* Credit programme;
- *(ii)* Women development;
- *(iii)* Agriculture labour and tree plantation;

(iv) Youth development;

(v) Livestock and poultry raising;

(vi) Family planning and environment;

(vii) Skill development training;

(viii) Non-formal education ;

(ix) Adult literacy etc.

Swanirvar Credit Programme

Besides the above programmes, Swanirvar Bangladesh provides credit to the organised group of members who own less than 0.40 acres of land or whose yearly income does not exceed Tk. 6000.00. There are separate groups for men and women and each group consists of five members. The Swanirvar credit programme differs from similar programmes of other NGOs in the sense that it does not depend upon the donor agencies for its funding but rather it utilizes local resources from commercial banks. Most of the Swanirvar credit programmes are supported by the Bangladesh Bank with support from public sector banks. Credits are given to the prospective loanees without collateral, but with a nominal interest rate of 13 per cent. The credit, along with interest and other dues, such as compulsory savings and contributions to the Swanirvar workers' Trust Fund, are repayable in 52 weekly installments. The yearly amount of credit disbursed along with number of beneficiaries may be seen in Table 7.10.

Credit disbursement increased from Tk.43.04 million in 1991-92 to Tk. 148.17 million in 1995-96 and Tk.146.84 million in 1998-99 showing about 241 per cent increase over the period. An amount of Tk. 770.03 million was disbursed between 1991 to 1999 to 2,11,228

Table 7.10: Progress of Credit Disbursement, 1991–92 – 1998–99

Year	*No. of members received credit*	*No. of family members benefited*	*Total amount of credit disbursed (in million Tk.)*	*Average size of loan disbursed (in Tk.)*
1991-92	15,335	76,727	43.04	2800
1992-93	18,066	90,330	52.05	2880
1993-94	26,972	1,34,860	80.27	2975
1994-95	36,184	1,80,920	124.57	3440
1995-96	27,971	1,39,705	148.17	5300
1996-97	30,620	1,53,100	107.19	3500
1997-98	19,400	97,000	67.90	3500
1998-99	36,710	1,83,550	146.84	4000

Source: Annual Report, Swanirvar, 1998-99, p.15.

loanees of whom 80 per cent were women. The average loan size varied from Tk. 2800 in 1991-92 to Tk. 5300 in 1995-96 and Tk.4000 in 1998-99.

The average loan size was, thus, very low and grossly inadequate by any standard and this kind of loan can only be utilized in rudimentary activities such as paddy processing, rickshaw pulling, small trading etc. This amount would at best, make a small dent in the colossal problem of scarce of financial resources of the rural poor. Under the poverty-focussed credit programmes, Swanirvar provides micro-credit to the rural poor mainly for the following activities (Table 7.11). As of December 1999, about Tk.1846.40 million was disbursed of which more than 64 per cent was disbursed in income and employment generating activities, while the rest was disbursed in unspecified activities.

Target Group

(*i*) Families owning agricultural land below 0.4 acres and whose household assets do not

Table 7.11: SWANIRVAR's MicroCredit Disbursement by Sub-Sector (As of December, 1999)

Sub-Sector	*Credit disbursement (in million Tk.)*	*% of Total*
A. Income and Employment-Oriented		
Agriculture	67.30	3.64
Fisheries	146.70	7.95
Livestock	422.10	22.86
Cottage Industry	170.30	9.22
Small Business	196.70	10.65
Food Processing	162.10	8.78
Transportation	117.00	6.34
Total (A)	1282.20	69.44
B. Social Welfare-Oriented		
Education	0	0
Health	0	0
Housing	0	0
Others	564.20	30.56
Total (B)	564.20	30.56
Grand Total (A+B)	1846.40	100.0

Source: CDF Statistics, Vol. 9, December, 1999, p.117.

exceed the market value of Tk. 15000 are considered as target group of Swanirvar Bangladesh.

(ii) Loanees should be a member of a Swanirvar Village Development Committee.

(iii) Emphasis is given in its target group to women.

Coverage

Upto December 1999, Swanirvar Bangladesh had

covered over 10,000 villages in 140 thanas of 39 districts throughout the country with about 0.69 million active members and 0.21 borrowers. An amount of Tk.1846 million was disbursed for different income generation activities.

Impact of Credit Programme

There is no up-to-date, scientific and reliable impact study of Swanirvar income generating activities. Although Swanirvar claims to have made some achievements in poverty alleviation through the creation of income-generating opportunities for the poor, its contributions in increasing income and employment generations have not been clearly documented by the recent assessment study. Moreover, its contribution in dispensing credit for poverty alleviation is not widespread in comparison to Grameen Bank and other NGOs such as BARC, ASA and Proshika. The Swanirvar poverty-focussed programme, although running since 1978, could not reach the level of Grameen Bank and other NGOs in terms of coverage, loan recovery and income and employment effects. However, the impact study carried out by the Bangladesh Institute of Development Studies (BIDS) in 1990 indicated that the Swanirvar credit programme generated considerable social and economic benefit for the poor. Another study report in 1987 indicated that the average family income increased by 125.63 per cent and the proportion of underemployed family labour dropped from 42.15 per cent to 19.6 per cent [Rahman, PK. M. (1995), P.441].

To sum up, there has been a substantial increase in the volume of micro credits and number of beneficiaries over the period. As of December 1999, a total of 6383 thousand beneficiaries were served by the four NGOs. Among the four NGOs, about 48 per cent of the beneficiaries were served by the BRAC, 23 per cent by PROSHIKA, 18 per cent by ASA and 11 per cent by Swanirvar Bangladesh. Of the total credit, about 56 per cent was provided by BRAC, 16 per cent by PROSHIKA, 25 per cent by ASA and 3 per cent by Swanirvar Bangladesh (Table 7.12). It is to be noted that women are increasingly targeted by these NGOs as beneficiaries of anti-poverty interventions. This is done either to improve their well-being directly or as a mechanism for indirectly targeting other groups such as children, disabled husbands etc. The main reason for giving greater privilege to women over men is that women need economic and social empowerment to improve their status within the household and community as well as to reduce their poverty.

Table 7.12: Micro Credit Disbursed by Four NGOs upto December 1999

Name of NGOs	*No. of member (in '000')*	*% of total number*	*Cumulative amount of credit disbursed (in million Tk.)*	*% of total amount*
BRAC	3057	47.90	40791.0	56.46
PROSHIKA	1453	22.76	11304.0	15.65
ASA	1179	18.47	18306.0	25.34
Sawnirvar Bangladesh	694	10.87	1846.0	2.55
Total	6383	100.0	72247.0	100.0

Source: CDF Statistics, Vol. 9, December 1999.

8

Food Aided Safety Net Programmes for Poverty Alleviation

Introduction

Apart from the traditional and growth oriented programmes that maximize trickle-down effects of growth, the Government of Bangladesh taken up various safety net programmes for raising productivity, employment and reducing poverty of the extreme poor and disadvantaged women. These programmes are mainly food-aided and supported by the Government, bilateral and donor agencies and directly serve the poor through transfer of income to labourers participating in labour-intensive activities such as infrastructure development, forestry, fisheries, etc. These programmes are implemented through the Ministry of Women and Children's Affairs and the Ministry of Disaster Management and Relief and both them provide food aid to the following projects, viz. (i) Test Relief (TR), (ii) Food for Work (FFW), (iii) Vulnerable Group Development (VGD), (iv) Water Management, (v) Forestry, (vi) Fisheries and (vii) Growth Centre connecting roads. Gratuitous Relief (GR) and Vulnerable Group Feeding (VGR) are also two important poverty reduction safety net programmes for the rural poor. Under the TR and FFW projects, a labourer is provided 3.5 kg. of rice or 5.25 kg. of wheat per day for six hours of work [BES, 1993-94] as wage for participation in labour-intensive works such as earthwork, construction of link roads, repair of roads, construction of embankments, and culverts, canal digging etc. These projects have positive impact on several dimensions of poverty and are largely taken up during the lean season in agriculture to create employment opportunities for the extreme poor labourers and to keep their income, nutritional status as well as food grain price in stable position. Well designed food aided programmes can help make the poorest of the poor and disadvantaged women self-reliant. The food aided programmes can be classified into two broad categories, namely, (a) Rural Development (RD) Programme and (b) Vulnerable Group Development (VGD) Programme.

These programmes have been largely underwritten by food aid provided by the World Food Programme (WFP), European Union, Canada, Australia and the GOB. The WFP, as the overall coordinating agency for international food aid to Bangladesh, plays a significant role in the dissemination and replication of successful integrated food assisted development projects. Its goal is to help reduce food insecurity in sustainable ways and alleviate poverty particularly in rural areas [WFP (1997)].

Rural Development (RD) Programmes

The success of government and NGO programmes has generally bypassed the poorest of the poor. The Rural Development Programmes which support food-for-work activities in water, road, fisheries and forestry sub-sectors are successful in reaching the target group (the hard core poor) and increasing income and employment opportunities for the hard core poor.

FFW and TR Programmes

The enormous challenge of poverty reduction facing Bangladesh requires faster employment generation. Thus greater efforts needs to be made to increase employment particularly for the rural poor men and women. The food for work (FFW) and Test Relief (TR) projects among others are likely to raise the income, employment and nutritional supplement of hard core poor and rural poor women. However, quantity of food grains distributed through these projects from 1990-91 to 1998-99 is shown in Table 8.1.

Table 8.1: Distribution of Food Grains in FFW and TR Projects from Public Stock 1990-91 to 1998-99.

(000 m tons)

Year	*FFW*			*TR*			*Total*
	Wheat	*Rice*	*Total*	*Wheat*	*Rice*	*Total*	*food-grains*
1990-91	420	38	458	45	70	115	573
1991-92	485	12	497	145	52	197	694
1992-93	163	205	368	12	104	116	484
1993-94	424	1	425	88	13	101	526
1994-95	493	7	500	118	9	127	627
1995-96	468	1	469	88	1	89	558
1996-97	332	127	459	6	128	138	597
1997-98	466	3	469	104	15	119	588
1998-99	690	8	698	53	37	90	788

Source: Database on Food situation, 1999, Food Planning and Monitoring Unit (FPMU), Ministry of Food, GOB

The Food for Works and Test Relief programmes utilized 573 thousand and 788 thousand metric tons of foodgrains valued approximately at Tk.4458.72 million and Tk.7404.90 million respectively, during 1990-91 and 1998-99. Under FFW programme about 458 thousand metric tons of foodgrains were distributed in 1990-91 to help the people below hard core poverty line which then rose to 698 thousand metric tons in 1998-99 indicating about 52 per cent increase over the years. This position is unsatisfactory with respect to allocation of foodgrain for Test Relief Programme and the allocation fell from 197 metric tons in 1991-92 to 90 metric tons in 1998-99. Table 8.1 further reveals that the distribution of foodgrains on account of FFW and TR shows a divergent trend. After registering a sharp increase in foodgrain distribution in 1991-92, the volume shows a sharp decline in 1992-93 which is followed by a sharp increase in 1994-95 and 1998-99.

Based on the rates of rice (3.5 kg.) and wheat (5.25 kg.) per day for six hours of labour and the total figures relating to the actual distribution of foodgrains for FFW and TR projects, the employment generated under these programmes have been estimated and shown in Table 8.2.

Table 8.2: Employment Generated Under FFW and TR Projects

Year	*No.of Workdays Generated (million)*
1990-91	119.43
1991-92	130.10
1992-93	121.62
1993-94	101.52
1994-95	120.88
1995-96	106.48
1996-97	137.24
1997-98	122.14
1998-99	154.37

The employment generated under the FFW and TR indicates an absolute fall in the 1992-96 period, with a marked decline in 1993-94 and 1995-96. The decline in employment opportunities during these years is the result of cuts in food aid to Bangladesh over the last few years [Rahman, PK.M (1995) P. 440]. The trend in employment situation may be seen in figure 8.1. According to the official estimate of WFP, a total of 13810 km. roads were created and 378,568 tons of wheat utilized for the road sector between 1990/91 and

Figure 8.1: Employment Generated Under FFW and TR Project

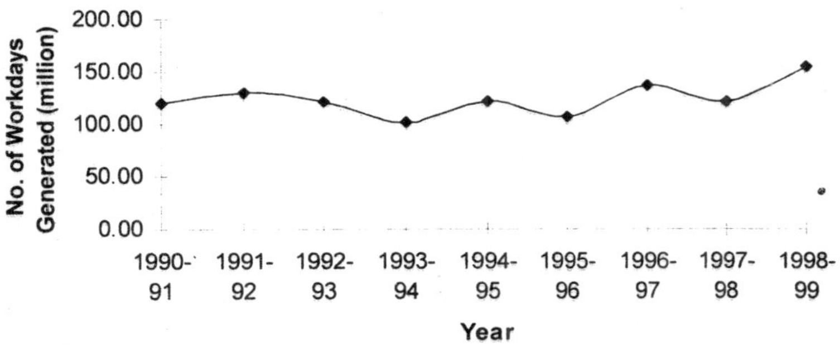

1996/97. The employment generated over this period was 71.62 million of which 15-16 per cent were for females. The progress in employment generation under road sector and achievement in other sectors are shown in Table 8.3. It appears from the table that employment generated under road sector registered an increase during 1990-94 which is then followed by a decrease. However, the highest employment was generated in 1998-99 and shows a very wide variation – from the highest of 17.20 million in 1992-93 to the lowest of 4.58 million workdays in 1996-97. Female employment constituted about 16 per cent of the total employment.

Water Sub-Sector (Bangladesh Water Development Board)

The main objective of the water sub-project is to limit damages caused by floods and improve water

Table 8.3 Achievement in Infrastructure Development and Employment Generated Under Road Sector, 1990/91-1996/97

Year	*No. of schemes imple-mented*	*Wheat distribution (tons) (utilised in scheme and monetized structure)*			*Infrastructure created*					*Workdays generated*	
		Utilized in schemes	*Monetized for structure*	*Total*	*Road (km)*	*Structure (meter)*	*School Grounds Dev. (Nos.)*	*Adarsha Gram Dev. (Nos.)*	*Homesteads Dev. (Nos.)*	*(million)*	*% Women*
1990-91	583	21,606	21,606	31,500	53,106	1,147		57		9.10	15
1991-92	926	29,778	29,778	34,760	64,538	1,844		11		12.00	15
1992-93	1,025	35,294	35,294	66,500	101,794	2.208		36	4	17.20	15
1993-94	1,097	34,574	34,574	24,866	59,440	2,290	155	53	2	14.40	15
1994-95	1,172	38,988	38,988	6,000	44,988	2,093	235	72	3	9.60	19
1995-96	669	23,377	23,377	6,000	29,377	731	305	28	7	4.74	16
1996-97	320	23,325	23,325	2,000	25,325	135	-	-	8	4.58	23
1997-98	387	-	-	-	2465	155	-	-	-	5.3	24
1998-99	558	-	-	-	3246	150	-	-	-	8.5	20

Source: Food Aid Reduces Poverty, WFP, Bangladesh, 1997, Table 21.

supply. This sub-project is also operated by public works and creates employment opportunities on which the poor depend for their livelihood. Several number of schemes have been implemented by the Bangladesh Water Development Board (BWDB) for rehabilitation of embankment and irrigation canals. Besides these, storage tanks have also been excavated by the Department of Public Health for water supply. Table 8.4 shows achievement of projects under BWDB between 1994-95 to 1998-99.

Food Aids to Forestry and Fisheries Sub-Projects

Greater emphasis has been accorded by the GOB to forestry and fisheries sub-projects for self employment generation. The successive plans have also paid due attention to these sub-projects as they essentially play important roles in our socio-economic development. These sub-projects are viable for generation of employment and income for the landless, unemployed youth and destitute women and eventually for poverty alleviation. Recently some NGOs and Private development organizations are involved in group formation, motivation, training of the poor women and marginal farmers. Well designed food assisted development interventions have also been made in both these sub-sectors mainly under the World Food Programme. The forestry sub-project involves road-side and block plantation and maintenance of trees, while construction, rehabilitation and management of inland fish ponds are carried out under the fishery sub-project. Foodgrain is used as wage for the labourers who participate in these activities. The volume of wheat distributed under these sub-projects is shown in Table 8.5.

Table 8.4: Number of Beneficiaries and Employment Generated in Water Sub-Sector

Beneficiaries	*1994-95*	*1995-96*	*1996-97*	*1997-98*	*1998-99*
No. of beneficiaries (earthwork)	184.000	169.000	144.000	185.767	231.661
% female workers (earthwork)	9%	17%	23%	25%	36%
No. of beneficiaries (dev. package)			2.000	30.000	35.000
% female beneficiaries (dev. package)			100%	100%	100%
Wheat earned/beneficiary/day (kg)	5.00	5.00	5.00	4.40	4.13
Cash earned/beneficiary/day (Tk.)				8.25	11.05
Embankments rehabilitated (km)	1.625	1.223	879	51159	6.511
No. of schemes	217	197	214	348	423
No. of workdays generated (million)	20.6	20.6	15.5	15.0	20.2
Canals rehabilitated (km)	1.037	937	879	678	558

Source: Annual Report 1999, World Food Programme, Bangladesh, p. 39.

Table 8.5: Volume of Wheat Distributed in Forestry and Fisheries Sub-Projects, 1990-91 to 1998-99

Year	*Wheat Distributed (in tons)*	
	Forestry	*Fisheries*
1990-91	7,368	8,377
1991-92	12,741	12,604
1992-93	22,860	15,946
1993-94	31,330	15,959
1994-95	41,362	22,619
1995-96	28,445	14,111
1996-97	28,228	12,553
1997-98	15,651	19,603
1998-99	28,608	41,000

Source: *(i)* Food Aid Reduces Poverty, World Food Program, Bangladesh, 1997
(ii) People First, World Food Programme, 1999.

Table 8.5 shows trends in wheat distribution in forestry and fisheries sub-sectors. For both sub-projects there appear to be an increasing trend in volume of wheat distribution during 1990-95, reaching a peak in 1994-95 and then declining in the following years except 1998-99. These projects are mainly dependent upon availability of foodgrains from donor agencies and thus the fluctuation in volume of wheat distribution is attributed to fluctuation in availability of wheat.

Both the sub-projects target the poor and expect to generate incomes by expanding their opportunities for gainful employment. But we have not been able to estimate the total employment effect of such interventions. However, the employment opportunities created under these two sub-projects are presented in Table 8.6.

Table 8.6: Employment Generated Under Forestry and Fisheries Sub-Projects, 1990-91 to 1996-97

Year	*Employment Generated in Forestry*		*Employment Generated in Fisheries*	
	Work days (in million)	*% women*	*Work days (in million)*	*% women*
1990-91	1.58	51	1.80	NA
1991-92	3.82	53	2.70	NA
1992-93	5.35	60	2.80	NA
1993-94	8.05	62	3.50	NA
1994-95	11.90	80	6.10	11
1995-96	8.57	86	2.70	13
1996-97	5.00	83	2.40	19
1997-98	3.3	87	3.2	24
1998-99	2.8	85	2.8	20

Source: *(i)* Food Aid Reduces Poverty, World Food Programme, Bangladesh, 1997, Table 24-27.
(ii) Annual Reports, 1999. World Food Programme, Bangladesh.

The employment opportunities created under forestry sub-sector shows an absolute increase during 1990-95 followed by a sharp decrease during 1995-99 and the share of women was more than 80 per cent between 1994 and 1999. The employment figure for fisheries sub-sector shows more or less the same level, with a marked increase in 1994-95 and the share of women was between 11 to 20 per cent during 1995-99. Thus, these two sub-projects have both income and employment effects, but there is no scientific and organized impact study to determine whether there has been any visible alleviation of poverty through these sub-projects over the period. However, the total volume of wheat distributed for RD projects by source is shown in Table 8.7.

Table 8.7: Volume of Wheat Distributed for RD Projects by Source

Year	*Resources Utilized (in metric tons of wheat or cash equivalent*									
	WFP	*EC*	*EC (IFADEP)*	*Australia*	*Canada*	*France*	*Belgium*	*Germany*	*GOB*	*Total*
1990-91	188755	31709	-	30640	74981	18425	-	5000	-	349510
1991-92	197594	88625	-	26300	76958	672	-	5000	-	395149
1992-93	110813	28167	-	24851	56828	6937	-	6434	-	234030
1993-94	116368	63630	-	25592	-	13045	-	514	-	219149
1994-95	115262	53960	-	28557	10401	15791	-	-	-	223971
1995-96	102681	30505	-	34585	732	23378	3000	-	-	194891
1996-97	84022	17779	-	11985	8785	10959	-	-	-	133530
1997-98**	80240	14160	-	15212	8581	10097	-	-	43310***	171600
1998-99*	89460	45798	25500	29124	19956	16000	-	-	78106***	303944

* Based on current commitments.

** RD Project distributions are as of 30 June 1998. Figures of final utilization not available at time of publication.

*** Cash converted into Wheat equivalent in tons. Includes carrying and contingency costs and support to local Project Implementation Committees.

Vulnerable Group Development (VGD) Programmes

The VGD is one of the largest multidimensional projects which aims at increasing the earning potential and social awareness of the disadvantaged rural women. It started first in 1974 as a relief project but in the 1990s, it was reoriented and its objective shifted from relief to skill development for promoting long-run self-reliance of rural poor women. Under this project, wheat ration amounting to 31.25 kg. per month is given as grant to most disadvantaged rural women, destitute, divorced and abandoned women for one year. Women having undernourished and lactating children and women having handicapped husbands are also targets for VGD project. Distribution of foodgrain from public stock for VGD project is shown in Table 8.8.

Table 8.8: Yearly Distribution of Foodgrain for VGD Project From Public Stock

Year	*Foodgrain distributed ('000' tons)*		
	Rice	*Wheat*	*Total*
1990-91	86	139	225
1991-92	26	204	230
1992-93	56	77	133
1993-94	0	167	167
1994-95	3	181	184
1995-96	0	173	173
1996-97	87	92	179
1997-98	100	129	229
1998-99	12	194	206

Source: Database on Food Situation Bangladesh, June 1999, Food Planning and Monitoring Unit (FPMU), M/O Food.

Besides government stock, direct food aid is also provided under World Food Programme (WFP) to VGD participants to increase their additional resources and to utilize them for food as well as other essential services. Under the VGD project, there are four sub-projects. These are:

(i) Income Generation (IG)

(ii) Women's Training Centre (WTC)

(iii) Group Leaders and Extension Workers (GLEW), and

(iv) Institutional Feeding (IF)

IG Sub-Project

In IG sub-project, an eighteen month ration is provided to women along with "development package" which includes skill development training and functional education. During the first twelve months of cycle, they are also provided with credit for purchasing income generating assets such as livestock, tools etc. The number of beneficiaries in IG sub-project is shown in Table 8.9.

It appears from Table 8.9 that the number of women who received wheat ration under IG sub-project declined by 14 per cent between 1990-91 and 1993-94 and then some increase was observed in the recent year (1998-99). There was a downward trend in the per centage of women who received skill training over the period. The government, multilateral and bilateral resources for IG sub-project amounted to 197,011 tons of wheat in 1990-91, 147,066 tons in 1992-93, 154,152 tons in 1994-95 and 159,565 tons in 1998-99 showing some downward trend by 19 per cent between 1990-91 and 1998-99. This trend may be seen in Table 8.10 and figure 8.2.

Women's Training Centre (WTC) Sub-Project

Under the Women's Training Centre (WTC) sub-project, a twelve month wheat ration is provided to rural

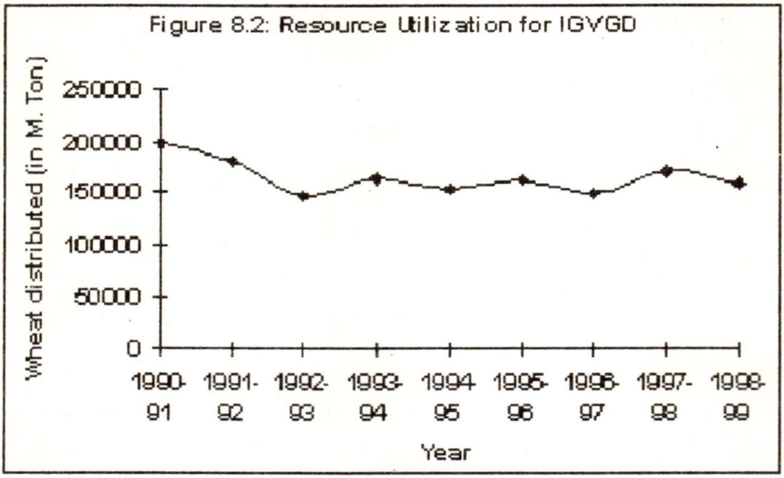

poor women. In addition, training on skill development, health, nutrition, literacy and numeracy are also given to ration receivers through 574 centres operated by the Department of Women's Affairs and NGOs. Food resources distributed for this sub-project amounted to 10,299 tons of wheat in 1990-91, 12,587 tons in 1992-93, 15,328 tons in 1994-95 and 12,124 tons in 1996-97 which exhibits no significant change in any direction. The number of beneficiaries of WTC sub-project is shown in Table 8.11.

As revealed by Table 8.11 there has been substantial increase in number of women who received wheat ration in 1995-96 with drastric fall in 1996-97 and then an increase to 42,052 women in 1998-99. It is also observed that all centres provide skill training to poor women but on the average half of the centres provide training on health, nutrition and education. Three-fourths of the centres provide training on literacy and numeracy. A significant finding which emerges from Table 8.11 is that WTC's development endeavours

Table 8.9: Number of Women in IGVGD Sub-Project from 1990-91 to 1996-97

Year	*Women who received wheat ration*	*Women (%) who participated on Savings Scheme*	*IG Activities*		
			Women (%) who received skills training		*Women (%) who received Credit*
			Poultry	*Other*	
1990-91	441,203	436,791 (99%)	60,439 (81%)	N/A	37,039 (49%)
1991-92	417,384	371,472 (89%)	57,929 (93%)	1,768 (3%)	37,151 (60%)
1992-93	370,907	318,980 (86%)	104,858 (90%)	1,768 (2%)	56,540 (64%)
1993-94	378,505	363,365 (96%)	107,594 (93%)	1,768 (2%)	74,623 (64%)
1994-95	402,970	386,859 (96%)	185,090 (58%)	*28,120 (9%)	79,834 (20%)
1995-96	399,091	397,200 (98%)	*213,210 (53%)		139,281 (35%)
1996-97	458,023	448,800 (98%)	313,846 (46%)		145,690 (32%)
1997-98	450,000	450,000 (100%)	337,500 (75%)		337,500 (-)
1998-99	450,000	450,000 (100%)	296,270 (66%)		169,328 (-)

* Women under BRAC Sericulture (14,390), GLEW (12,500) and EPI (1,230).

Source: Food Aid Reduces Poverty, WFP, Bangladesh, 1997, Table 8

Table 8.10: Resource Utilization for IGVGD

(in tons)

Year	*Wheat distributed and monetized*
1990-91	197,011
1991-92	181,241
1992-93	147,066
1993-94	163,281
1994-95	154,152
1995-96	161,332
1996-97	148,083
1997-98	169,940
1998-99	159,565

Source: *(i)* Food Aid Reduces Poverty, WFP, Bangladesh 1967, Table 7.
(ii) People First, World Food Programme, February, 1999.

revolve around economic emancipation of poor through training on skill development and other social aspects.

Group Leader Extension Workers (GLEW) Sub-project

Food resources are also provided to GLEW workers who are involved in local group formation and awareness raising activities in areas where VGD projects are not available. The number of groups formed, and the number of women in the GLEW groups who received training and credit from 1994-95 to 1998-99 are shown in Table 8.12

During 1994-99, the number of women in the GLEW groups increased by more than two times but the number of female group members that received training for income generation was 4470 in 1998-99 which was only 16 per cent of the total number of members in GLEW Sub-Projects. Moreover, per centage figure of trained

Table 8.11: Number of Women Beneficiaries and Centres in the WTC Sub-Project from 1990-91 to 1996-97

Year	*Number of Centre enrolled*	*Number of women who received wheat ration*	*Per centage of the Centres which*				
			Provided skill terLaining	*Had saving activities*	*Had credit programme*	*Provided health, training on nutrition education*	*Provided literacy and numeracy training*
1990-91	258	29,718	100	69	31	N/A	N/A
1991-92	354	41,426	100	72	31	73	86
1992-93	350	41,177	100	81	43	54	75
1993-94	468	37,128	100	96	50	35	58
1994-95	546	40,908	100	99	46	47	76
1995-96	614	44,150	100	99	70	42	74
1996-97	574	37,537	100	99	62	62	61
1997-98	637	39,855	100	99	70	64	65
1998-99	738	42,052	100	100	60	63	61

Source: (*i*) Food Aid Reduces Poverty, WFP, Bangladesh, 1997, Table 11.
(*ii*) Annual Report, 1999, World Food Programme, Bangladesh.

Table 8.12: Number of Women Under GLEW Sub-Project, 1994-95 to 1998-99

Year	*Number of groups formed*	*Number of group meeting held*	*Average attendance in the meeting*	*Number of women in the GLEW groups*	*Number of women who received training*				*Number of women who received credit*	
					Income generation training		*Other training*			
					Nos.	*(%)*	*Nos.*	*(%)*	*Nos.*	*(%)*
1994-95	500	16,224	19	12,500	1,600	13%	1,350	11%	1,250	10%
1995-96	500	19,971	20	12,500	1,971	16%	771	6%	2,399	19%
1996-97	998	47,200	22	25,000	2,880	12%	1,600	6%	3,500	14%
1997-98	996	39,900	22	24,000	3,220	13%	925	4%	3,500	15%
1998-99	996	39,910	23	28,300	3,550	13%	920	3%	4,450	16%

Source: *(i)* Food Aid Reduces Poverty, WFP, Bangladesh, 1997, Table 16.
(ii) Annual Report, 1999. World Food Programme, Bangladesh.

Table 8.13: IF Centres Donor-Wise Resource Utilization from 1990-91 to 1997-98

Year	*Food utilized (in tons)*								
	WFP			*Canada Wheat*	*FU Wheat*	*Total*			
	Wheat	*Pulses*	*Oil*			*Wheat*	*Pulses*	*Oil*	*All Commodities*
1990-91	5,546	452	244			5,546	452	244	6,242
1991-92	4,082	115	45			4,082	115	45	4,242
1992-93	2,654				2,279	4,933			4,933
1993-94	2,485	276	104		766	3,251	276	404	3,631
1994-95	2,485	298	111	788		3,273	298	111	3,682
1995-96	2,401	151	48	755		3,156	151	48	3,355
1996-97	1,505					1,505			1,505
1997-98	2,021					2,021			2,021

Source: Food Aid Reduces Poverty, WFP, Bangladesh, 1997 Table 13.

women are marked by sharp fluctuations. Similar pattern is also observed in case of proportion of women who received microcredit. A significant finding which emerges from Table 8.12 is that there is a wide gap between the number of group members and the members receiving training and microcredit for income generation.

Institutional Feeding (IF) Sub-Project

Under the IF Sub-Project, food rations (wheat, pulses and oil) were given to residential institutions for vulnerable children by different donor agencies from 1990-91 to 1997-98. Table 8.13 shows a steady decline in quantity of foodgrains distributed over the period. It decreased from 6,242 tons in 1990-91 to 2,021 tons in 1997-98 showing about 68 per cent decline. This decline is, however, largely attributed to a decline in the number of beneficiaries (vulnerable children).

The number of children provided with food ration was marked by a sharp fall between 1990-91 and 1997-98. The decrease ranged from 53,904 children to 22,000 children over the period. But more than 90 per cent of the children were given general education to help them read and write in a manner that was meaningful and practical by all means. But the per centage of centres providing vocational training decreased at a sharper rate after 1995-96 (Table 8.14).

The total volume of wheat distributed for VGD Projects is shown in Table 8.15 and then trend may be seen in Fig. 8.3.

Food for Education Programme (FFEP) in Poverty Alleviation

Illiteracy remains one of the main social problems in Bangladesh. Although considerable progress has been

Table 8.14: Number of Children and Centres in the IF Centres Sub-Project from 1990-91 to 1996-97

Year	*Number of centres*	*Number of children provided with food ration*	*Percentage of children provided with general education*	*Percentage of centres providing vocational training*
1990-91	548	53,904	80	66
1991-92	554	55,123	81	61
1992-93	543	54,248	82	76
1993-94	236	32,634	79	75
1994-95	235	32,584	82	83
1995-96	232	31,159	91	75
1996-97	171	22,000	93	32

Source: Food Aid Reduces Poverty, WFP, Bangladesh, 1997, Table 14.

made during the last decade, literacy rates remain low, particularly for females. Literacy is an important social factor for alleviation of poverty. However, the GOB is committed towards the goal "Education for All" by 2000 set by the international forum. The strategy of universal primary education calls for an increase in enrolment and attendance rates in age group 6-10 and reduction of dropout rates in the primary schools. But many poor parents still cannot send their children to school due to poverty and a large number of enrolled children dropout from school before completion of five-year cycle of primary education and join the labour market as child labourers for earning their livelihood. Therefore, as a current strategy of education for all, the FFEP was designed to attract poor children to schools instead of joining the labour market. Under this programme, a poor family with one child in primary school is entitled to

Table 8.15:: Volume of Wheat Distributed for VGD Project by Source

Year	*Resources Utilized (in metric tons of wheat or cash equivalent)*									
	WFP	*EC*	*EC (IFADEP)*	*Australia*	*Canada*	*France*	*Belgium*	*Germany*	*GOB*	*Total*
1990-91	82849	39042	-	15027	47837	-	4123	5261	21648	215787
1991-92	91248	21600	-	18962	12400	-	-	4940	21682	200832
1992-93	72836	27927	-	20921	22965	7370	-	3665	15163	170847
1993-94	74714	32975	-	19932	22980	3688	-	5976	15603	175868
1994-95	60031	28299	-	19738	20143	5659	-	-	39580	173450
1995-96	58399	11066	-	23813	22321	6673	-	-	59261	181533
1996-97	34242	15102	11220	20325	11620	4622	-	-	65000	162131
1997-98	49484	20477	24551	21648	10097	4886	-	-	60000	197143
1998-99	34900	40000	18750	27747	16409	6000	-	-	60000	203806

Source: People First, World Food Programme, 1999. Table 3, p. 33.

Figure 8.3: Trend in Wheat Distribution for VGD Project

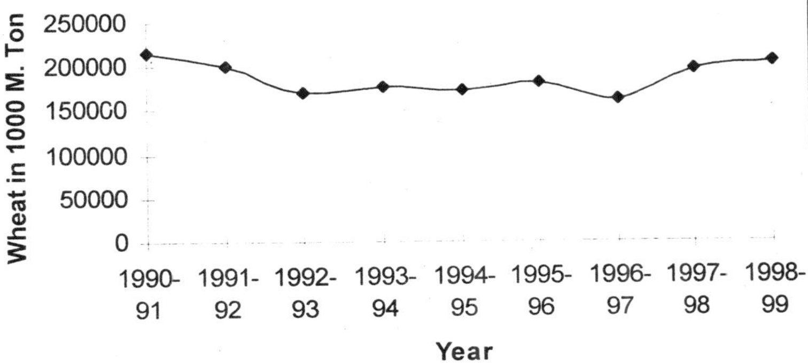

get 15 kg. of wheat or rice of equivalent price and a family with two or more children in school gets 20 kg. per month. For wheat entitlement, every school-aged child should enroll his/her name in primary school and the attendance rate of students should be at least 85 per cent of the total working days in a month. Table 8.16 gives the yearly distribution of foodgrain from public stock for food-for-education programme.

Table 8.16 illustrates the increasing trend in foodgrain distribution for FFEP during 1993-99. The volume of foodgrains distributed increased from 79.5 thousand metric tons in 1993-94 to 286.7 thousand metric tons in 1998-99 indicating about 261 per cent increase over the period. It, however, reached to a peak of 357.7 thousand metric tons in 1997-98. The trend may be seen visually in Fig. 8.4.

As this programme is designed to help the poor and low-income families, it plays an important role in

Table 8.16: Volume of Foodgrain Distributed from Public Stock for FFE Programme

(in 000 in tons)

Year	*Rice*	*Wheat*	*Total*
1993-94	0.2	79.3	79.5
1994-95	6.0	168.5	174.5
1995-96	3.9	237.3	241.2
1996-97	209.6	68.0	277.6
1997-98	71.0	286.7	357.7
1998-99	59.6	227.0	286.7

Source: Database on Food Situation Bangladesh, Food Planning and Monitoring Unit (FPMU), Ministry of Food, June 1999.

Figure 8.4: Volume of Foodgrain Distributed from Public Stock for FFE Program

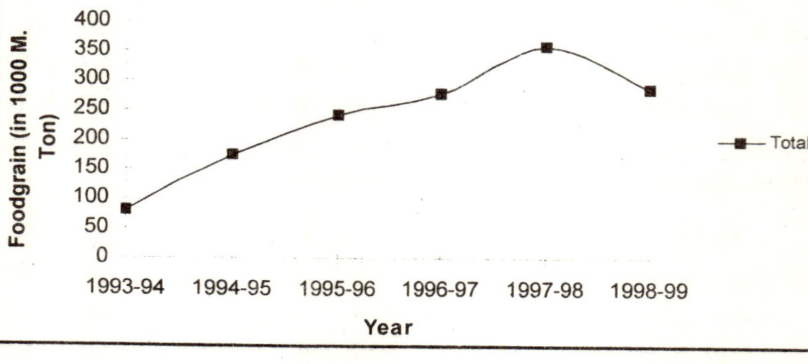

increasing income and thus poverty alleviation. It is also helpful in improving enrolment and attendance rate of students in the FFE-schools. An official estimate of Primary and Mass Education Division (PMED) indicated that annual income of the targeted family with one school children increased by Tk.1470.60 in 1993-94 and by Tk.1807.20 in 1995-96. This figure for two or more children was around Tk.2410.00 per year per family. Thus monthly food aid given to poor families directly help them in improving their level of subsistence and hence their standard of living. In addition to income benefit of target groups, there has been sharp increase in enrolment and attendance in FFE schools. The dropout rate decreased remarkably in these schools [PMED (1996)].The number of beneficiaries along with their income is presented in Table 8.17.

An early evaluation of the programme made by the International Food Policy Research Institute (IFPRI), indicated that the FFEP is highly successful in achieving its objectives in respect of increasing enrolment, attendance rate and reducing dropout rate. The findings of the evaluation have been summarized in Table 8.18.

In addition to economic and social empowerment or benefits, the FFEP generates temporary employment opportunities for the poor. The programme creates extra demand for at least two labourers one for carrying and another for distribution of foodgrains. Thus this programme has both income and employment effects on the poor. However, the volume of temporary employment generated between 1993-94 and 1995-96 is shown in Table 8.19.

The picture that emerges from the above discussions would appear to reflect the following noteworthy features regarding food aided programmes for poverty alleviation. The poor men and women still have limited access to farm employment. Although food aided programmes have created some employment opportunities for them in non-farm activities, these are rudimentary in nature and provide low wages. The impact assessment survey,

Table 8.17: Number of Beneficiaries from FFEP, 1993-94 to 1995-96

Period	*Total families benefited.*			*Total amount distributed*		*Yearly income increased per family*	
	One child family	*Two or more children family*	*Total*	*In terms of wheat (m. tons)*	*In terms of Taka (in Lakh Taka)*	*One-child family (Taka)*	*Two or more children family (Taka)*
1993-94	395640	154241	549881	79661	6506.33	1470.60	2941.20
1994-95	1172634	244298	1416932	177498	18681.88	1807.20	2409.60
1995-96	1685187	277309	1962496	242118	25726.26	1807.20	2409.60

Source: Food for Education Programme, Primary and Mass Education Division, GOB, 1996.

Table 8.18: Changes in Enrolment, Attendance and Dropout Rates

Period	*FFE School*			*Non-FFE Schools*		
	change in enrolment (%)	*Attendance Rate (%)*	*Dropout Rate (%)*	*Change in enrolment (%)*	*Attendance Rate (%)*	*Dropout Rate (%)*
Before (April 1992 To April 1993)	7.7	61.3	18.5	8.6	60.8	17.1
After (April 1993 to April 1994)	28.1	77.6	10.9	6.6	61.0	15.2

Source: PMED, GOB, 1996.

Table 8.19: Employment Generated Under FFEP

Period	*Total No. of distribution centres (Primary level institutions)*	*Total persons employed per month (2 persons per center)*	*Annual labour day (2 prs per centre per month)*	*Total wages earned per annum (Tk. 100.00 per person per month)*	*Per Capita wages earned per annum (Tk. 100.00 per month)*
1993-94	4914	9828	117936	11793600.00	1200.00
1994-95	12182	24364	292368	29236800.00	1200.00
1995-96	16159	32318	387816	38781600.00	1200.00

Source: PMED, GOB, 1996.

however, demonstrates higher incomes, higher savings and higher social empowerment for the beneficiary group as compared to the non-beneficiary group. However, it fails to provide any satisfactory insight regarding income transformatory effect on poverty alleviation and the number of poor that have successfully moved out of the poverty line. It seems that food distribution, as well as credit operation alone does not satisfactorily address the whole problem of poverty alleviation.

An important question that needs to be answered is whether or not the economic empowerment achieved through the various food aided programmes is sustainable without further intervention. Different evaluation studies have provided only vague and partial information in this regard. One such study is the impact evaluation study report on third round of longitudinal survey series, which followed a cohort of women who participated in the VGD programme in 1992-93. This survey was conducted in 1996, which was two years after the completion of the VGD cycle. The findings of this report showed that the calorie intake level in 1996 was lower than the 1994 level. This programme was undertaken with the hope that VGD members would continue to engage in their savings scheme even after the VGD cycle was terminated. But in contrast, the survey revealed that VGD members closed their bank accounts soon after the VGD cycle was over (WFP, 1997). Such findings seem to cast doubt on the sustainability of long-term benefits of food aided programmes. However, it goes without saying that the food aided programmes are successful in reaching out to the target group.

Apart from the food aided safety net programme, the government has taken up some special safety net programmes for poverty alleviation of the landless and homeless, distressed widows, poor women abandoned by their husbands and unemployed youth. These are (i) Boyoska Vata (old age Pension), (ii) Grihayan Tahbil (Housing Fund), (iii) Asrayan (Shelter for the homeless) and (iv) Karma Sangsthan Bank (Employment Bank). An amount of Tk.260 million and Tk.500 million was allocated in the revised budget of 1997-98 and 1998-99 for Boyoska Vata, while Tk.500 million in 1997-98 and Tk.80 million in 1998-99 were allocated for Grihayan Tahbil. For Asrayan project, about Tk.100 million was fixed as expenditure for the period 1997-98 to 2001-2002. Karma Sangsthan Bank provides microcredit to unemployed youth for creation of productive employment particularly in the field of cottage industry, poultry, dairy farm etc. This project was started in September 22, 1998 and up to March 2000, about Tk.56.6 million was distributed as microcredit. However, the recovery rate was only 66 per cent. The number of beneficiaries during this period was 1369 in 24 districts [BER (2000)]. But the main weakness of the special safety net programmes is that they failed to recognize the potential of the poor as a productive force. The idea and practice of poverty alleviation as an act of charity has to be changed and replaced by recognition of the fact that the poor themselves can be an important factor in development. The prime objective of any viable poverty alleviation programme should be to mobilize the poor masses so as to bring them into the mainstream of the economic development process.

9

Formal Sector Micro Finance Institutions in Poverty Alleviation

Introduction

The idea of Micro Finance (MF) for poverty alleviation has originated from the concept that access to MF for livelihood is a human right and this idea has been accepted internationally. In recognition of the importance of microfinance for poverty alleviation a World Summit on MF was also held in Washington D.C. in February 1997 to glorify its merits to the world leaders. And subsequently there was a call for mobilisation of $20 billion as microcredit among the poor developing nations as well as poverty stricken areas of developed countries [Asaduzzaman, M. (1999)]. The provision of micro finance has been made with the hope that it would help generate income for poverty alleviation through creation of self-employment opportunities. Micro finance in this regard is recognised as an effective policy for poverty alleviation in most of the developing nations, particularly in the South Asian region. The main feature of MF is that it is collateral free and the landless poor can easily avail it for their socio-economic development.

The government of Bangladesh has also been giving emphasis on the MF support to the poor through NGOs and rural banks for rural economic development in general, and poverty alleviation in particular. Two government owned specialised banks such as the Bangladesh Krishi Bank (BKB) and Rajshahi Krishi Unnayan Bank (RAKUB) and four nationalised commercial banks (BCBs) such as Sonali Bank, Agrani Bank, Janata Bank and Rupali Bank have stepped into the sphere of micro financing by providing MF support to various programmes/projects for poverty alleviation. So far, these banks finance as many as 69 programmes/ projects under the micro finance schedule with their own sources and funds provided by the Central banks as well as different donar agencies. Of the total 69 programmes/ projects, 65 are still in operation and the rest 4 have been completed on the expiry of their project period [Sohrabuddin, M. (1999)]. In the present context 2 specialised banks and 4 nationalised commercial banks are considered as formal sector micro finance institutions (MFIs) and these banks constitute the main sources of formal sector micro financing in Bangladesh. A few other institutions such as Private Commercial Banks (PCBs) also belong to the formal sector. Of all the PCBs, Islamic Bank of Bangladesh Ltd. has a special credit scheme under the title of Small Business Investment Project (SBIP) for poverty alleviation. But the PCBs have not been taken under the preview of the analysis due to non-availability of data and insignificant contribution to the micro-finance programmes/projects. Thus the analysis in this chapter is confined to two specialised and four nationalised commercial banks.

Household Expenditure Survey (HES), 1995-96 indicated that the major share of household income (64%) is spent on food items and 35 per cent of the total income in rural areas comes from agriculture sector.

These phenomena indicate a hardship of life. Since agriculture is the main source of rural income, its growth is likely to have direct bearing on poverty alleviation in rural areas. Thus recognising the importance of agriculture in the rural economy, commercial and agricultural banks provide institutional credit mainly for financing the cost of modern agriculture (seed, fertilizer and irrigation) and to some extent for non-farm activities such as fisheries, livestock, rural transport, small scale industries etc. The credit operations by the two specialised and three national commercial banks except Rupali Bank are briefly described below. Reliable and detailed information regarding Rupali Bank's microcredit was not available and thus it was not considered in the analysis.

Role of Formal Sector Micro Finance Institution for Poverty Alleviation

Sonali Bank

Sonali Bank is the largest commercial bank in the country and it provides a huge amount of microcredit to rural poor to improve agricultural production and to undertake various income generating activities particularly by the small entrepreneurs. Upto December 1999, a cumulative amount of Tk.35,317.8 million was disbursed by the rural branch of Sonali bank to nearly 5.97 million beneficiaries [BER (2000), p.119].

The major programmes/projects of Sonali bank for poverty alleviation are (a) Rural Poor Co-operative Project (RPCP), (b) Integrated Rural Women Development (IRWD), and (c) Agro Based Micro Enterprise (ABME). The RPCP was started in 1994 and it is jointly funded by the Sonali Bank and the ADB.

An amount of Tk.2428.50 million has been disbursed without collateral since its inception. This project aims at creating exployment opportunities for rural landless poor men and women by providing credit as well as skill development training to them. This project has been implemented in 82 thanas of greater Rajshahi, Pabna, Kustia and Jessore [Sohrabuddin, M. (1999)].

The Integrated Rural Women Development project was started in 1980 and it is run by Sonali Bank's own fund. So far an amount of Tk.807.60 million has been disbursed with interest rate of 8 per cent and the average loan size is estimated at Tk.7000.00. This project is a remarkable intervention for poverty alleviation through the creation of gainful employment opportunities for women.

In order to promote agro-based micro industries in the country, the agro-based enterprise project was initiated in 1993 with funding from Sonali Bank. An amount of Tk.484.70 million has been disbursed among the beneficiaries without collateral but at an interest rate of Tk.13.75 per cent. Besides these projects, there are other important projects known as BARD-Sanali Bank Functional Research Project and RDA-Sonali Bank Functional Research Projects. These projects started in 1994. Some selected thana of Comilla, Narayanganj and Sylhet districts were under BARD-Sonali Bank Project, while some selected thana of Bogra, Gaibandha, Jhenaidah and Kustia were under the RDA-Sonali Bank Project [Khan, M.H. (1997)].

Janata Bank

There are several microcredit programmes/projects of Janata Bank for poverty alleviation among which

(a) Small Farmers and Landless Labourers Development Project (SFDP), (b) Co-operative Credit for Rural Poor (CCRP) and (c) Marginal and Small Farm System Crop Intensification Project (MSFSCIP) are important. These programmes/projects are mainly financed by the Janata Bank. The SFDP was started in 1976 in collaboration with BRDB. At present the coverage of the project has been extended to 51 thanas of 7 districts – Comilla, Bogra, Mymensingh, Barisal, Borguna, Patuakhali and Bhola. Under this credit programme, group guarantee and group savings are taken as collateral and credits are sanctioned by the branch managers on the basis of the plan submitted by the group. The average size of the loan per member ranges between Tk.3,000 and Tk.10,000 depending on the nature of the activities. The main objectives of the project are to increase production, employment and income of small farmers and landless labourers through various income generating activities (IGAs). So far, 70,914 rural poor members have enrolled and received Tk.259.33 million as credit [Khan, M.H.(1997)].

The co-operative credit programme for rural poor was initiated in 1980 for employment generation of the co-operative members through different income generating activities. The programme was launched in three districts, namely, Noakhali, Luxmipur and Feni. It is implemented by Janata Bank in association with the BRDB. The credit is disbursed to co-operative group members for farm and non-farm activities through their central association (Thana Central Co-operative Association – TCCA). The average loan size is found to be Tk.5000 at beneficiary level depending on the nature of activities.

The MSFSCIP credit scheme has been in operation since 1991 in the district of Kurigram. This project was designed to prevent further landlessness and marginalisation of the poor farm households by improving of their on-farm and off-farm activities and productivities. Upto 1996 this scheme was run by the Department of Agriculture Extension in collaboration with an NGO called Rangpur Dinajpur Rural Service (RDRS), while German Technical Cooperation (GTC) provided technical support to the target groups. Now it is fully run with support from the Janata Bank [Sohrabuddin, M. (1999)].

Agrani Bank

The Productive Employment Project (PEP), the Marginal and Small Farm Systems Crop Intensification Project (MSFSCIP), Small Enterprises Development Project (SEDP) and the Netrokona Integrated Agricultural Production and Water Management Projects (NIAPWMP) are the major micro credit programmes of Agrani Bank for poverty alleviation.

The Productive Employment Project (PEP) was launched by the Agrani Bank in collaboration with the BRDB. The financial assistance was made from Swedish International Development Agency (SIDA) and Norwegian Agency for Development corporation (NORAD). Initially this project was implemented in six thanas of Faridpur and Kurigram districts and gradually it has expanded in all thanas of those two districts. The main objective of this project was to improve the socio-economic condition of the rural poor through provision of skill development training, training for raising awareness and providing credit facilities. Daridra

Bimochon Karmasuchi (DABIK) was also implemented by the Bank's own initiative for poverty alleviation [Khan, M.H. (1997)].

The MSFSCIP was undertaken by the Bank in 1991 in collaboration with Bangladesh Bank, RDRS, GTZ and IFAD. This project has now been extended in 9 thanas of Kurigram district with the primary objective to establish a sustainable relationship between the Self Help Groups (SHG) and the Bank. Credit facilities are provided to Self-help groups for collective as well as individual activities in the form of Seasonal Agricultural Loan (SAL), Agricultural Investment Loan (AIL) and Non-Agricultural Investment Loan (NAIL). Maximum ceiling of loan was Tk.8000.0 at individual level, while it was Tk.80,500.0 at collective level. Upto December 1998, a total of Tk.50.88 million was disbursed among 3189 borrowers at the interest rate of 14 per cent [Sohrabuddin, M. (1999)].

The Small Enterprises Development Project (SEDP) was initiated in May 1995 by the Bank in association with NORAD. Under this project the credit facilities have been extended in 40 thanas of greater Faridpur and Mymensingh districts. The main objective of the project is to improve the socio-economic conditions of the people in the project areas through self-employment generation. The components of micro-enterprises are rice mill, nursery, repairing workshop, hatchery, fishery, weaving, handicrafts etc. About Tk. 325.78 million have been disbursed to 12929 entrepreneurs upto December 1998 [Sohrabuddin, M. (1999)].

There is another Agrani-IFAD co-sponsored project called 'Netrokona Integrated Agricultural Production and

Water Management Project (NIAPWM)' in Netrokona district. This project has been designed to improve the standard of living of the small and marginal farmers in general and women in particular. An amount of Tk. 100.0 million will be disbursed over the next five years of the project period to the target group members for purchasing seeds, fertilizers, agricultural equipment and minor irrigation pumps etc. Under this programme the bank extends its services directly to the target group members as well as through some selected NGOs. As of June 1999 an amount of Tk.5.6 million and Tk.13.10 million have been disbursed through banks and six selected NGOs respectively to the target group members [Sohrabuddin, M. (1999)].

Bangladesh Krishi Bank (BKB)

There are 16 microcredit programmes which are run by the BKB for poverty alleviation. Out of these 16 programmes, 6 are for non-crop activities such as goat rearing, cow fattening etc., 5 for non-farm activities such as processing, manufacturing, trade and commerce, cottage industries, construction and small income generating activities, and 5 for both types of activities. However, the major programmes/projects of Bangladesh Krishi Bank (BKB) are (i) Landless and Marginal Farmers Credit programme (LMFCP), (ii) Swanirvar Credit Programme (SCP), (iii) Small Holders Livestock Development Project (SHLDP), (iv) BKB-ADP assisted Rural Women Employment Creation Project (RWECP), and (v) Employment Programmes for Educated and Training Youth. The LMFCP has been implemented in 49 districts of the country and credits are given from BKB's own fund in the field of processing, manufacturing, Homestead Agriculture, Small and

Cottage Industries etc. Almost Tk.1865 million has been disbursed upto June 1999 among 2,48,082 members without collateral but with an interest rate of 12 per cent per annum.

The coverage of Swanirvar credit programme has extended in 31 districts. Collateral free credit is provided from BKB's own fund in the field of Processing, Manufacturing, Homestead Agriculture, Trade and Commerce, Small and Cottage industries etc. As of June 1999, an amount of Tk. 525.0 million has been disbursed among 84117 members at the annual interest rate of 17 per cent.

The SHLDP is funded by IFAD in 16 districts. BRAC and PROSHIKA are two executing agencies of the project. An amount of Tk.17.0 million has been disbursed upto June 1999 among 196442 members without collateral. The rate of interest is 15 per cent [Sohrabuddin, M. (1999)].

The ADB-assisted Project for employment generation for rural women has been implemented in 12 thanas of the country upto 1996 since 1993. The main aim of this project is to create employment opportunities for target groups through the interventions of local NGOs [Khan, M.H. (1997), p.216].

Rajshahi Krishi Unnayan Bank

This bank also plays a very important role in poverty alleviation through organising rural poor, and by imparting training to the target groups as well as providing collateral free credit to them. There are several programmes/projects under this bank among which (i) Swanirvar Credit programme (SCP), (ii) Women

Entrepreneurship Development Programme (WEDP) and (iii) RAKUB self-help credit Programme (RSCP) are important.

The Sawnirvar Credit Programme has been implemented in 28 thanas of 9 districts – Pabna, Joypurhat, Natore, Rangpur, Kurigram, Nilphamari, Gaibandha, Thakurgaon and Panchagarh. An amount of Tk.5000.0 is provided to each member of the target group without collateral for activities like processing of agricultural produces, horticulture and forestry, fishing and livestock, service oriented items and rural trading etc. The interest rate of credit is 11 per cent per annum.

The WEDP has been implemented in 8 districts – Rangpur, Dinajpur, Gaibandha, Rajshahi, Natore, Pabna, Sirajgonj and Joypurhat – for the development of women. Credits are provided to women without collateral for non-farm activities such as cottage industries, handicrafts etc. However, the interest rate is 16 per cent.

The RSCP has been undertaken in 15 districts of Rajshahi Division except Kurigram. Thus the coverage of this programme is very large but confined within the Rajshahi Division only as this bank was established to cater to the needs of this particular division. Groups consisting of 8 to 12 members are formed for males and females separately and they are mainly composed of landless, marginal and small farmers. After group formation, the group members deposit their weekly savings regularly for six months for getting entitlement to apply for loans. Under this programme, credits are provided by the bank for activities such as crop production, livestock, fish culture, irrigation, orchard, poultry farming, small trading, rice husking etc. The average size of loan per group member ranges between Tk.2000.0 and Tk.10000.0 and the interest rate is 16 per cent per annum. The status of microcredit disbursed by four nationaled scheduled banks and two specialised banks are shown in Table 9.1. It is observed that upto December 1999 about Tk.63956.0 million was disbursed to 10.24 million beneficiaries.

Linkage Effects Associated with the Institutional Credit and Growth Performance of Agriculture

Access to institutional credit for agricultural development through technological transformation and increasing production could not make a significant contribution to the growth performance in this sector.

As revealed by Table 9.2 there has been a substantial expansion of credit for agricultural development between 1990-91 and 1998-99. It increased from Tk.5956.0 million in 1990-91 to Tk.32453.6 million in 1998-99 showing nearly five times increase. Sharp increase has, however, taken place after 1993-94. A significant finding which emerges from the same table is that more than 60 per cent of the total credit on agriculture is provided by the specialised banks such as Bangladesh Krishi Bank and Rajshahi Krishi Unnayan Bank, while the nationalised commercial banks provide nearly one-third of the total credit. Contribution of private banks in this sphere is insignificant. A particularly noteworthy and alarming finding is that only 8-10% of the total credit has been given to the poor marginal farmers (upto 0.50 acres) indicating that the distribution of credit has been uneven among the groups, benefiting mainly medium and large farmers (Table 9.3).

Table 9.1: Status of Micro-Credit Disbursement by Nationalized Scheduled Bank and Specialized Bank

(Tk.in million)

Scheduled Bank	*Cumulative amount of credit disbursed upto June 1996*	*1996-1997*	*1997-1998*	*1998-1999*	*1999-2000*	*Cumulative amount of credit disbursed upto December 1999*
1	2	3	4	5	6	7
Sonali Bank:						
Amount disbursed	25556.5	2582.7	2949.3	2554.8	1674.5	35317.8
No.of Beneficiaries	4028000	382000	730000	500000	334900	5974900
Agrani Bank:						
Amount disbursed	5653.2	714.6	1001.8	1957.5	647.7	9327.1
No.of Beneficiaries	2192478	95604	114723	240600	135530	2778935
Janata Bank:						
Amount disbursed	8953.1	1259.1	950.6	1422.1	466.4	13051.3
No.of Beneficiaries	247168	40200	28775	25670	19705	361518

(Table Contd...)

Table 9.1: Contd...

1	*2*	*3*	*4*	*5*	*6*	*7*
Rupali Bank:						
Amount disbursed	166.5	5.3	4.8	8.6	3.3	188.5
No.of Beneficiaries	-	-	-	-	-	-
BKB:						
Amount disbursed	1597.9	834.5	983.0	1444.3	629.1	5488.8
No.of Beneficiaries	538445	60451	16924	376638	58983	1051441
Rajshahi Krishi Unnayan Bank:						
Amount disbursed	246.4	61.1	68.5	109.1	97.0	580.0
No.of Beneficiaries	34394	7323	7480	9778	17743	76718
Total:						
Amount disbursed	42173.6	5457.3	5958.0	7496.4	3518.0	63955.5
No. of Beneficiaries	7040485	585578	897902	1152686	566861	10243512

Source: Bangladesh Economic Review, 2000, p.119.

Table 9.2: Amount of Credit Disbursed for Agricultural Development,1990-91 to 1998-99

(Fig. in million)

Year	*Total credit disbursed by different banks*	*Credit disbursed by NCB*	*Credit disbursed by specialised banks*	*Private banks*	*BSBL and BRDB*
1990-91	5956.0	1786.6	3612.3	35.0	522.1
1991-92	7945.9	2670.6	5.34.9	36.3	204.1
1992-93	8418.6	2588.7	5638.5	37.8	153.5
1993-94	11007.9	3452.6	7423.4	-	131.9
1994-95	16054.4	4571.3	9580.9	1150.6	751.6
1995-96	16358.2	4378.4	9510.4	1341.9	927.8
1996-97	16724.3	4466.2	9580.6	1551.3	1126.2
1997-98	18145.3	4436.5	10576.3	1716.9	1415.6
1998-99	32453.6	7377.7	19068.4	2394.4	3613.1

Source: Scheduled Banks Statistics, Bangladesh Bank, Jan-March, 1997 and July-Sept, 1998.

Table 9.3: Agricultural Credit Disbursed to Marginal Farmers

(Fig. on credit in million Tk)

Year	*Total credit disbursed by banks*	*Credit disbursed to marginal (upto 0.5 acres) farmers*	*Credit to marginal farmers as % of total disbursement*
1990-91	5956.0	572.0	9.60
1991-92	7945.9	663.0	8.34
1992-93	8418.6	890.0	1057
1993-94	11007.9	797.0	7.24
1994-95	16054.4	1190.0	7.41
1995-96	16358.2	831.0*	-
1996-97	16724.3	-	-
1997-98	18145.3	-	-

* From June-December, 1995.

Source: *(i)* Scheduled Bank Statistics, Bangladesh Bank,January-March,1997, Pp. 148-152.

(ii) Bangladesh Economic Review, 1996. MoF, p.84.

Thus the share of the marginal farmers in total credit disbursed is substantially lower than their share in farm population.

In short, the Banking Institutions play an important role in economic development of the country by providing institutional credit to the development programmes, and a number of policy measures have been taken up for economic development in the desired direction. The nationalised, specialised and private banks have attached some priority to rural credit with the primary objective of attaining agricultural development as well as poverty alleviation. Recognizing the importance of agriculture in the economy, the banking sector provides credit mainly for financing the cost of modern agriculture (seed, fertilizer, and irrigation) and to some extent for non-farm activities such or fisheries, livestocks, rural transport, small scale industries etc. But the development of this sector is essential for the economic development of the country and for alleviation of rural poverty. In view of the agricultural transformation and developments in rural economy, commercial and agricultural banks in the rural areas provide institutional credit to the farmers. Thus the banks seem to be the most suitable financial institutions that play the pivotal role in carrying out the task of development of the rural economy as well as poverty alleviation.

What Has Happened to Output of Main Crops and Wage Rate

The credit for agriculture and irrigation was designed to raise the output of foodgrains and to raise the income of landless through creation of extra demand for labour in this sector and thereby increasing wage rates. But the wage rate is a function of demand for and supply of labour. The demand for labour is, however, determined by the level of output and technology in use, while the supply depends largely on the growth of population. The situation with respect to growth of food production, average yield of major crops, employment generation and wage rate of labour in this sector is far from flattering both in absolute and relative terms. The available figures on these aspects are a clear indication of the depressed conditions of agriculture in Bangladesh. The total rice production increased from 17.86 million tons in 1990-91 to 23.07 million tons in 1999-2000 showing about 3.2 per cent increase per annum. During the same period, the total foodgrain production increased from 18.86 million tons to 24.90 million tons indicating about 3.5 per cent increase per annum [Table 9.4].

It is discouraging to note that the growth of agriculture sector is very slow and show a divergent trend. Decline in production in 1993-94 and 1994-95 lowered agricultural growth. However the growth performance of agriculture and its sub-sector is shown in Table 9.5.

Table 9.5 reveals that the rates of agricultural growth were fairly low and it registered a decline in 1993-94 and 1994-95. The growth rate of food crops showed a marked negative growth since 1994-95 with highest positive growth in 1996-97.

Employment in this sector increased only at the rate of 0.6 per cent, while the population growth rate during the same period was estimated at 1.90 per cent. Moreover, the pace of generation of employment opportunities seemed to have lagged behind the growth in labour force.

The rural non-farm and industrial sectors also did not grow at a rate sufficiently high enough to absorb the surplus labour from the agriculture sector. At the same time the mechanisation of agriculture tended to slacken the growth of demand for labour. As a result, significant increase in the index of real wages of agricultural labourers could not be achieved. Table 9.6 show and Figure 9.1 show the trend in real wage index of agricultural labour from 1990-91 to 1998-99. It shows only 2 per cent increase in 1998-99 compared to 1969-60.

The position of real wage index of agriculture labour is equally unsatisfactory with respect to its increase due

Table 9.4: Total Foodgrains Production, 1990-91 to 1999-2000

(Fig. in million ton)

Foodgrain	*1990-1991*	*1991-1992*	*1992-1993*	*1993-1994*	*1994-1995*	*1995-1996*	*1996-1997*	*1997-1998*	*1998-1999*	*1999-2000*
Aus	2.33	2.18	2.07	1.85	1.79	1.68	1.87	1.87	1.62	1.73
Aman	9.17	9.27	9.68	9.42	8.50	8.79	9.55	8.85	7.74	10.30
Boro	6.36	6.80	6.59	6.77	6.54	7.22	7.46	8.14	10.55	11.04
Total rice	17.86	18.25	18.34	18.04	16.83	17.69	18.88	18.86	19.91	23.07
Wheat	1.00	1.07	1.18	1.13	1.25	1.37	1.45	1.80	1.91	1.83
Total foodgrain	18.86	19.32	19.52	19.17	18.08	19.06	20.34	20.66	21.81	23.63
(%) change	(0.6)	(2.4)	(1.0)	(-1.8)	(-5.7)	(5.4)	(6.7)	(1.6)	(5.6)	(14.16)

Source: Bangladesh Economic Review, 2001, Table 7.3, p.49.

Table 9.5. Growth Performance in Agriculture Sector and Agriculture Sub-Sectors (%) at Constant (Base:1995-96) Price

Year	*Agricultural growth (%)*	*Growth in sub-sector (%)*			
		Crop	*Fisheries*	*Live stock*	*Forestry*
1990-91	1.2	0.8	7.9	2.3	3.2
1991-92	1.4	1.1	8.2	2.3	2.3
1992-93	1.4	1.0	8.5	2.4	3.0
1993-94	-0.7	-1.7	7.9	2.4	2.8
1994-95	-1.9	-3.4	6.8	2.5	2.8
1995-96	2.0	1.7	7.4	2.5	3.5
1996-97	5.6	6.4	7.6	2.6	4.0
1997-98	1.6	1.1	9.0	2.6	4.5
1998-99	3.3	3.2	10.0	2.7	5.2
1999-00	5.5	8.1	8.9	2.7	6.9

Source: Bangladesh Economic Review, 2001, p. 47.

Table 9.6: Real Wage Indices of Agricultural Labour (Base 1969/70=100)

Year	*Real wage index of agriculture*
1990-91	95
1991-92	98
1992-93	105
1993-94	106
1994-95	103
1995-96	104
1996-97	109
1997-98	107
1998-99	102

Source: Bangladesh Economic Review, 2000, Ministry of Finance, Table 12, p.141.

Figure 9.1: Real Wage indices of Agricultural Labour

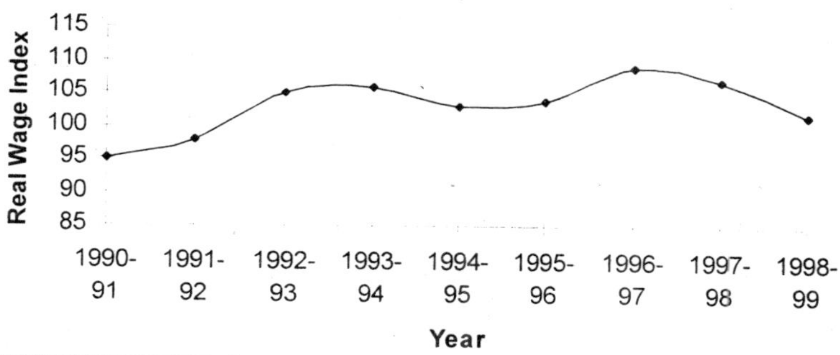

to credit operation in agriculture sector. However, available data relating to food production, creation of job opportunities, increase in wage rate of agriculture labour indicated limited impact of agricultural credit on these indicators as well as poverty reduction. As for the small and marginal farmers, increasing agricultural credit does not favour them as they have limited access to it. The indirect effect of modern technology (fertilizer, mechanised irrigation, power tiller, weeding machine etc.) could not favour the rural poor, since the effect of demand for inputs such as fertilizer, pesticides, power tiller etc., is transmitted to urban areas where these inputs are produced.

During the distribution of agricultural credit, the number of landless agricultural labourers, marginal and small farmers was not given any significant consideration. As a result, favourable impact on the economic condition of poor farmers could not be achieved. As the impact of the programmes are evaluated on the basis of total cost or total amount of credit disbursed and total benefit in terms of total food production, effect of programmes on the poor tend to be ignored. Furthermore, because of difficulties of measurement, many of the displacement effects are not taken into consideration. The distributional aspect of costs and benefits, therefore, should not be ignored by the policy makers and planners while preparing any credit operation plan for economic development of the poor. Available information from different sources on incidence of poverty do not show a significant impact of the credit operation on poverty alleviation.

The success of most of the bank's credit programmes are evaluated mainly by high recovery rate, savings, repayment of weekly installments etc. But performance in respect of creation of employment opportunities for rural poor, increase in crop production, rate of return from investment of micro-credit in different activities, skill development, the number of borrowers moving out of poverty and in how much time, etc. has not been examined. In the absence of such information, it is difficult to claim that the bank's microcredit programmes are successful in alleviating rural poverty.

10

Agricultural Development and Poverty Reduction

Introduction

The government through its line Ministries such as the Ministry of Local Government Rural Development and Cooperatives, Ministry of Women and Children Affairs, Ministry of Social Welfare, Ministry of Fisheries and Livestock etc. and the decentralized state agencies provide financial and support services to activities related to poverty alleviation. But the Ministry of Agriculture can play a more vital role in improving the economy of Bangladesh by helping to alleviate rural poverty. Agriculture should be introduced as a priority area since it is the largest sector of the economy accounting for about 32 per cent (FY 98) of GDP and 8 per cent of the total export earnings [BER (2000)]. This sector provides about 63 per cent of the total rural employment. Although the contribution of agriculture to GDP has been declining, its contribution to employment, achievement of self-sufficiency in food, fulfillment of nutritional demand, overall economic development and reduction of rural poverty still remains high. A large number of people (about 103.02 million), most of which are poor, live in rural areas and about 65.0 million of them depend in one way or another on agriculture for their income and employment. More than 35 per cent of the total number of rural households depend on agriculture labour. Millions of rural households have only between 0.01 to 0.49 acres of land. Under the present cultivation methods, this size of land is not sufficient to feed a family or to provide farm employment for all family members. The early strategies for poverty alleviation through growth and trickle down process did not respond to the rural reality. Thus the landless and small farm households have to depend on seasonal farm works and non-farm activities for their survival. About 75 per cent of them are estimated to obtain less than the minimum calorie requirement (2122 kcal.) thus suffering from malnutrition. Keeping these in view, Tk.21425.38 million has been allocated for the crop sub-sector in the Fifth Five Year Plan. The important objectives envisaged in this plan include attainment of self-sufficiency in food production to ensure food security, increase in production of nutritious crops to ensure stable supply of nutrition for the people, etc. Increase in agricultural production may help improve nutritional status which is eventually necessary to increase the productive capacity of the poor [ADP (1999)]. As a strategy for achieving these objectives, the government has also taken up certain programmes which include HYV seed production and distribution, expansion of irrigation facilities, crop diversification, introduction of mechanization and extension of other support services. Increase in agricultural production through spread of new technology can increase the aggregate volume of the marketable surplus which will lead to enhanced demand for trade, better transport and service sector employment and this increase may be further reinforced by linkage effects through demand spillovers to local markets. All these phenomena appear to have been effective for poverty reduction [BIDS]. Intensification of agriculture sector is essential for employment and income generation of the rural poor. Rural construction, personal services, manufacturing, non-farm activities etc. are the major channels through which the poor may benefit from agricultural development.

Agrarian Structure

Agricultural Economy and Its Structural Changes

Agricultural structure is one of the important factors for economic development and reduction of rural poverty. The concept of agricultural structure varies widely from one expert to another. Some of the experts have defined it as a net-work of relations among various groups of persons whose livelihood depends on agricultural activities. It also encompasses the land tenure system, ownership pattern, system under which land is operated and its product is shared between tenant and land owner, etc. [Momin, M.A. (1992)].

Structure of agricultural economy has been changing rapidly and it is now more diversified than before. The crop sub-sector is gradually loosing ground while the other sub-sectors such as forestry, livestock and fisheries are gradually gaining more importance in the agricultural economy. The share of crop sub-sector in agricultural value added was 80 per cent in 1973-74 and it declined to 71.5 per cent in 1989-90, 57.8 per cent in 1998-99 and further reduction is expected in future. The projected share is 47 per cent in 2020. The share of livestock, fisheries and forestry sub-sectors was only 20 per cent in 1973-74 and it increased to 28.5 per cent in 1989-90 and 42.2 per cent in 1998-99 [Table 10.1]. These figures indicate that structural change has occurred having accelerated during the 1990s. However, the crop sub-sector still dominates the agricultural economy. But the non-crop sub-sectors are the dominant factors behind the growth of agriculture sector. The improved performance of non-crop sub-sectors is essential for improvement in the livelihood of the poor households by expanding self-employment opportunities. This is because, the crop sub-sector is much more land-intensive than the non-crop sub-sectors and land is scarce and unevenly distributed. Thus we must recognize the importance of the non-crop sub-sectors, for achieving higher growth in agriculture as well as for alleviating poverty [Hossain, M. (2000)].

Table 10.1: Structural Transformation of the Agriculture Sector, 1973-74 to 1998-99

(Per cent share of agricultural incomes)

Sub-sectors	*1973-74*	*1989-90*	*1998-99*	*2020(P)*
Crops	80.0	71.5	57.8	47.0
Forestry	4.2	9.8	10.9	11.8
Livestock	7.6	9.3	12.9	19.9
Fisheries	8.2	9.5	18.4	21.3
Total	100	100	100	100

Source: Hossain, M. CPD-IRDB 2000; Agriculture, Table 1.

Agriculture Census Report-1996 offers the following senerio regarding the dynamics of population in the recent past. High population growth leads to splitting up of holdings as well as land size. This phenomenon results in further fragmentation, increase in the number of holdings, increase in agricultural land under homestead area and simultaneously decreases the area under cultivation. It also accelerates landlessness is also accelerated because small holders cannot survive on their land and hence they are forced to sell their land. Table 10.2 shows that the operated area decreased from 23.02 million acres in 1983-84 to 20.48 million acres in 1996 indicating about 11 per cent decrease. Thus 2.54 million acres of land have gone out of agriculture over the period. This means that on the average nearly 2,00,000 acres of land are going out of agriculture every year and the area of land for agriculture has been shrinking even since the main reasons behind the decline

Table 10.2: Changes in Resource Base and other Related Factors for Agriculture

Indicator	*Agriculture Census Year*		*% Change over*
	1983-84	*1996*	*1983-84*
No. of holdings (in million)	13.82	17.83	(+) 29.02
No. of farm holdings (in million)	10.05	11.80	(+) 17.41
Operated area (in million acres)	23.02	20.48	(-) 11.93
Operated area per farm (in acres)	2.26	1.69	(-) 25.22
Operated area per holding	1.67	1.15	(-) 31.99
Operated area (in million acres) of farm holdings	22.68	19.96	(-) 11.99
Per capita operated area (in acres)	0.27	0.17	(-) 37.04
Per centage of landless households (%)	8.67	10.18	(+) 17.42
Per centage of agriculture labour households	39.80	35.90	(-) 16.49
Per centage of farms reporting irrigation	43.30	64.2	71.01
Per centage of irrigated to cultivated area	19.90	48.3	114.46
Cropping intensity	171	179	(+) 4.68

Source: Reports of the Census of Agriculture (National Vol. 1), 1983-84 and 1996.

of arable land is the increase in area under municipalities, towns and cities. The 1996 agriculture census indicated that during the 1983-84 to 1996 period, the area under municipality, towns and cities had increased by 1.50 million acres which is about 59 per cent of the total decline of operational areas. The homestead area increased from 0.966 million acres to 1.32 million acres showing about 36.48 per cent increase over the same period. The homestead area in rural areas is nearly 6.4 per cent of the total operational areas and 14 per cent of the land taken out of crop cultivation have gone under homestead area. Infrastructure development such as roads, educational and other institutions also take a sizeable amount of land out of agriculture [Hossain, M. (2000)]. The possibility of further expansion of operational area is more or less exhausted which is reflected in the diminishing figures for the operational area per farm and per head. The per capita operational area reduced from 0.27 acres to 0.17 acres over the same period. The absolute landless (% of holdings owning no land) increased from 8.67 per cent in 1983-84 to 10.18 per cent in 1996. The total holding as well as farm holdings have increased by 29.04 per cent (or 2.24% annually) and 17.05 per cent (or 1.31% annually) respectively over the period. The growth of holding is much higher than the population growth. The number of non-farm households increased from 3.77 million or 27 per cent of all rural households in 1983-84 to 6.03 million or 34 per cent in 1996. The number of agriculture labour households declined from 40 per cent in 1983-84 to 36 per cent in 1996. This indicates a movement of agriculture labour from farm to non-farm activities such as rural trade, transport sectors etc. However, the intensity of cropping has been increasing rapidly as more and more land is brought under double cropping and this has been made possible by the rapid expansion of irrigation facilities which is reflected in the increase in the ratio of irrigated to the cultivated area. Irrigation is one of the key indicators of agricultural development through its effects on the pattern and efficiency of land use. The adoption of HYV and chemical fertilizers is also closely related to the availability of water supply and irrigation facilities.

A close analysis of size class and distribution of landholdings presents a very uneven character which presupposes the most skewed distribution of land. The position regarding distributional pattern of farm households may be viewed in Table 10.3.

As shown in Table 10.3, small farm households operating upto 2.49 acres of land constituted about 52 per cent in 1960, 70 per cent in 1983-84 and 80 per cent in 1996 of the total farm households. According to the 1996 Agricultural Census Report, the small farm holdings (80%) operated only 42 per cent of the total operated land; the medium farm holdings (operating 2,50 to 7.49 acres of land) constituted 18 per cent of the total farm holdings and shared about 42 per cent of the total farm area. The large farm households which operate more than 7.5 acres of land constituted nearly 3 per cent of the total farm holdings but operated slightly more than 17 per cent of the total farm area. A clear picture that emerges from the same table is the small domination of the farm holdings having registered a clear gain in numbers as well as operated area. Medium and large farmers, on the other hand, have indicated a distinct decline both in numbers and area under operation. The average farm size in all size groups has

Table 10.3: Distribution of Farm Households and Their Operated Land by Size in Different Agriculture Census Years

(Fig.in '000')

Items	*Agriculture Census Year*			*% change*	*% change*	*% change*
	1960	*1983-1984*	*1996*	*in 1983-84 over 1960*	*in 1996 over 1960*	*in 1996 over 1983-8*
1	2	3	*4*	*5*	*6*	*7*
Total farm household	6148 (100)	10045 (100)	11798 (100)	(+) 63.4	(+) 91.9	(+) 17.5
Small farm	3179 (51.71)	7066 (70.34)	9423 (79.87)	(+) 22.3	(+) 196.4	(+) 33.4
Medium farm	2315 (37.62)	2483 (24.72)	2077 (17.61)	(+) 7.3	(-) 10.3	(-) 16.4
Large farm	656 (10.67)	496 (4.94)	297 (2.52)	(-) 24.4	(-) 54.7	(-) 40.1
Total operated area (acres)	21726 (100)	22678 (100)	19957 (100)	(+) 4.4	(-) 8.1	(-) 12.0

(Table Contd...)

Table 10.3: Contd...

1	2	3	4	5	6	7
Small farm	3530 (16.20)	6573 (28.98)	8219 (41.81)	(+) 86.2	(+) 132.8	(+) 25.0
Medium farm	9928 (45.70)	10226 (45.10)	8282 (41.50)	(+) 3.0	(-) 16.6	(-) 19.0
Large farm	8268 (38.10)	5879 (25.92)	3456 (17.32)	(-) 28.9	(-) 58.2	(-) 41.2
Operated area/ farm (acres)	3.54	2.26	1.69	(-) 36.2	(-) 52.3	(-) 25.2
Small farm	1.11	0.93	0.87	(-) 16.2	(-) 21.6)	(-) 6.5
Medium farm	4.29	4.12	3.99	(-) 4.0	(-) 22.4	(-) 3.2
Large farm	12.60	11.85	11.64	(-) 6.0	(-) 7.6	(-) 1.8
Gini index[1]	0.490	0.548	0.540	(+) 11.84	(+) 10.2	(-) 1.46

Source: Report of the Census of Agriculture (National Vol. 1), 1983-84 and 1996.
Note: Figure in the parenthesis is the % of total.

declined reflecting the increase in population pressure and the small farm size decreased from 1.11 acres in 1960 to 0.93 acres in 1983-84 and then to 0.87 acres in 1996. A similar declining trend is also noticed in case of medium and large farm sizes. It is, therefore, apparent that significant changes occurred in the size classes and the pressure of population on land is very high which tends to diminish the per capita landholding and consequently leads to an increase in the number of small and marginal farms. Small landholding per capita coupled with concentration of land in a few lands characterize the land distribution in rural Bangladesh and therefore, greatly hinders in bringing out optimum benefits of available land. To counter this problem, the government of Bangladesh came out with a number of land reform measures first in 1972 and then in 1984. The focal point of land reform measures is to ensure a more equitable distribution of land and to derive optimum benefits from the land redistributions among the landless peasants. These were advocated in consideration of both equity and efficiency and also to ensure higher standard of living and to improve social status for those directly engaged in tilling. An evaluation of land reform measures between the two reference periods (1972-1984) does not show any positive impact of land reforms on the small and landless poor although some changes in the pattern and distribution of farm and its size classes are observed. The Gini index indicated a sharp increase in inequality in the distribution of operational land between 1960 and 1983-84, while between 1983-84 and 1996, it showed a slight decrease from 0.5483 to 0.5396. This improvement in the distribution of operational holdings may be explained by (a) increased growth of population and agricultural households dependent upon land for subsistence, (b) effects of the inexorable operation of Muslim law of inheritance which leads to sub infeudation, and (c) absentee ownership and squeezing of big farms by letting out part of own land to small tenants on share-cropping basis.

Normative Measure of Inequality in Land Distribution

The normative measure of inequality in distribution of operated land as propounded by Atkinson (1973) has been estimated because the earlier measure of inequality had the following limitations; (i) Gini-coefficient gives an ambiguous interpretation of inequality if the Lorenze curves intersect, and (ii) it gives greater weight to middle range of distribution. Moreover, this index makes no explicit use of any concept of social welfare. Inequality index as suggested by Atkinson, on the other hand, gives an idea of the direction as well as magnitude of the potential gains that may be achieved from redistribution of operated land equally among the farmers. This measure is based on an explicit specification of social welfare and value judgement. In this method, a social welfare function is considered and an inequality aversion parameter $\in$, representing the weight attached by the society to inequality in the distribution, is introduced. The value of this parameter ranges from 0 to α. The zero value of $\in$ means that the society is indifferent to inequality, while a high value of $\in$ means more weight is attached to the transfer at the lower end of the ladder on the landholding scale. At the other extreme $\in = \alpha$ implies that society is concerned with the transfer to the lowest income group. The higher the degree of inequality, the lower is the level of social welfare for a given total land. A set of Atkinson indices (I_A) has been estimated for the rural areas by considering some weight towards the bottom level of operated land and is presented in Table 10.4.

Table 10.4: Atkinson Index (I_A) of Inequality in Operated Landholding.

$\in$	*Value of the (I_A)*	
	1983-84	*1996*
0.5	0.2526	0.2414
1.5	0.5992	0.5521
2.5	0.7474	0.6893
3.5	0.8041	0.7476
4.5	0.8299	0.7761

The index I_A for operated landholding is 0.5991 for 1983-84 and 0.5521 for 1996 corresponding to the parameter $\in$ = 1.5 which signifies that the same level of social welfare can be achieved with only (1.00-0.5991 =) 40.09% in 1983-84 and (1.0-0.5521=) 44.79% in 1996 of total operated land if it is equally distributed. Alternatively, the gain from redistribution to bring about

Figure 10.1: Sensitivity of Atkinson Index (IA) to variation in E

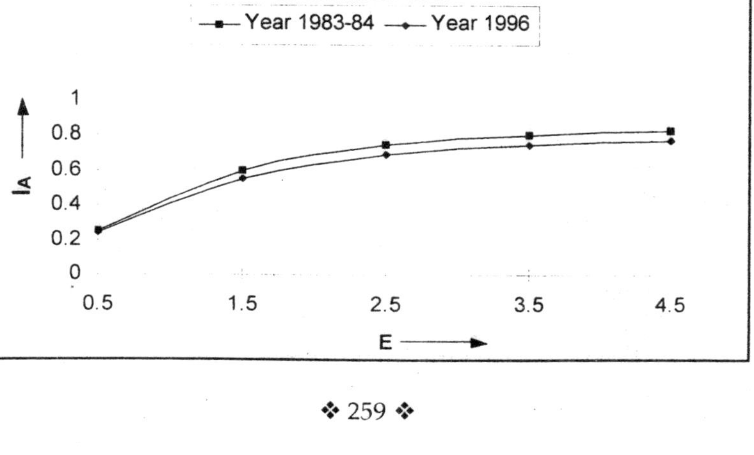

equality in operated landholding would be equivalent to an increase of 59.91 per cent in 1983-84 and 55.21 per cent in 1996 of the total operated land. Figure 10.1 illustrates graphically the sensitivity of I_A to changes in $\in$.

Agricultural Development

Spread of new technology, access to inputs and water resources, and development of farm and non-farm activities can be made through agriculture extension, and research and support services. In order to alleviate poverty through higher production, and increasing income and employment opportunities, 167 projects for crop, food, fisheries, forestry and livestock sub-sectors have been implemented by different executing agencies of the Ministry of Agriculture in the Fifth Five Year Plan. These projects are important in promoting the expansion of new technology in agriculture with particular focus on marginal and small farmers. Targeted projects have become an important element of poverty alleviation strategy and these projects are being implemented for improving the socio-economic status of the rural poor. Crop Diversification, Comprehensive Crop, Rehabilitation, Marginal and Small Farmer's System Crop Intensification, Minor Irrigation, Poverty Alleviation through Integrated Area Development, Barind Integrated Development projects etc. are the main projects. All these projects in their approach combine the elements of increased agricultural production, proper utilisation of land and assist small and marginal farmers. However, the ADP allocations for productive input package programmes consisting of seed, fertilizer, and irrigation technology with other support services and for various programmes of non-crop sub-projects are shown in Table 10.5. The main goals and objectives of these projects are to boost up agricultural production and ensure food security.

Table 10.5: ADP Allocation in Agriculture Sector, 1999-2000

Sub-sector	*No. of Project*	*Allocation (in million Tk.)*		
		GOB	*Project Aid*	*Total*
Crop	78	3780	-	3780
Food	12	250	280	530
Forestry	26	480	1180	1660
Fisheries	29	1250	-	1250
Livestock	22	450	680	1130
Total Agriculture	167	6210	2140	8350

Source: ADP, 1999-2000, Planning Commission, GOB.

Of the total allocation of agriculture sector about 45 per cent was allocated for crop sub-sector. The number of projects in this sub-sector is also high compared to other sub-sectors. Forestry and fisheries sub-sectors rank second and third respectively in respect of ADP allocation.

Table 10.6 reveals that the net irrigated area and net fertilized area as per centage of cultivated area have shown a divergent trend. After registering an increasing trend with the increase of land size upto 2.49 acres, the proportion of irrigated area and fertilized area shows a sharp decline in medium and large holdings. Similar trend is also observed in case of cropping intensity.

It is evident from the above table that there is a preponderance of small holdings in the country and high inequality in landholding distribution. There has been a substantial increase in irrigated area, cropping

Table 10.6: Basic Indicators of Agricultural Development by Farm Size, 1996

Land size group (in acres)	*Indicators*		
	Net irrigated area as % of cultivated area	*Net fertilized area as % of cultivated area*	*Cropping intensity*
0.05 – 0.49	47.24	66.04	194
0.50 – 0.99	55.80	79.92	193
1.00 – 1.49	54.58	80.97	189
1.50 – 2.49	50.53	80.03	182
Total small holdings (0.05 – 2.49)	52.32	78.95	187
Medium holding (2.50 – 7.50)	46.53	77.65	171
Large holdings (7.50 acres and above)	43.84	75.17	154
Total farm holdings	48.37	77.73	174

Source: Census of Agriculture-1996, Tables 1 and 2.

intensity and adoption of modern inputs like HYV seeds and chemical fertilizers and these are critical factors in agricultural development and employment generation.

Growth Performance of Area, Output and Yield of Major Crops

The major dynamic element of income generation, employment opportunity and poverty alleviation in rural areas is the high growth of agricultural output. It is the end result of spread of new technology, institutional support, extension services, and credit for agricultural development in the rural economy. In the process, it leads to changes in agriculture sector as a whole as well as in other sectors of the economy. Agricultural development as a result of increase in irrigated area, fertilized area and cropping intensity over the periods can readily be measured statistically by examining the growth performance of crop output.

We will now examine growth rates of area, output and yield of major crops such as rice, wheat, pulses and oilseeds. As a time series increasing by a constant per centage has the growth properties of compound interest, an initial principle of Y_0, the area/output/yield increase at the rate r, will at the end of T years have grown to

$$Y_t = Y_0 (1 + r)^T \quad (10.1)$$

Since time enters this expression as an exponent, the trend is exponential and when (10.1) is expressed in logarithms, the expression becomes.

$$\log Y_t = \log Y_0 + T \log(1+r) \quad (10.2)$$

But if we set $\log Y_0 = A$ and $\log(1+r) = B$, we get

$$\log Y_t = A + BT \quad (10.3)$$

This functions gives a uniform rate of change.

To calculate the compound growth rates least squares technique was applied and the compound growth rate or the magnitude of r is readily obtained from (Anti log B-1) x 100.

The steeper the regression line – that is, larger the value of B – the higher the compound rate of growth r. Another useful characteristic of expression (10.3) is that the period of time required for the trend magnitude, Y, to be double is easily obtained by:

$$P = \frac{\log 2}{B} \quad (10.4)$$

In order to have an idea of the time profile of growth of different crops the entire study period (1980-81 to 1996-97) has been divided into two periods i.e. period I (1980-81 to 1989-90) and period II (1990-91 to 1996-97). Broadly speaking period I represents the period of time before the spread of new technology and implementation of several targeted projects by different executing agencies of Ministry of Agriculture while period II

Table 10.7: Trend in Growth Rates of Area, Output and Yield of Major Crops

	Crop	*Entire period (1980-81 to 1996-97)*	*Period I (1980-81 to 1989-90)*	*Period II (1990-91 to 1996-97)*
	Area	-4.52	-3.09	-6.83
Aus	Output	-4.30	-2.19	-4.70
	Yield	0.25	0.92	2.30
	Area	-0.20	-1.16	-0.12
Aman	Output	1.46	0.79	-0.40
	Yield	1.86	1.98	-0.28
	Area	5.99	8.42	1.34
Boro	Output	6.69	8.78	2.13
	Yield	0.66	0.34	0.77
	Area	1.33	0.70	3.27
Wheat	Output	0.81	-1.43	5.57
	Yield	-0.51	-2.12	2.22
	Area	3.96	11.19	-0.76
Pulses	Output	4.13	10.93	+0.30
	Yield	0.17	0.17	-0.24
	Area	3.00	8.16	-0.46
Oilseeds	Output	2.81	6.84	0.89
	Yield	-0.19	-1.21	1.37

Source: Data on acreage and output, obtained from the Bangladesh Economic Review, 1999. Table 20.

represents the time period after spread of new technology and implementation of several targeted projects for agricultural development. Table 10.7 shows the trend of growth rate of area, output and yield of major crops in Bangladesh. The analysis is based on macro data obtainable from the secondary published source [BER, 1999, Table 21].

Aus Rice: The area under the cultivation and output of aus rice accounted for about 14.14 per cent and 9.07 per cent of the total foodgrains area and output respectively in 1997-98. For the entire period under study (i.e. 1980-81 to 1996-97) aus rice output as well as area shows a declining trend and a marked negative growth. However, the yield rate shows an upward trend registering a positive growth rate of around 0.25 per cent for the entire period. This rate for period I was 0.79 per cent while for period II, it was 2.30 per cent per annum thus indicating a significant increase.

Aman Rice: Aman rice plays an important role in augmenting foodgrains in Bangladesh and it accounted for 52.48 per cent and 42.83 per cent of the total foodgrain area and output. But the area under aman rice shows a decrease, while the output and yield rate per annum indicate a moderate increase between 1980-81 and 1996-97 – being about 1.46 per cent for output and 1.86 per cent for yield for the entire period. The rate of growth of area, output and yield has declined sharply in period II (1990-91 to 1969-97) and registered a negative growth. The diversion of land towards boro rice and other crops seem to have been responsible for this discouraging situation. The condition with respect to output and yield was relatively better in period I (i.e. 1990-81 to 1989-90) as compared to period II.

Particularly noticeable is the negative growth rate of area, output and yield of aman rice in period II. The growth rates were –0.12 per cent, -0.40 per cent and –0.28 per cent, respectively while these figures in period I were -0.16 per cent, 0.79 per cent and 1.98 per cent respectively.

Boro Rice: The rate of growth of area, output and yield of boro rice is fairly high and shows a sharp rise in period I and then registers a decline in period II but is still positive. For the entire period under study, the area, output and yield have increased at the rate of 5.99 per cent, 6.69 per cent and 0.66 per cent per annum respectively. These rates showed a big jump to 8.42 per cent, 8.78 per cent and 0.34 per cent in period I and then the growth rate for area and output fell to 1.34 per cent and 2.13 per cent repectively although the yield rate increased to 0.77 per cent per annum in period II. Thus, Boro crop contributes significantly to the overall food production accounting for 26.10 per cent and 39.38 per cent of the total foodgrains area and output respectively.

Wheat: The rate of growth of area, output and yield shows an acceleration from period I to period II and it has increased from 0.70 per cent, -1.43 per cent and –2.12 per cent per annum in period I to 3.27 per cent, 5.57 per cent and 2.22 per cent respectively in period II. For the entire period these rates were 1.33 per cent, 0.81 per cent and –0.51 per cent respectively. The significantly high rate of wheat output in period II was sustained mainly by the relatively rapid growth of the area of cultivation under it. It is highly encouraging to note that the growth rate of wheat productivity shows a clear and marked improvement in period II as compared to period I.

Pulses: The pulses registered a fairly high growth rate in period I – around 11.19 per cent for area under cultivation 10.93 per cent for output and 0.17 per cent for yield, while for the entire period these figures were 3.96 per cent 4.13 per cent and 0.17 per cent respectively. It is discouraging to note that in period II, the growth rates for these items declined and the rates for area as well as yield showed a negative growth. The high growth rate in output of pulses was achieved in period I mainly due to the rapid increase of area under pulses and the growth rate of area has exceeded that of output of the crop. A particularly noteworthy and alarming situation from the nutritional point of view has been the marked decline in the area and output of pulses.

Oilseeds: For the entire period of the study, the area, output and yield of oilseeds increased at the rate of 3.0 per cent, 2.81 per cent, and –0.19 per cent respectively, these figures for period I were 8.16 per cent, 2.81 per cent and –1.21 per cent respectively. And for period II, these were –0.46 per cent, 0.89 per cent and 1.37 per cent respectively per annum. If we compare the relative growth rate of area and output of oilseeds, it will be observed that the growth rate of area has exceeded that of output of the crop.

To sum up, the growth rate has been uneven among the crops. An important finding, which emerges from Table 10.7, is that all crops except aman, and pulses have registered clear increase in yield rate. Even the aus rice which shows a decline in output and area under cultivation has registered an upward trend in yield rate. The decline in output of aus rice seems mainly due to diversion of cultivated area to more productive or lucrative crops. A most alarming fact is that the area, output and yield of aman rice declined sharply throughout the study period and registered negative growth rates in the nineties (period II), whereas previously this crop accounted for about 52.48 per cent and 43.0 per cent respectively of the total foodgrains area and output. Another discouraging fact is the marked decline in the yield and output of pulses which is the main source of protien. This is alarming from the nutritional point of view. During 1990-91 to 1996-97 (period II), the output and yield of pulses showed negative growth indicating that pulses have been loosing ground to other crops since 1990-91. During this period large amount of credit has been disbursed, new technologies have spread, and several targeted projects have been implemented for agricultural development as well as poverty alleviation. But the impact of these factors has been uneven among crops, benefiting mainly yield of aus, boro, wheat and oilseeds. Table 10.7 further reveals that the pattern of agricultural growth has been quite different in period I (i.e. 1980-81 to 1989-90) and period II (i.e. 1990-91 to 1996-97). Although, land productivity in the case of aus, boro, wheat and oilseeds has increased in period II as compared to period I, the per capita productivity of foodgrains decreased from 170.0 kg in 1990-91 to 151.0 kg in 1994-95 followed by some increase in 1996-97 to a level of 163 kg per annum. The present level of land productivity continues to lag behind the growth rate of population except for aus and wheat, and thus, development achieved in the agriculture sector is not sufficient to dent the rural poverty.

Land Ownership Size and Poverty

Since agriculture is the main source of rural income, ownership of land asset is likely to have a more direct bearing on poverty alleviation. Ownership of land asset is possibly the most important indicator of a rural household's economic status than any other socio-economic indicator. A wide disparity in living standards is observed when the rural households are classified according to land ownership size. Food consumption and nutritional status are also found to vary among different landholding sizes. There is a positive correlation between land ownership size and monthly per capita income. The absolutely landless households had an income of Tk.347 per person per month in 1997 as against Tk.1628 for households owning more than 7.5 acres of land. The per capita income of small farm households (owning 0.05-2.49 acres) was Tk.578 and for medium farm households (2.50-7.49 acres) it was Tk.952. A similar pattern was also observed in respect of incidence of poverty. It decreases with the increase in land ownership size. The incidence of poverty as estimated by BBS in 1995-96 was quite high (66 per cent) in the landless class. For small landholding size class, the proportion of poor was 53.3 per cent, for medium it was 32.1 per cent and this figure for large holding size was 20.5 per cent (Table 10.8).

Table 10.8: Incidence of Poverty by Land Ownership Size Class

Land Ownership Size Class (in acres)	*Absolute Poverty 2122 k.cal/per day*	*Hard core poverty 1805 k.cal/per day*	*Ultra poverty 1600 k.cal/per day*
Landless	66.0	44.3	25.4
0.01 – 0.49	58.6	32.2	19.5
0.50 – 1.49	40.8	20.4	10.5
2.50 – 2.49	33.7	14.9	8.3
2.50 – 7.49	32.1	13.2	6.4
7.50+	20.5	7.1	3.2
All groups	47.5	26.1	14.1

Source: Household Expenditure Survey, 1995-96, BBS.

It is interesting to note that in spite of having relatively higher proportion of irrigated area, area under

HYV and higher cropping intensity in small compared to medium and large farm holdings, the incidence of poverty in small size class is disproportionately high. Thus, a Agricultural development, could not significantly reduce poverty in this size class. Share-cropping is the most common form of tenancy in small size class in Bangladesh. The share croppers are mostly comprised of landless and small farm holdings and they are subsistence farmers. The share-croppers bear almost all costs of inputs – seeds, fertilizers, pesticides and irrigation facilities. But the terms and conditions of product sharing of owner to tenant are 50:50. They hardly receive more and sometimes get even less return. On the other hand, the share-croppers have to bear the full risks of production, and have to supply all inputs of production such as draft animals, plough, labour and other agricultural implements. The above facts support the hypothesis of disincentive effects of crop sharing arrangement and this factor may be identified as one of the reasons for high incidence of poverty among the small farm and landless households.

Crop production increased from 30.07 million metric tons in 1990-91 to 33.63 million metric tons in 1998-99 showing about 1.48 per cent increase per annum over the period, while foodgain production increased from 18.86 million metric tons to 21.81 million metric tons over the same period [BER, 2000]. These figures indicate positive development in crop-sub sector which appears to have been effective for reduction of poverty. But the increase in crop production fails to generate and expand opportunities for the poor and to meet the minimum requirement of food except rice [Table 10.9]. It appears from the table that the consumption of cereals in 1990s is higher than the minimum requirement of food intake as prescribed by the Bangladesh Nutritional Council. There

Table 10.9: Per capita Consumption of Different Food Items Compared to the Norm for Having Balanced Nutrition, 1991-92 and 1995-96

(Grams per day per person)

Food items	*Minimum intake required for Balanced nutrition*	*Rural area*			*Urban area*		
		1991-1992	*1995-1996*	*May 1999**	*1991-1992*	*1995-1996*	*May 1999**
Rice	390	481	479	443	416	391	382
Other cereals	100	42	43	48	55	51	69
Tubers & vegetables	225	176	201	211	209	206	216
Pulses	30	17	13	25	22	19	24
Oils & fats	20	9	8		16	17	
Spices	10	26	35		36	45	
Fruits	50	16	25	106	23	39	130
Sugar/gur	10	9	9		11	10	
Fish	45	32	42		48	52	
Meat & eggs	34	12	12		20	30	
Milk	30	18	27	32	23	36	33
Total	944	838	894	919	879	896	938

Sources: *(i)* Bangladesh National Nutrition Council for the norm of minimum food intake required balanced nutrition. Report of the Household Expenditure Survey, Bangladesh Bureau of Statistics for per capita food consumption in rural and urban areas.

(ii) *Poverty Monitoring Survey-1999, BBS, 1999.

is marginal shortfall in tubers and vegetables, and fish, but substantial decrease in production of pulses, oil seeds and livestock products which are the main sources of protein and other micronutrients. In spite of having higher production the total food intake in 1990s for both rural and urban areas is lower than the minimum requirement for balanced nutrition. This means that gains in production do not work in favour of poor due to unequal distribution of land and other productive assets and unfavourable "exchange entitlement of labour power" or labour exchange rate for a group of commodities.

List of Some Selected Projects

Sl. No	*Programmes/project*	*Main Objectives*	*Benefits*
	1	*2*	*3*
Investment Project			
1.	CIDA funded Crop Diversification Programme (DAE, BARI, DAM, BADC & PIU Components).	Integrated extension, research and marketing activities for increased production of pulses oil seeds, potato and maize.	The consumption level of pulses and oilseeds is expected to increase from 2 kg/per capita each to 2.5 kg and 2.2 kg respectively at the end of 1994-95. The production of HYV potato will be increased by expanding 29 per cent acreage in the project area. Access to agricultural credit, seed, fertilizer, irrigation equipment, marketing facilities, training, motivation and demonstration, etc. will be provided under the project.
2.	Comprehensive Crop Rehabilitation programme in the Southern Districts.	To increase agri production through utilization of fallow land and develop horticulture and afforestation in 38 thanas of the greater districts of Barisal & Patuakhali and 5 thanas of Gopalgonj district.	Fallow land of 43 thanas will be brought under cultivation for increasing crop production, horticulture development and afforestation. Access to land, agricultural inputs, agricultural credit and motivational activities will be created under the project.

(Table Contd...)

1		2	3
Investment Project			
3	Horticulture Research and Development in Bangladesh with ADB Assistance (DAE, BARI & BADC Components).	Improved methods for cultivation of fruits, vegetables, spices, etc. and their promotional activities as nutritional crops.	Production of vegetable, fruits and spices is expected to increase through supply of seed/seedlings/grafts/ gooties. Modern technology will be evolved and their use will be increased. Improved marketing and inputs distribution facilities will be created under the project.
4	Crop Storage-cum-Credit Project with Swiss Assistance	Evolving model for improving the economic condition of the small farmers and sharecroppers by agril. Credit and storage facilities.	Small and Marginal farmers of selected districts will be benefited to store their crops against bank loans to avoid distress sales. The target farmers' access to storage and marketing facilities will be provided under the project.
Investment Project			
5	Marginal and Small Farmer's Systems Crop Intensification Project with IFAD Funding.	Assisting Marginal and Small Farmers in Kurigram district to increase their productive intensity and volume of production.	Out of the 24,000 collaborative farmers targeted under the project, 1100 marginal farmer groups and 625 small farmers groups have been formed with about 20,000 members, credit disbursement already started to marginal groups. Establishment of 5625 demonstration plots have been completed mainly on vegetables and other minor crops. Access to agricultural inputs, motivation, demonstration. training marketing facilities, women involvement etc. will be created under the project.

(Table Contd...)

	1	2	3
6	Agriculture Support Services Project with IDA Assistance.	Increased agricultural production and initiate diversification process aimed at introducing high value export crops.	Motivation, demonstration and training of farmers for introducing high value export crops will be provided.
Investment Project			
7	Continuation and Expansion of Rice Research and Training Programme of BRRI.	Development of new HYV rice and rented production technology.	So far, BRRI has developed 25 new improved varieties and more than 5,000 persons were trained on modern rice production technologies, most of them were farmers.
8	Research Project under BARI for its ongoing research programmes.	Carry out research on Agricultural Sciences to keep conformity with the changing technologies.	Multi-crop research programmes will be continued for varietal improvement suited to different agro-ecological conditions.
9	Agro-Service Center.	Establishment of demonstration farm to disseminate modern production technique of vegetables and seedlings, etc.	Small and Marginal farmers are being provided with graft, gooties, seedlings, etc. and they are provided with marketing facilities for their produce.
10	Projects for Production, Proceument and Distribution of Improved Seeds of Paddy, Jute, Potato etc.	Muliply, procure preserve and distribution of improved seeds in BADC farms and through contact growers.	Contact growers are provided with production technology and increased support service by BADC.
11	Minor Irrigation Development Projects.	Wider and equitable access to minor irrigation through technology for increasing production.	Irrigation coverage has increased and irrigated areas are provided with HYV seeds for higher production.

(Table Contd...)

1	2	3
Investment Project		
12 Strengthening of Soil Resources Development Institute (SRDI).	To provide detailed inforamtion on soil & land type under Thana guide for making Land & Soil Inventory.	Detailed information of land and soil have been collected from 220 thanas for preparation of Thana soil Guidelines, Soil problems are identified and correcting measures are suggested.
13 Poverty Alleviation through Integrated Area Development Programme.	Improving the people of 11 Thanas (Selected) through improved cultural practices, training of poor farmers, improved infrastructural facilities, creation of employment opportunities, homestead farming, etc.	To increase the production of horticultural crops in the homestead and increase the income of small and marginal farmers through improved marketing facilities and inputs supply.
14 Agricultural Rehabilitation Programme, 1991.	To provide production support (seed, fertilizer irrigation equipment and power-tiller) to the cost to small & Marginal farmers of the affected area.	Small and Marginal Farmers of the affected areas were provided with agricultural inputs free of cost to retain them in agricultural production.
Investment Project		
15. Barind Integrated Area Development Project (Phase-II).	To increase agricultural production through installation of 235 DTWs, excavation of ponds, afforestation, crop diversification, etc.	Access to irrigation facilities and other agricultural inputs by farmers, maintaining ecological balance and improving quality of life of the local people.
TAPPs (Thana Cereal)		
16 Transfer and Identification of Crop Technology at Thana Level.	To Provide high input technology and optimum utilization of existing irrigation facilities of cereal production in identified thanas.	Farmers will be benefited by adopting improved technology through demonstration and training.

(Table Contd...)

	1	2	3
17	Mango Improvement and Development (Phase-II).	Strengthen capabilities by developing manpower and facilities and also disseminate improved mango production technology to the growers.	To increase the production of mangoes through the adoption of improved technology.
18	Development of Rainfed Rice Production in Bangladesh	To accelerate varietal, crop management and cropping for the T. Aman based rice areas of Bangladesh.	To increase the production of rainfed T. Aman.
Investment Project			
19	Strengthening to National Vegetable Seed Production Programme.	To construct three seed centres, establish equipped breeding units, improve land and irrigation facilities, promote seed production, provide training, etc.	Availability of improved vegetable seeds will be ensured to the farmers.
20	Assisting Transformation to Irrigated Agriculture.	Monitor supply of minor irrigation equipment and other inputs, assist BADC Irrigation Wing, adjust crop recommendations, improve capabilities to conduct research, etc.	No direct benefits to the farmers. However, policy thrust will be given through this project on expanded irrigated agriculture.
21	Support for Horticulture Export Development Project	To assist the farmers especially the small and marginal farmers in producing and marketing (internal and external) horticultural crops.	Farmers especially the small and marginal farmers will be benefited availing facilities for exporting horticultural products.

Source: Hussain, A.M. (1993): Programmes Under Implementary By The Ministry of Agriculture in Poverty Alleviation; Government of Bangladesh in Poverty Alleviation (Proceedings of National Seminar held in Dhaka, February 17-19, 1993).

Reference

1. The Gini index is the ratio of the difference between the line of absolute equality (diagonal) and the Lorenz Curve to the trangular region underneath the diagonal.

11

Statistical Evaluation of Socio-economic Development and Poverty: A Portrait of 64 Districts

Introduction

It was mentioned earlier that Bangladesh has had a long experience of national level planning and has already implemented five Five Year Plans. But those plans followed the "top down" planning approach and were implemented through government bureaucracies. The main objectives of these plans and programmes were to bring about dispersed regional socio-economic development, thus improving quality of life of general masses and thereby reducing poverty. Equitable socio-economic development of regions cannot be achieved without balanced and appropriate interactive development of various sectors of the economy across these regions. For instance, although hundreds of billions of taka have been spent in the last two decades on various development programmes for socio-economic development in the country, these programmes have failed to bring about equitable development across the regions and significant improvement in the quality of life of the general masses. It has also been observed that regional disparities in terms of development in different sectors of the economy are still wide. Many districts exhibit the characteristics of a backward economy, such as low level of urbanization and industrialization, heavy dependence on agriculture, low level of development in education, health, infrastructure and other socio-economic factors. For instance, the population pressure is significantly higher in Dhaka, which has a population density that is 6 times that of Bandarban. The score of human development index (HDI) shows a large variations at district level ranging from 0.542 in Rangamati to 0.241 in Sherpur [UNDP (1996)]. There are considerable inter-district variations in the level of incidence of poverty too. Thus, the backward and least developed districts will not benefit from the present system of economic planning unless the economic policy and resource allocation are tempered with equity and social justice. Deliberate allocation of resources from the centre particularly for the least developed districts is essential for equitable economic development and poverty alleviation.

Development is a multidimensional process and its impact cannot be measured fully by any single indicator. Moreover, a number of factors analysed separately or individually will not give an integrated and comprehensive picture of reality. There is a need for constructing a composite index of development based on different socio-economic factors. In this chapter, an attempt has been made to quantify the level of socio-economic development in sixty four districts by constructing composite indices for agriculture, rural industry, infrastructure and social services, education and population sectors in order to examine (i) how much progress has been made in each district, and (ii) how the districts stand up against each other with regard to their levels of development.

Objectives of the Analysis

The main goal or objective of this chapter is to provide an integrated picture of the socio-economic development that has taken place in the district level economy and to find out distributive patterns of gain for development through poverty situation analysis. In order to facilitate the analysis, data on various development indicators have also been identified and obtained from different published and unpublished sources. However, the main sources of data are the Bangladesh Bureau of Statistics (BBS), Handloom Board, Rural Electrification Board, Directorate of Population and Family Planning etc. The analysis is performed for 64 districts with the hope that it will enable us to present an overall view of development and provide an understanding of the factors associated with development and reduction of poverty. Knowledge of the level of development at district level in various sectors is helpful in identifying where a given district stands in relation to others. However, the specific objectives are:

(i) To estimate the composite indices of socio-economic development for each district;

(ii) To classify districts into different levels of development on the basis of their composite indices;

(iii) To examine the statistical significance of overall change in development indices over two periods;

(iv) To measure rank correlation between two indicators;

(v) To estimate proportion of area and population in the least developed districts by region.

Method of Analysis

The level of development for each of the 64 districts has been evaluated with the help of a composite index based on different development indicators. The selected indicators depict various facets of development of the economy. The main idea of evaluating composite index (CI) is to rank the districts on the basis of level of development and to examine the impact of development on reduction of poverty.

The level of development is examined separately for agricultural, industrial, infrastructure and social services, education and population sectors. Based on critical difference (CD) obtainable from distance matrix (DM) and composite indices of development, model districts could be identified for fixing up the potential targets of different indicators for the least developed districts. However, model districts for different indicators have not been identified in the present analysis.

The districts have been considered as the unit of analysis and thus all the sixty-four districts of the country have been included in the analysis. The analysis uses data for the year 1996 on 31 socio-economic indicators out of which 7 indicators are directly related to agricultural development, 9 indicators to rural industrial development, 7 indicators to infrastructure and social services sectors, 4 indicators to education and the rest 4 indicators are related to population[1].

Development Indicators Under Consideration

(a) Agricultural Sector

Agriculture sector plays an important role in the national economy. It is the dominant sector for rural development in terms of contribution to GDP (32.24%) and employment of the rural labour force (64%). Agricultural sector includes crops, livestock, forestry and fishery. But, about 24 per cent of the GDP is contributed by the crop-sub-sector alone and the rest 8 per cent is contributed by other sub-sectors [BBS (1998)]. The development of agriculture sector is, thus, largely dependent upon the improved practices for crop such as adoption of HYVs, modern irrigation, multiple cropping etc. The other sub-sectors are also important for providing greater employment opportunities. But relevant and reliable information particularly on livestock, forestry and fishery for 64 districts are not available. However, the following indicators have been taken into consideration for the present analysis.

- *(i)* Average operated area/household (in acre)
- *(ii)* Cropping intensity (%)
- *(iii)* Per centage of irrigated area
- *(iv)* Per centage of area under HYV
- *(v)* Per centage of agricultural labour household
- *(vi)* Per centage of tenant households
- *(vii)* Per centage of landless households

(b) Rural Industrial Sector

Although Bangladesh is not industrially developed, contribution of this sector to GDP is about 10 per cent of the total. This sector can also divert heavy dependency on agricultural sector and provides employment to a large number of poor people. The large-scale industries, which contribute about 6 per cent of the GDP, are mainly concentrated in Dhaka and Chittagong divisions and majority of the districts have no large-scale industry. However, Bangladesh has a large number of small scale, handloom and cottage industries in rural areas, which contribute about 4 per cent of the GDP. These industries play important roles in shaping a self-reliant rural economy through creation of gainful employment for the rural poor. Districtwise information on large-scale industries and other related factors are not available. However, the following available indicators from industry sector have been selected for the analysis.

(i) Number of small scale industries/lakh population

(ii) Number of cottage industries/lakh population

(iii) Number of handlooms/lakh population

(iv) Per centage of labour in small-scale industries to total labour force

(v) Per centage of labour in cottage industries to total labour force

(vi) Per centage of labour in handloom to total labour force

(vii) Investment in small-scale industries in lakh taka

(viii) Investment in cottage industries in lakh taka

(ix) Per centage of outstanding credit given by schedule and agricultural banks

(c) Infrastructure and Social Services Sectors

The provision of physical infrastructure such as communication, road transport, electrification, educational institutions, hospital, dispensary, post-office, bank and other financial institutions, communication etc. is essential for the socio economic development. Districts with few post-offices, cooperative and banking facilities will obviously present fewer opportunities for people to deposit or borrow money and to perform economic activities. Districts with less number of educational and health institutions tend to have less opportunity to improve literacy rate as well as to maintain good health and to increase economic mobility. The following development indicators for the infrastructure and social services sectors have been considered for this analysis:

1. No. of post-offices/lakh population
2. No. of banks/lakh population
3. Per centage of villages electrified by Rural Electrification Board
4. Length of road/100 sq.km. of district area
5. No. of primary schools in one sq.km. radius
6. No. of secondary schools in two sq.km. radius
7. No. of rural dispensaries and union health and family welfare centres/lakh population.

(d) Education Sector

Education is very important to the poor in two ways. Firstly, it enhances the labour market opportunities. Secondly, good education is not merely inputs that can raise earnings, but it also contributes to economic development. Educated people are more productive and contribute more to the country's economic development. The adult literacy rate, which is essential for skill development, varies sharply from district to district. Gender differentials in literacy and adult literacy rates are also significant in Bangladesh. According to 1991

Census, about 85 per cent of the population live in rural areas. Therefore, development of education, particularly Primary and Secondary education, in rural areas is an urgent social need for development of the country. However, the following indicators from education sector have been included

(i) Per centage of male literacy rate (7 years and above)

(ii) Per centage of female literacy rate (7 years and above)

(iii) Per centage of adult male literacy rate (15 years and above)

(iv) Per centage of adult female literacy rate (15 years and above)

(e) Population Sector

It is generally believed that rapid population growth and higher population density pose a serious challenge to the attainment of economic and social goals including alleviation of poverty. Higher fertility causes high dependency ratio and large household size adversely affects the possibility of substantial socio-economic progress as it imposes heavy burden on the development programmes. However, the following indicators from population sector have been included:

(i) Average household size

(ii) Density of population/sq.km

(iii) Population growth rate, 1991-96

(iv) Per centage of urban population.

Mathematical Exposition of the Composite Index

Let X_{ij} be the jth developmental indicator of the ith district. The whole set of indicators can be represented in matrix notation as $[X_{ij}]$.

where i = 1,2,..........n and j = 1,2,.......k

As the selected developmental indicators are measured in diffeent units, there is a need for standardization of the indicators. Let Z_{ij} be the jth standardized indicator of the ith district, which may be written as below:

$$Z_{ij} = (X_{ij} - \overline{X}) / s_j \qquad (11.1)$$

where $s_j^2 = \sum_{i=1}^{n} (X_{ij} - \overline{X}_j)^2 / n$ and $\overline{X}_j = \sum_{i=1}^{n} X_{ij} / n$

The whole set of standardized indicators can also be represented in a matrix form as $[Z_{ij}]$. The best-standardized value for each indicator (i.e. with maximum or minimum standardized value depending upon the direction of the indicator) is identified and represented by Z_{mj}. The square root of sum of squares deviations of Z_{ij} from the corresponding best value Z_{mj} for ith district is taken for all selected indicators in the following manner:

$$a_i = [\sum_{j=1}^{K} (Z_{ij} - Z_{mj})^2]^{1/2} \qquad (11.2)$$

where a_i indicates the pattern of development of the ith district.

The value of a_i is useful in identifying the "model" district. It also helps in fixing the potential target of each indicator. The composite index of development of the district (C_i) is then computed using the following formula as propounded by Narain, Rai and Sarup (1991).

$$C_i = a_i/A \tag{11.3}$$

where $A = \bar{a} + 2s_a$ and $\bar{a}$ and s_a are the mean and standard deviation respectively of a_i.

The value of the composite index (CI) thus obtained lies between 0 and 1. A value of CI close to 0 indicates the highest level of development whereas a value close to 1 signifies the lowest level of development.

The Development Distance Between Districts

The development distance among different districts based on all the indicators are obtained and model districts are identified for fixing up the potential target of different indicators for the poorly developed districts. However, by using the standardized variates $[Z_{ij}]$, the developmental distance between districts as suggested by Narain et.al. (1991) may be computed as below:

$$D_{ip} = [\sum_{j=1}^{K}(Z_{ij} - Z_{pj})^2]^{1/2} \tag{11.4}$$

where D_{ip} is the developmental distance between ith and pth districts, (i=1,2,....n and p=1,2,....,n).

In this case, $D_{ii} = 0$, $D_{ip} = D_{pi}$, and the distance between the districts may be expressed in matrix notation as follows:

$$DM = \begin{bmatrix} 0 & d_{12} & d_{13} & \cdots & \cdots & d_{1n} \\ d_{21} & 0 & d_{23} & \cdots & \cdots & d_{2n} \\ \cdots & \cdots & \cdots & \cdots & \cdots & \\ \cdots & \cdots & \cdots & \cdots & \cdots & \cdots \\ d_{n1} & d_{n2} & d_{n3} & \cdots & \cdots & 0 \end{bmatrix} \quad (11.5)$$

The minimum distance (d_i) in each row of the above matrix is identified for computation of critical distance (CD) in the following manner:

$$CD = \bar{d} \pm 2s_d \quad (11.6)$$

where $\bar{d}$ and s_d are the mean and standard deviation of d_i respectively.

A simple ranking of the districts on the basis of composite indices may be worked out for classification of districts in respect of the level of development. On the other hand, classification of districts from an assumed distribution of the mean of the composite indices will give a more meaningful characterization of different levels of development. It appears appropriate to assume that the mean of the composite index has a Beta distribution in the range (0,1). Let us assume that $(0,Z_1)$, (Z_1,Z_2) and $(Z_2,1)$ be linear intervals having the same probability weight of 0.33 [Narain et al (1991)]. The fractile groups can be used to characterize the various categories of development such as (i) developed, (ii) developing and (iii) least developed. For instance, the districts with composite indices between 0 and Z_1 may be put in category 1 as developed and those having composite indices between Z_1 and Z_2 may be treated as developing. In a similar fashion, the districts with indices between Z_2 and 1 are considered as least developed or poorly developed districts. The value of Z's may be obtained from the Incomplete Beta Function [Pearson, K. (1933)].

Measurement of Changes in Development

It is of great interest for the researchers to examine the significant changes in development over different time periods. For instance, we are interested to see the changes in economic development of the country at the beginning and end of a Five Year Plan; before and after an economic intervention and so on. For such an analysis, the Slippage test proposed by Rai, S.C. (1987) may be used and the method of this test is discussed below:

Having computed the composite indices for two time periods (say), the districts are arranged in ascending order for each time period. The development indices are then ranked by allotting 1 to the smallest index value, 2 to the next higher value and so on. Let q_i be the sum of ranks of the ith period for the districts. The following test statistic is then computed.

$$Q = [12/nt(t+1) \times \sum[\theta_i^2 - 3n(t+1)] \qquad (11.7)$$

The test statistic Q is distributed as χ^2 with (t-1) d.f., and the null hypothesis (H_o) to be tested may be set as:

H_o: There is no change in the development indices of the districts over time, and alternative hypothesis is

H_1: There is change in the development indices of the districts over time.

Estimated Composite Indices of Development

It will be quite interesting and useful to examine the level of development of different districts separately for agricultural, industrial, infrastructure and social services, education and population sectors. The composite index of development is, therefore, estimated for 64 districts separately for each sector. The districts are then ranked on the basis of the level of composite index. The estimated composite indices along with their ranks for each of the 64 districts are set out in Table 11.1.

Agriculture Sector

Column 1 of Table 11.1 relating to the composite index (CI) of development in agricultural sector shows that the district of Joypurhat ranked first, while the district of Bhola ranked last. The CI of these two districts was found to be 0.4525 and 1 respectively. The level of development in Joypurhat was 2.25 times higher than that of Bhola. This indicates that there was great disparity in the level of development in agriculture sector between the districts. For relative comparison, 64 districts were classified into three levels of development. A simple ranking of the districts on the basis of CI and its three ranges between (0,1) obtainable from Beta distribution would be sufficient for classification of districts according to their level of development. The districts with CI between 0 and 0.73 may be put in category 1 as developed, districts with CI between 0.73 and 0.83 may be placed in category II as developing and districts with CI between 0.83 and 1 may be put in category III as the least developed. Of the 64 districts, 17 or 27% districts were observed to be in category I, 27 or 42% in category II and 20 or 31% in category III. The list of district by level of development is shown in Table 11.2. The least developed districts listed in column 3 of this table need improvement

Table 11.1: Composite Indices and their Ranks by District and Sector

Name of district	Sectors									
	Agriculture		*Rural Industry*		*Infrastructure & Social Services*		*Education*		*Population*	
	CI	*Rank*	*CI*	*Rank*	*CI*	*Rank*	*CI*	*Rank*	*CI*	*Rank*
1	*2*	*3*	*4*	*5*	*6*	*7*	*8*	*9*	*10*	*11*
01. Barisal	0.740	21	0.829	8	0.720	16	0.348	6	0.794	38
02. Barguna	0.834	45	0.931	54	0857	47	0.0436	12	0.758	21
03. Bhola	1.000	64	0.922	50	1.018	64	0.631	27	0.726	16
04. Jhalokati	0.770	30	0.898	36	0.605	4	0.118	2	0.764	24
05. Patuakhali	0.809	39	0.917	46	0.828	45	0.429	11	0.767	27
06. Pirojpur	0.865	52	0.924	51	0.535	2	0.090	1	0.740	18
07. Bandarban	0.947	60	0.860	15	0.971	61	0.825	56	0.573	4
08. Brahmanbaria	0.749	25	0.864	20	0.867	49	0.696	42	0.843	51
09. Chandpur	0.699	11	0.918	47	0.723	17	0.513	17	0.915	59
10. Chittagong	0.803	38	0.718	3	0.805	36	0.556	19	0.639	8
11. Comilla	0.627	6	0.861	17	0.679	8	0.364	9	0.875	55

(Table Contd...)

Table 11.1: Contd...

	1	*2*	*3*	*4*	*5*	*6*	*7*	*8*	*9*	*10*	*11*
12.	Cox's Bazar	0.775	32	0.658	1	0.948	59	0.761	49	0.971	63
13.	Feni	0.593	4	0.902	38	0.527	1	0.389	10	0.884	56
14.	Khagrachari	0.881	58	0.833	27	0.916	57	0.788	54	0.575	5
15.	Lakshmipur	0.800	37	0.935	56	0.734	18	0.461	14	0.761	22
16.	Noakhali	0.835	44	0.908	40	0.815	39	0.490	15	0.799	39
17.	Rangamati	0.859	50	0.856	13	0.969	60	0.649	30	0.565	3
18.	Dhaka	0.748	24	0.666	2	0.811	38	0.270	3	0.999	64
19.	Faridpur	0.745	22	0.870	24	0.822	42	0.557	20	0.767	26
20.	Gazipur	0.740	20	0.857.	14	0.803	35	0.596	21	0.515	2
21.	Gopalgonj	0.746	23	0.811	6	0.671	6	0.331	5	0.769	28
22.	Jamalpur	0.787	35	0.910	43	0.740	20	0.940	64	0.770	29
23.	Kishorgonj	0.750	27	0.894	32	0.870	50	0.667	33	0.786	32
24.	Madaripur	0.810	40	0.914	45	0.779	29	0.704	44	0.813	45
25.	Manikgonj	0.719	15	0.912	44	0.705	12	0.718	45	0.812	44
26.	Munshigonj	0.866	53	0.861	16	0.603	3	0.497	16	0.817	46
27.	Mymensingh	0.825	43	0.902	39	0.796	34	0.631	28	0.864	54
28.	Narayangonj	0.762	29	0.811	5	0.700	11	0.436	13	0.647	9

Table 11.1: Contd...

	1	2	3	4	5	6	7	8	9	10	11
29.	Narshingdi	0.632	7	0.782	4	0.644	5	0.703	43	0.860	53
30.	Netrokone	0.758	28	0.941	58	0.872	51	0.579	38	0.804	42
31.	Rajbari	0.734	18	0.866	22	0.820	40	0.803	55	0.955	61
32.	Shariatpur	0.836	46	0.909	42	0.901	55	0.731	47	0.788	35
33.	Sherpur	0.720	16	0.929	53	0.768	25	0.875	60	0.785	31
34.	Tangail	0.701	12	0.900	37	0.770	27	0.674	35	0.787	37
35.	Khulna	0.974	62	0.870	23	0.929	58	0.352	7	0.421	1
36.	Bagerhat	0.867	54	0.873	25	0.822	41	0.329	4	0.678	11
37.	Chuadanga	0.719	14	0.895	34	0.754	21	0.619	24	0.709	12
38.	Jessore	0.634	8	0.862	19	0.673	7	0.693	41	0.761	23
39.	Jhenaidah	0.556	3	0.862	18	0.758	24	0.629	26	0.909	58
40.	Kushtia	0.617	5	0.897	35	0.856	46	0.772	51	0.596	6
41.	Magur	0.472	2	0.886	29	0.714	14	0.667	32	0.804	41
42.	Meherpur	0.711	13	0.852	12	0.754	22	0.768	50	0.723	14
43.	Narail	0.678	10	0.881	26	0.715	15	0.358	8	0.758	20
44.	Satkhira	0.788	36	0.866	21	0.872	52	0.522	18	0.791	36

(Table Contd...)

Table 11.1: Contd...

1		2	3	4	5	6	7	8	9	10	11
45.	Bogra	0.675	9	0.886	30	0.712	13	0.641	29	0.961	62
46.	Dinajpur	0.727	17	0.918	48	0.735	19	0.670	34	0.718	13
47.	Gaibandha	0.821	42	0.955	64	0.822	43	0.720	46	0.854	52
48.	Joypurhat	0.460	1	0.848	11	0.679	9	0.742	48	0.832	50
49.	Kurigram	0.879	57	0.954	63	0.977	62	0.893	62	0.787	33
50.	Lalmonirhat	0.868	55	0.937	57	0.902	56	0.686	39	0.733	17
51.	Naogaon	0.738	19	0.951	62	0.858	48	0.612	23	0.803	40
52.	Natore	0.780	33	0.926	52	0.769	26	0.677	37	0.767	25
53.	Nawabgonj	0.850	47	0.944	59	0.889	54	0.937	63	0.825	47
54.	Nilphamari	0.855	48	0.945	61	0.787	31	0.890	61	0.794	37
55.	Pabna	0.814	41	0.818	7	0.779	30	0.779	53	0.826	49
56.	Panchagarh	0.882	59	0.918	49	0.791	33	0.690	40	0.749	19
57.	Rahshahi	0.858	49	0.842	10	0.741	28	0.625	25	0.627	7
58.	Rangpur	0.878	56	0.933	55	0.790	32	0.832	57	0.771	30
59.	Sirajgonj	0.773	31	0.841	9	0.687	10	0.866	59	0.665	10
60.	Thakurgaon	0.749	26	0.991	31	0.809	37	0.777	52	0.723	15
61.	Habigonj	0.782	34	0.909	41	0.886	53	0.662	31	0.826	48
62.	Maulvibazar	0.954	61	0.886	28	0.825	44	0.600	22	0.812	43
63.	Sunamgonj	0.993	63	0.940	60	0.978	63	0.836	58	0.890	57
64.	Sylhet	0.861	51	0.894	33	0.754	23	0.676	36	0.941	60

Table 11.2: Distribution of District by Level Development in Agriculture Sector

Development (0-0.73)		*Development (0.73-0.83)*		*Least Development (0.83.1.0)*	
1.	Joypurhat	18.	Rajbari	45.	Borguna
2.	Magura	19.	Noagaon	46.	Sharitpur
3.	Jhenaidah	20.	Gazipur	47.	Nowabgonj
4.	Feni	21.	Barisal	48.	Nilphamari
5.	Kustia	22.	Faridpur	49.	Rajshahi
6.	Comilla	23.	Gopalgonj	50.	Rangamati
7.	Narshindi	24.	Dhaka	51.	Sylhet
8.	Jessore	25.	Brahman Baria	52.	Pirojpur
9.	Bogra	26.	Thakurgan	53.	Munshigonj
10.	Narail	27.	Kishoregonj	54.	Bagerhat
11.	Chandpur	28.	Netrokona	55.	Lalmonirhat
12.	Tangail	29.	Narayangong	56.	Rangpur
13.	Meherpur	30.	Jhalakhati	57.	Kurigram
14.	Chuadanga	31.	Sirajgonj	58.	Khagrachari
15.	Manikgonj	32.	Sirajgonj	59.	Panchagar
16.	Sherpur	33.	Cox's Bazar	60.	Bandarban
17.	Dinajpur	34.	Habigonj	61.	Maulovi Bazar
		35.	Jamalpur	62.	Khulna
		36.	Shatkhira	63.	Sunamgonj
		37.	Laksmipur	64.	Bhola
		38.	Chittagong		
		39.	Patuakhali		
		40.	Madaripur		
		41.	Pabna		
		42.	Gaibanda		
		43.	Mymensingh		
		44.	Noalhali		

in all the seven indicators and more specifically in area under HYV, per capita availability of cultivated land, cropping intensity, area covered by small and marginal farmers, number of landless labourers, tenant and landless households. It is interesting to note that out of 20 least developed districts, 3 districts from Chittagong division, 2 from Dhaka division, 7 from Rajshahi division, 3 from Barisal division, 2 from Khulna division and 3 from Sylhet division fell in this category.

Rural Industrial Sector

The estimated composite index for rural industrial sector provides a comprehensive picture of the development status of small and cottage industries of each of 64 districts. Almost all the districts of Bangladesh are observed to be poorly developed in this respect in relation to other sectoral developments. The lowest value of the composite index was 0.66, which is far away from 0 but closer to 1 (column 3 of Table 11.1). The highest value appeared to be 0.955. The disparity between the lowest and the highest values was 0.30. However, in respect of rural industrial development, the districts of Dhaka and Cox's Bazar were found to be in the first position whereas the district of Gaibandha was in the last position. The district of Chittagong ranked second in this respect. For relative comparison, the districts with composite indices between 0 and 0.86 were considered as developed districts. The districts with CI between 0.87 and 0.91 were considered in category II as developing and those with CI $\geq$ 0.91 were taken in category III and classified as least developed. Only 20 districts were in category I, 25 districts, the largest number, were in category II and 19 districts were in category III. One of the important reasons for Dhaka being first in rural industrial development is that more than 60 per cent of total credit disbursed by the schedule and agricultural banks was distributed in Dhaka division

Table 11.3: Distribution of District of Level of Development in Rural Industrial Sector

Level of Development					
Development (0-0.86)		*Development (0.86-0.91)*		*Least Development (0.91-1)*	
1.	Cox's bazar	1.	Satkhira	1.	Patuakhali
2.	Dhaka	2.	Rajbari	2.	Chandpur
3.	Chittagong	3.	Khulna	3.	Dinajpur
4.	Narsingdi	4.	Faridpur	4.	Panchagarah
5.	Narayangonj	5.	Bagerhat	5.	Bhola
6.	Gapalgonj	6.	Narail	6.	Pirojpur
7.	Pabna	7.	Khagrachari	7.	Natore
8.	Barisal	8.	Moulvibazar	8.	Sherpur
9.	Sirajgonj	9.	Magura	9.	Borguna
10.	Rajshahi	10.	Bogra	10.	Rangpur
11.	Joypurhat	11.	Thakurgaon	11.	Lakshmipur
12.	Meherpur	12.	Kishoegonj	12.	Lalmonirhat
13.	Rangamati	13.	Sylhet	13.	Netrokona
14.	Gazipur	14.	Chuadanga	14.	Nawabgonj
15.	Bandarban	15.	Kustia	15.	Nilphamari
16.	Munshigonj	16.	Jhalokati	16.	Sunamgonj
17.	Comilla	17.	Tangail	17.	Noagaon
18.	Jhenaidah	18.	Feni	18.	Kurigram
19.	Jessore1	19.	Mymensingh	19.	Gaibandha
20.	Brahmanbaria	20.	Noakhali		
		21.	Hobigonj		
		22.	Shariatpur		
		23.	Jamalpur		
		24.	Manikgonj		
		25.	Madaripu		

and more than 50 per cent in Dhaka district alone. The list of district by level of development in rural industrial sectors in shown in Table 11.3. In rural industrial sector, all the least developed districts require improvements of varying degree in indicators like small industries, handloom, cottage industries and credit for them. It is evident from this table that none of the districts from Sylhet division fell in category I, whereas, 5 districts from Dhaka division, 4 from Chittagong, 4 from Rajshahi, and one district from both Khulna and Barisal divisions fell under this category. On the contrary, 19 or 30% districts in Bangladesh had CI values between 0.915 and 1 and were observed to be very poorly developed. It is interesting to note that out of 19 least developed districts, 10 or 53 per cent belonged to Rajshahi division, 4 to Barisal, 2 to Chittagong, 2 districts to Dhaka and 1 to Sylhet division.

Infrastructure and Social Services Sector

Columns 5 and 6 of Table 11.1 present the value and ranks of CI for each of the 64 districts in respect of infrastructure and social services sectors. The level of development in these sectors indicated that Feni occupied the first position but the district of Bhola ranked the last. The values of the composite indices for these two districts were 0.5270 and 1 respectively. The level of development in the former was almost 2 times higher than in the latter district. The second best district was Pirojpur and the level of disparity between the districts ranking first and the second was not too high. Sunamgaonj, Kurigram, Bandarban, and Rangamati were also found to be poorly developed with CI values close to 1. For relative comparison the districts with CI between 0 to 0.75 may be put in category I as developed.

The districts, which have CI values between 0.75 to 0.84, may be considered in category II as developing and those with CI between 0.84 to 1 may be considered in category III as least developed (Table 11.4). It transpires from

Table 11.4: Distribution of District by Level of Development in Infrastructure and Social Sectors

Level of Development					
Development (0-0.75)		*Development (0.75-0.86)*		*Least Development (0.86-1)*	
1.	Feni	1.	Jhenaidah	1.	Brahmanbaria
2.	Pirojpur	2.	Sherpur	2.	Kishoregonj
3.	Munshigonj	3.	Natore	3.	Netrokona
4.	Jhalokati	4.	Tangail	4.	Satkhira
5.	Narshingdi	5.	Rajshahi	5.	Hobigonj
6.	Gopalgonj	6.	Madaripur	6.	Nawabpur
7.	Jessore	7.	Pabna	7.	Shariatpur
8.	Comilla	8.	Nilphamari	8.	Lalmonirhat
9.	Joypurhat	9.	Rangpur	9.	Khagrachari
10.	Sirajgonj	10.	Panchagarh	10.	Khulna
11.	Narayangonj	11.	Mymensingh	11.	Cox's Bazar
12.	Manikgonj	12.	Gazipur	12.	Rangamati
13.	Bogra	13.	Chittagong	13.	Bandarban
14.	Magura	14.	Thakurgaon	14.	Kurigram
15.	Narail	15.	Dhaka	15.	Sunamgonj
16.	Barisal	16.	Noakhali	16.	Bhola
17.	Chandpur	17.	Rajbari		
18.	Lakshmipur	18.	Bagerhat		
19.	Dinajpur	19.	Faridpur		
20.	Jamalpur	20.	Gaibandha		
21.	Chuadanga	21.	Moulvibazar		
22.	Meherpur	22.	Patuakhali		
23.	Sylhet	23.	Kustia		
		24.	Borguna		
		25.	Naogaon		

Table 11.4 that 23 or 36% districts were in category I, 25 or 39% in category II and 16 or 29% in category III. Improvement in infrastructure and social services sectors is required uniformly in all the sixteen least developed districts for indicators concerning banking facilities, post office, educational institutions and health care centres, electrification of villages and length of road. Out of 16 least developed districts, 3 districts were from Dhaka division, 5 from Chittagong, 3 from Rajshahi, 2 from Khulna, 1 from Barisal and 2 from Sylhet division.

Education

It may be seen from column 7 of Table 11.1 that the district of Pirojpur occupied the first position, while Jamalpur occupied the last in literacy rates. The CI for education sector varied from the lowest of 0.0898 to the highest of 0.9404. The variation in the level of development in literacy between the districts was found to be highest as compared to the other sectors. The level of development of Pirojpur in literacy was 10 times higher than that of Jamalpur. The districts with CI between 0 - 0.56 may be put in category I as developed, between 0.56 - 0.74 in category II as developing and those with CI between 0.74 – 1.00 in category III as least developed (Table 11.5). It is evident from Table 11.5 that 20 or 31% districts belonged to category I, 28 or 44% were in category II and 16 or 25% districts were in category III. These sixteen districts need improvement in literacy and adult literacy in general and female literacy in particular.

Population

In Population sector Khulna ranked the first, while Dhaka ranked the last. The values of CI for these two

Table 11.5: Distribution of District by Level of Development in Education Sector

	Level of Development	
Development (0-0.56)	*Development (0.56-0.74)*	*Least Development (0.74-1)*
1. Pirpjpur	1. Gazipur	1. Cox's Bazar
2. Jhalokhati	2. Moulvibazar	2. Meherpur
3. Dhaka	3. Naogaon	3. Kustia
4. Bagerhat	4. Chuadanga	4. Thakurgaon
5. Gopalgonj	5. Rajshahi	5. Pabna
6. Barisal	6. Jhenaidah	6. Khagrachari
7. Khulna	7. Bhola	7. Rajbai
8. Narail	8. Mymensingh	8. Bandarban
9. Comilla	9. Bogra	9. Rangpur
10. Feni	10. Rangamati	10. Sunamgonj
11. Patuakhali	11. Hobigonj	11. Sirajgonj
12. Borguna	12. Magura	12. Sherpur
13. Narayangonj	13. Keshoregonj	13. Nilphamari
14. Lakshmipur	14. Dinajpur	14. Kurigram
15. Noakhali	15. Tangail	15. Nawabgon
16. Munshigonj	16. Sylhet	16. Jamalpur
17. Chandpur	17. Natore	
18. Satkhira	18. Netrokona	
19. Chittagong	19. Lalmonirhat	
20. Faridpur	20. Panchagarh	
	21. Jessore	
	22. Brahmanbaria	
	23. Narshingdi	
	24. Madaripur	
	25. Manikgonj	
	26. Gaibandha	
	27. Shariatpur	
	28. Joypurhat	

districts were 0.4213 and 1 respectively and the difference between them is vast. The main reason for which Dhaka is last is that it has the highest population density due to large-scale migration of the people to Dhaka Metropolitan City from other districts. The districts with CI between 0 - 0.73 may be put in category I as developed, between 0.73 – 0.83 may be placed in category II as developing and those with CI between 0.83 – 1.00 may be put in category III as least developed districts. Out of 64 districts, 17 or 27% were in category I, 33 or 54% in category II and 14 or 22% in category III. The least developed districts in this sector require reduction in the indicators like decadal growth of population, population density and household size for their socio-economic development. Distribution of districts by level of development in population sector is presented in Table 11.6.

Regional Disparity in Development

Physical Characteristics of Regions

It is important to find out the relative share of area and population affected due to poor development in selected sectors in different regions. For regional analysis of development, 64 districts comprising Bangladesh have been stratified into six administrative regions, namely, Dhaka, Chittagong, Rajshahi, Khulna, Barisal and Sylhet on the basis of administrative, physical and locational characteristics. These are also known as administrative divisions. Dhaka division forms the central region and the capital of the country is located in this region. It consists of 17 districts covering an area of 31119 sq.km. (21.23%) and with a population of about 37767 thousand (30.18%). Chittagong division located in the south-eastern region has 10 districts with

Table 11.6: Distribution of District by Level of Development in Population Sector

Level of Development					
Development (0-0.56)		*Development (0.56-0.74)*		*Least Development (0.74-1)*	
1.	Khulna	1.	Pirojpur	1.	Brahmanbari
2.	Gazipur	2.	Panchagarh	2.	Gaibandha
3.	Rangamati	3.	Narail	3.	Narshaindi
4.	Bandarban	4.	Borguna	4.	Mymsinsingh
5.	Khagrachari	5.	Lakshmipur	5.	Comilla
6.	Kustia	6.	Jessore	6.	Feni
7.	Rajshahi	7.	Jhalokhati	7.	Sunamgonj
8.	Chittagong	8.	Natore	8.	Jhenaidah
9.	Narayangonj	9.	Faridpur	9.	Chandpur
10.	Sirajgonj	10.	Patuakhali	10.	Sylhet
11.	Bagerhat	11.	Gopalgonj	11.	Rajbari
12.	Chuadanga	12.	Jamalpur	12.	Bogra
13.	Dinajpur	13.	Rangpur	13.	Cox's bazar
14.	Meherpur	14.	Sherpur	14.	Dhaka
15.	Thakurgaon	15.	Kishoregonj		
16.	Bhola	16.	Kurigram		
17.	Lalmonirhat	17.	Tangail		
		18.	Shariatpur		
		19.	Satkhira		
		20.	Nilphamari		
		21.	Barisal		
		22.	Noakhali		
		23.	Naogaon		
		24.	Magura		
		25.	Netrokona		
		26.	Moulvibazar		
		27.	Manikgonj		
		28.	Madaripur		
		29.	Munshigonj		
		30.	Nawabgaonj		
		31.	Hobigonj		
		32.	Pabna		
		33.	Joypurhat		

an area of 32771 sq.km.(22.36%) and population of 23894 thousand (19.49%). It shows marked variation in topographic, geographic and socio-economic characteristics from those of other regions. The physical feature of this region consists of some scenic blending of hills and valleys and patches of green forest. This region is well linked to the capital city and has the largest seaport of the country. Rajshahi division forms the north-western region. There are 16 districts in this region with an area of 34511 sq.km. (23.55%) and 30125 thousand population (24.58%). This region has less fertile soil and rainfall and has less irrigation facilities. The economy of this region is more rural and agricultural than that of other regions and has less link with the developed administration. Khulna division, which forms the south and southwestern region, has 10 districts with an area of 22274 sq.km. (15.20%) and a population of 14521 thousand (11.85%). It is largely a deltaic region with vast low-lying alluvial plain lands intersected by many rivers. The region has the largest single block of forest called Sundarban and is situated at the extreme southern part of the region. The second seaport (Mongla) is situated in this region. Barisal division with 7 districts and covering an area of 13297 sq.km. (9.07%) forms the southern region. The physical, cultural, socio-economic and locational characteristics are similar to that of Khulna division. Sylhet division consists of 4 districts having an area of about 12596 sq.km. (8.59%)' and about 7819 thousand population (6.38%), and forms the northeastern region of the country. Like Chittagong division, its physical feature consists of hills and valleys, springs and plain lands intersected by rivers, beels and haors. This region possesses some important natural resources like gas, forest land etc. The economy of this region is largely dependent upon the agriculture and tea industry. The number of districts, area and population covered under different levels of development in selected sectors by region have been set out in Tables 11.7 to 11.11.

Relative Share of Area and Population in Development

On the basis of selected indicators in agricultural sector, the level of development in Sylhet division is the worst compared to other divisions. Three districts of this division covering an area of 79 per cent and population of 78 per cent are found to be in least developed category and none of the districts from this division fall under the developed category (Table 11.7). The development of Chittagong division in respect of agriculture is moderate compared to other regions. About 39 per cent of the area and 5 per cent of the population of Chittagong division belong to the least developed category, while majority of the area (44%) and the population (60%) fall under the developing category. Khulna division ranks first and about 45 per cent of the total area and 60 per cent of its population fall under developed category. Four districts from Dhaka, three districts from Chittagong and three districts from Rajshahi belong to this category. There are twenty-seven districts in Bangladesh covering an area of 34.68 per cent and with a population of 38.06 per cent that belong to category II which represents medium level development.

Based on selected indicators for rural industry sector, ten districts in Rajshahi division covering an area of 62 per cent and population of 60 per cent belong to category III as poorly developed in respect of rural industrial development (Table 11.8). This situation is more deplorable in Barisal division where more than 73

Table 11.7: Area and Population under Different Levels of Development in Agriculture Sector by Division

Division	*Level of Development*								
	Developed (category I)			*Developed (category II)*			*Least Developed (category III)*		
	No. of districts	*Area (%)*	*Population (%)*	*No. of districts*	*Area (%)*	*Population (%)*	*No. of districts*	*Area (%)*	*Population (%)*
Dhaka	4	23.46	20.60	11	69.68	73.11	2	6.86	2.29
Chittagong	3	16.93	34.40	5	43.77	60.36	3	39.30	5.24
Rajshahi	3	21.23	18.55	6	41.10	40.57	7	37.67	40.88
Khulna	6	45.17	59.74	1	17.32	12.32	2	37.51	27.94
Barisal	-	-	-	3	50.82	55.46	3	49.18	44.56
Sylhet	-	-	-	1	20.94	22.44	3	79.06	77.56

Table 11.8: Area and Population under Different Levels of Development in Rural Industrial Sector by Division

Division	*Level of Development*								
	Developed (category I)			*Developed (category II)*			*Least Developed (category III)*		
	No. of districts	*Area (%)*	*Population (%)*	*No. of districts*	*Area (%)*	*Population (%)*	*No. of districts*	*Area (%)*	*Population (%)*
Dhaka	6	24.26	41.25	9	62.33	50.09	2	13.41	8.66
Chittagong	6	71.35	66.00	3	19.01	17.80	2	9.64	16.20
Rajshahi	4	23.88	26.32	2	13.70	14.13	10	62.42	59.55
Khulna	3	23.54	31.27	7	76.46	68.73	-	-	-
Barisal	1	20.99	29.55	1	5.70	8.94	4	73.31	61.51
Sylhet	-	-	-	3	70.86	74.70	1	29.14	25.30

Table 11.9: Area and Population under Different Levels of Development in Infrastructue and Social Services Sector by Division

Division	Level of Development								
	Developed (category I)			*Developed (category II)*			*Least Developed (category III)*		
	No. of districts	*Area (%)*	*Population (%)*	*No. of districts*	*Area (%)*	*Population (%)*	*No. of districts*	*Area (%)*	*Population (%)*
Dhaka	6	24.92	31.26	8	53.61	59.28	3	21.47	14.96
Chittagong	4	21.89	41.19	2	24.06	36.69	5	54.05	22.12
Rajshahi	4	28.46	30.55	9	56.36	55.38	3	15.18	14.07
Khulna	5	29.09	37.51	3	33.86	33.76	2	37.05	28.70
Barisal	3	36.53	52.61	2	37.88	27.34	1	25.59	20.05
Sylhet	1	27.71	31.99	1	22.22	20.22	1	50.07	47.79

Table 11.10: Area and Population under Different Levels of Development in Education Sector by Division

Division	*Level of Development*								
	Developed (category I)			*Developed (category II)*			*Least Developed (category III)*		
	No. of districts	*Area (%)*	*Population (%)*	*No. of districts*	*Area (%)*	*Population (%)*	*No. of districts*	*Area (%)*	*Population (%)*
Dhaka	5	21.66	35.82	9	63.83	52.54	3	14.51	11.64
Chittagong	6	45.95	77.88	2	24.54	12.34	3	29.51	9.78
Rajshahi	-	-	-	9	57.63	56.18	7	42.37	43.82
Khulna	4	59.72	44.87	4	30.24	39.43	2	10.49	15.70
Barisal	5	75.41	79.95	1	25.59	20.05	-	-	-
Sylhet	-	-	-	3	70.86	74.70	1	29.14	25.30

Table 11.11: Area and under Different Levels of Development in Population Sector by Division

Division	*Level of Development*								
	Developed (category I)			*Developed (category II)*			*Least Developed (category III)*		
	No. of districts	*Area (%)*	*Population (%)*	*No. of districts*	*Area (%)*	*Population (%)*	*No. of districts*	*Area (%)*	*Population (%)*
Dhaka	2	8.03	9.91	11	58.98	51.01	4	25.99	37.08
Chittagong	4	56.69	30.64	2	12.38	17.12	5	30.93	52.24
Rajshahi	5	33.02	32.08	9	52.21	50.14	2	14.77	17.78
Khulna	5	53.20	49.52	4	38.00	39.74	1	8.80	10.74
Barisal	1	25.59	20.05	5	74.41	79.95	-	-	-
Sylhet	-	-	-	2	43.16	42.72	2	56.84	57.28

per cent of its area and 62 per cent of its population fall in the least developed category. Chittagong division ranks the first, while Dhaka occupies the second position in this respect. None of the districts from Sylhet and Khulna divisions fall in developed and least developed categories respectively. Twenty-five districts covering 38.94 per cent of the area and 35.90 per cent of population of Bangladesh belong to the developing category. It is clear that there is wide disparity in the development of rural industrial sector among regions and about 26 per cent of the population of the country belong to districts having poor level of development out of which about 56 per cent people have come from the north-western region.

It is evident from Table 11.9 that majority of the districts (25 or 39%) in Bangladesh fall in category II as developing in respect of infrastructure and social services development. In this respect Barisal ranks the first, while Sylhet ranks the last. The position of Chittagong is relatively better than Dhaka, Rajshahi and Khulna divisions. But out of five, four districts of Chittagong division covering 54 per cent of the area and 22 per cent of the population fall in the least developed category. Eight districts from Dhaka with about 54 per cent area and 59 per cent population as well as nine districts from Rajshahi covering about 56 per cent area and 55 per cent population belong to category II. Infrastructure and social services sectors in these districts are at the middle level of development and could improve in future. However, six districts from Dhaka, four from Chittagong, four from Rajshahi, five from Khulna, three from Barisal and one from Sylhet fall in category I as developed.

On the basis of the selected indicators on educational development, Rajshahi division ranks the last, while Barisal ranks the first. There are nine districts in Rajshahi covering 58 per cent area and 56 per cent population that fall in category II as developing and 7 districts with 42 per cent area and 44 per cent population that belong to least developed category (Table 11.10). None of the districts from Rajshahi and Sylhet fall in category I as developed in respect of educational development, while 74 per cent area and 80 per cent population in Barisal, 59 per cent area and 45 per cent population in Khulna, 46 per cent area and 78 per cent population in Chittagong and 22 per cent area and 36 per cent population in Dhaka divisions are found to be in developed category. None of the districts from Barisal fall in category III. Twenty-eight districts in Bangladesh are observed to be in developing stage in respect of development in education. Of these, nine districts are from Dhaka and nine from Rajshahi division. Largest disparity in educational development is observed among different regions and about 20 per cent population of the country belong to the districts having poor level of development out of which about 55 per cent people come from north-western region.

In population development, Sylhet division is observed to be in the worst condition although its share of population is the lowest and none of its districts fall in developed category. Dhaka division ranks next to Sylhet and it shares the highest proportion of the population. Only two districts from Dhaka belong to category I as developed, eleven to category II as developing and four to category III as poorly developed. The value of CI of Dhaka district is estimated at 1, which signifies the worst position in respect of population development. The position of Chittagong and Rajshahi divisions is third and fourth respectively. About 74 per cent area and 80 per cent population of Barisal division fall in developing category and none of the districts belong to least developed category (Table 11.11).

Inter-Relationship Among Different Sectors

In order to measure the degree of relationship among agriculture (AGRI), rural industry (RIN), physical infrastructure and social services (INFRA), education (ED), and population sectors (POP), spearman rank correlation has been estimated. The ranks of the districts in respect of human development index (HDI) as estimated by the UNDP (1995) and incidence of poverty (head count ratio) as estimated by the BBS (1995) were also taken into consideration to measure inter-relationship between the two sectors. The estimated rank correlation coefficients between the sectors are shown in Table 11.12.

Table 11.12: Spearman Rank Correlation Coefficients

Sector	*Correlation Coefficients (r)*					
RIN	0.3189 (.010)					
INFRA	0.5538 (0.000)	0.2120 (0.093)				
EDU	0.1015 (0.425)	0.2089 (0.098)	0.2853 (0.022)			
POP	-0.2633 (0.036)	0.0799 (0.530)	-0.1263 (0.320)	0.0857 (0.501)		
HDI	0.0468 (0.713)	0.3845 (0.002)	0.1888 (0.135)	0.5580 (0.000)	0.2107 (0.095)	
POV	0.2546 (0.042)	0.6110 (0.000)	0.1871 (0.139)	0.4128 (0.001)	0.0396 (0.7560)	0.4955 (0.000)
	AGRI	RIN	INFRA	EDU	POP	HDI

Note: Figure in the parenthesis is the p values i.e. level of significance.

The correlation coefficients between the rankings of development of agriculture and rural industry, between agriculture and physical infrastructure and social services, between agriculture and incidence of poverty are observed to be positive and their respective values are 0.3189; 0.5538 and 0.2546. These values are significant at 5 per cent level and the findings indicate a significant correlation or interdependence between them. The ranks of agriculture sector show disagreement with the ranks of population sector. The correlation coefficient between rankings of agriculture and population sectors is estimated to be -0.2633 and is significant at 5 per cent level. The magnitude of correlation coefficients between rankings of rural industry and HDI as well as incidence of poverty are worked out as 0.3845 and 0.6610 respectively and these values are highly significant at 1 per cent level. This implies that developed districts in respect of HDI are also developed in rural industry and have lower incidence of poverty. The correlation coefficient between rankings of physical infrastructure and social services and educational development is estimated to be 0.2853 and is significant at 2 per cent level but lower in magnitude. Education and HDI are highly correlated and the correlation coefficient is estimated at 0.5580 which is significant at 1 per cent level. This is expected since literacy rate which is included in education sector is also included in estimating HDI. The districts which are educationally developed have higher value of HDI and these factors contribute positively in reducing poverty. The rank correlation coefficients between education and poverty and between HDI and poverty are 0.4128 and 0.4955 respectively and these coefficients are significantly different from zero.

To sum up, for high economic development and reduction of poverty, agriculture, rural industry and infrastructure and social services should be developed simultaneously and they should go hand in hand. Population pressure is working as a hindrance to development in all the sectors and in some sectors it is negatively influencing the progress of development. Although the various development programmes have simulated growth in various sectors, their impact appears to have been eroded by the rapid population growth. Human capital development has the largest impact on poverty reduction and human capital is positively influenced by the development of agriculture, rural industry, physical and social infrastructure sectors. Thus, packaging of these sectors will not only enhance economic growth, but also accelerate the rate of poverty reduction. While allocating resources, the government should be more careful in adopting a balanced approach recognizing the role of these sectors for poverty alleviation.

Level of Development and Incidence of Poverty: A Regional Analysis

The economy of Bangladesh in general and the rural economy in particular have been experiencing severe strain/constraints mainly due to natural calamities like recurrent drought, flood, water logging, tornado, cyclone etc. With frequent disasters, it is very difficult to bring about any significant economic development and to help the poor graduate themselves from poverty to prosperity. A major portion of development resources is spent in maintaining the essential supplies as relief and social services to a large number of distressed people. However, three poverty indices known as head count (P_0), poverty gap (P_1) and squared poverty gap (P_2) were estimated for 64 districts to measure poverty and are shown in Table 11.13.

Table 11.13: Estimated Poverty Measures By Districts With Fixed Calorie Intakes (2122 kcal.)

Locality	*Head Count Index (P_0)*	*Poverty Gap Index (P_1)*	*Squared Poverty Gap Index (P_2)*
1	*2*	*3*	*4*
Barisal	49.70	0.12	0.04
Barguna	52.21	0.20	0.10
Bhola	56.69	0.19	0.09
Jhalokati	53.00	0.17	0.08
Patuakhali	50.10	0.20	0.10
Pirojour	48.10	0.17	0.08
Bandarban	50.00	0.17	0.09
Brahmanbaria	54.80	0.21	0.11
Chandpur	52.29	0.18	0.08
Chittagong	36.27	0.11	0.05
Comilla	50.73	0.20	0.10
Cox's Bazar	39.40	0.13	0.06
Feni	41.48	0.14	0.07
Khagrachhari	47.09	0.17	0.08
Lakshmipur	49.20	0.18	0.09
Noakhali	52.83	0.20	0.10
Rangamati	39.80	0.13	0.06
Dhaka	23.29	0.07	0.03
Faridpur	47.19	0.19	0.09
Gazipur	47.20	0.17	0.08
Gopalgonj	47.70	0.17	0.09

Table 11.13: Contd...

1	*2*	*3*	*4*
Jamalpur	56.91	0.23	0.12
Kishoregonj	45.67	0.19	0.10
Madaripur	51.39	0.19	0.09
Manikgonj	50.87	0.19	0.10
Munshigonj	39.28	0.14	0.07
Mymensingh	53.29	0.22	0.11
Narayangonj	37.07	0.13	0.06
Narsingdi	40.64	0.15	0.07
Netrokona	53.32	0.23	0.12
Rajbari	48.04	0.18	0.09
Shariatpur	54.40	0.20	0.10
Sherpur	58.98	0.21	0.10
Tangail	43.25	0.18	0.10
Khulna	47.69	0.18	0.09
Bagerhat	54.69	0.20	0.10
Chuadanga	50.00	0.19	0.09
Jessore	43.60	0.17	0.09
Jhenaidah	48.80	0.18	0.09
Kushtia	53.85	0.22	0.12
Magura	52.51	0.21	0.11
Meherpur	46.95	0.16	0.08
Narail	42.41	0.16	0.07
Satkhira	45.02	0.17	0.08
Bogra	50.70	0.20	0.11
Dinajpur	47.70	0.20	0.11
Gaibandha	62.00	0.27	0.15
Joypurhat	45.56	0.16	0.08
Kurikram	65.20	0.31	0.19

(Table Contd...)

Table 11.13: Contd...

1	*2*	*3*	*4*
Lalmonirhat	57.97	0.25	0.14
Naogaon	45.89	0.17	0.10
Natore	49.90	0.20	0.10
Nawabganj	52.69	0.21	0.11
Nilphamari	61.18	0.28	0.15
Pabna	48.45	0.20	0.11
Panchagar	61.90	0.29	0.17
Rajshahi	43.11	0.16	0.09
Rangpur	56.89	0.25	0.14
Sirajganj	55.49	0.23	0.12
Thakurgaon	53.63	0.23	0.13
Habiganj	50.40	0.19	0.10
Maulavibazar	35.08	0.14	0.07
Sunamganj	49.80	0.20	0.10
Sylhet	50.40	0.21	0.11
Bangladesh	49.27	0.19	0.10

Source: BBS (1998). Analysis of Basic Needs Dimension of Poverty, Vol. III, Table 6.6, p. 106.

The head-count index (P_0) shows the per centage of household/ population below the poverty line; the income-gap index (P_1) reflects the average distance below the poverty line and measures the depth of poverty; and the squared poverty-gap (P_2), in which the above distances are squared to make the measure sensitive to changes in inequality among the poor, measures the severity of poverty [Foster, Greer and Thorbecke (1984)].

The incidence of poverty in Kurigram, Nilphamari, Gaibandha, Panchagarh, Lalmonirhat, Sirajgonj,

Rangpur, Kushtia, Jamalpur, Sherpur, Mymensingh and Bhola districts is found to be higher than other districts as well as the Bangladesh average. The per centage of households below the poverty line in these districts stands at 65.20, 61.18, 62.00, 61.90, 57.97, 55.49, 56.86, 53.85, 56.91, 58.98, 53.29 and 56.69, respectively as against the corresponding value of 49.27 per cent for Bangladesh [Table 11.13]. The highest incidence of poverty is observed to be in Kurigram and the lowest in the Dhaka district, the capital city of Bangladesh. The estimated squared poverty gap (P_2) also indicates that the severity of poverty in Kurigram is the highest, while it is the lowest in Dhaka. Among all the districts, only 44 per cent have a value of P_0 lower than the Bangladesh average. Ten districts are in their worst condition, with P_0 above 55 per cent. The overall socio-economic development in these districts is also found to be the lowest. The ranks relating to the composite index (CI) and incidence of poverty suggest a moderate correlation ($r = 0.44$) between the level of development and the level of incidence of poverty which is significantly different from zero at 1 per cent level. The overall socio-economic development, thus, plays an important role in reducing poverty.

The economic status of households/individuals is also reflected by the per capita consumption expenditure. The per centage share of expenditure on food and non-food items may be used as a tool for measuring the standard of living of households/individuals. A higher per centage share of expenditure on food items as compared to non-food items is generally considered as a sign of under development. An accepted phenomenon of Engle's Law of income and expenditure is that higher the income, the lower is the per centage of income spent on food items and vice versa.

The average monthly per capita consumption expenditure on total items as well as on food and non-food items along with their per centage share is presented in Table 11.14. It is evident from the table that twenty two districts have higher level of monthly per capita consumption expenditure than that of Bangladesh average of Tk.663.19 which indicates that the economic status of these districts is relatively better than the other districts. The per capita consumer expenditure of forty-two districts is, however, below the level of the Bangladesh average and the district of Rangpur has the lowest monthly per capita consumption expenditure of Tk.503.49. The per centage share of expenditure on food to total expenditure is higher in all the districts as well as for Bangladesh average (Table 11.14) except Dhaka, Tangail, Naogaon and Bogra. This in fact indicates that all districts in Bangladesh need improvement in all sectors of varying degree for overall development of the country. It is also clear that any policy taken for socio-economic development as well as poverty alleviation must focus on the least developed districts in general and north-western as well as hilly districts in particular.

Conclusion

The foregoing analysis provides an objective assessment of which particular districts are lagging behind in development, in what respect and by how much. The data analyzed here clearly indicate that great disparity in development exists among the districts. Wide disparity is observed between the regions and

Table11.14: Monthly Per Capita Expenditure on Food and Non-Food Items By District

Locality	*Total*	*Expenditure in Tk.*		*Share of Expenditure (%)*	
		Food	*Non-food*	*Food*	*Non-food*
1	*2*	*3*	*4*	*5*	*6*
Division	618.42	384.10	234.32	62.11	37.89
Barisal	618.74	397.45	221.28p	64.24	35.76
Barguna	621.91	379.45	242.45	61.02	38.98
Bhola	607.55	376.59	230.24	61.99	38.01
Jhalokhati	592.82	398.58	203.24	65.72	34.28
Patuakhali	641.32	377.37	263.95	58.84	41.16
Pirojpur	626.92	384.99	241.92	61.41	38.59
Chittagong Division	671.60	398.25	273.35	59.30	40.70
Bandarban	629.82	375.71	254.11	59.65	40.35
Brahmanbaria	582.63	370.01	212.62	63.51	36.49
Chandpur	637.29	390.57	246.72	61.29	38.71
Chittagong	753.25	435.46	317.79	57.81	42.19
Comilla	663.36	389.39	273.97	58.70	41.30
Cox's Bazar	804.86	458.09	346.76	56.82	43.08
Feni	645.74	357.90	287.85	55.42	44.58
Khagrachari	689.03	403.66	285.37	58.58	41.42
Lakshmipur	614.27	378.18	236.09	61.57	38.43
Noakhali	633.26	377.90	255.36	59.68	40.32
Rangamati	719.42	438.73	280.69	60.98	39.02
Dhaka Division	684.01	377.81	306.20	55.23	44.77
Dhaka	1272.56	572.16	700.32	44.96	55.04
Faridpur	619.55	350.99	268.57	56.65	43.35
Gazipur	677.63	370.82	306.81	54.72	45.28
Gopalgonj	682.67	385.01	297.66	56.40	43.60

(Table Contd...)

Table11.14: Contd...

1	*2*	*3*	*4*	*5*	*6*
Jamalpur	540.40	312.90	227.49	57.90	42.10
Kishoregonj	759.24	434.24	325.00	57.19	42.81
Madaripur	624.55	368.87	255.76	59.05	40.95
Manikgonj	627.33	367.07	260.26	58.51	41.49
Munshigonj	788.55	405.35	383.20	51.40	48.60
Mymensingh	632.16	351.73	280.43	55.64	44.36
Narayangonj	859.00	443.64	415.36	51.65	48.35
Narshingdi	730.18	432.08	298.10	59.17	40.83
Netrokona	534.35	321.92	212.43	60.25	39.75
Rajbari	616.13	337.96	278.34	54.84	45.16
Shariatpur	615.13	386.89	228.24	62.90	37.10
Sherpur	521.95	314.84	207.06	60.33	39.67
Tangail	576.97	276.38	300.59	47.90	52.10
Khulna Division	632.58	353.15	278.37	55.83	44.10
Khulna	593.87	353.53	240.35	59.53	40.47
Bagerhat	537.24	343.94	193.29	64.02	35.98
Chuadanga	753.16	382.23	370.93	50.76	49.25
Jessore	694.72	361.45	333.27	52.03	47.97
Jhenaidah	695.84	356.04	339.80	61.17	48.83
Kustia	599.43	340.84	258.59	56.86	43.14
Magura	568.67	316.75	251.92	55.70	44.30
Meherpur	636.09	354.06	282.02	55.66	44.34
Narail	619.82	370.19	249.62	59.73	40.27
Satkhira	369.65	357.57	282.08	55.90	44.10
Rajsahi Division	632.22	342.69	289.52	54.20	45.80
Bogra	873.97	403.65	470.32	46.19	53.81
Dinajpur	713.95	357.06	356.89	50.01	49.99
Gaibandha	613.25	333.90	279.35	54.45	45.55

Table11.14: Contd...

1	2	3	4	5	6
Joypurhat	757.22	394.60	362.62	52.11	47.89
Kurigram	525.16	303.63	221.54	57.82	42.18
Lalmonirhat	542.67	298.69	243.98	55.04	44.96
Naogaon	855.18	396.42	456.76	46.59	53.41
Natore	638.23	330.87	303.36	51.84	48.16
Nawabgonj	586.37	348.73	237.64	59.47	40.53
Nilphamari	555.56	321.54	234.01	57.88	42.12
Pabna	628.76	377.45	251.31	60.03	39.97
Panchagarh	549.95	314.03	235.92	57.10	42.90
Rajshahi	631.79	361.43	270.36	57.21	42.79
Rangpur	503.49	276.35	227.13	54.89	45.11
Sirajgonj	561.82	347.08	214.75	61.78	38.22
Thakurgaon	603.01	317.15	285.86	52.59	47.41
Sylhet Division	711.91	423.64	293.28	59.09	40.91
Hobigonj	684.48	416.37	268.11	60.83	39.17
Maulvibazar	746.67	437.73	308.94	58.62	41.38
Sunamgonj	637.33	383.20	254.13	60.13	39.87
Sylhet	811.19	463.32	348.30	57.09	42.91
Bangladesh	663.19	376.35	286.84	56.75	43.25

Source: Analysis of Basic Needs Dimension of Poverty (Estimated), BBS, 1998.

districts in educational development. The composite index (CI) varies from the lowest of 0.0898 in Perojpur to the highest of 0.94 in Jamalpur and Nawabgonj. The southern and southwestern regions, which include Barisal and Khulna divisions, are found to be better developed in terms of literacy as compared to other regions. The district of Dhaka ranks the first in respect of population problem, while Khulna ranks the last in this respect. The disparity in this sector is about 2.4 times between the former and the latter district. The disparity in development in agriculture as well as in infrastructure and social sectors between the districts are almost similar and one-fourth of the total number of districts are found to be in the least developed category. The central and hilly regions are also found to be poorly developed in these two sectors. The level of development in rural industrial sector is much lower than the level of development of other sectors. However, the hilly region and a few other districts are observed to be better developed in respect of rural industry. This is mainly due to presence of handloom and cottage industries in hilly districts.

The overall development in the country is positively and highly associated with literacy. The progress in literacy in general and adult literacy in particular influences the development in the positive direction. The development of rural industry also contributes positively to overall development. The infrastructure and social services facilities have positive impact on the overall socio-economic development. An important feature of development is that the districts which are developed in agriculture are also developed in rural industry. The rank correlation between these two sectors is found to be positive. Population pressure appears to be the main obstacle to socio-economic development in Bangladesh and impact of various development programmes are being eroded by the high population growth. The overall results suggest that the level of overall development is higher in districts where the level of other dimensions of development are also higher and vice-versa. It may also be the case that the magnitude of developmental indicators is higher/lower because the overall development is higher or lower. In this sense, the overall socio-economic development and other dimensions of development most probably have mutually reinforcing and synergetic effects.

Recommendations for Development and Planning

On the basis of the analysis made in this study the following important recommendations have been made for development in different sectors.

(i) Our economy is mainly based on agriculture. Therefore, intensive use of land is an important strategy for rural development. The development has to be based on an increase in production and thereby increase in labour productivity. In order to achieve these goals of higher productivity and cropping intensity, spread of HYV crops, diffusion of modern technology, adoption of modern inputs etc. are essential. Special emphasis should be given in these respect to poorly developed regions – central and south-eastern regions and some least developed districts of north-western region.

(ii) Rural industrialization is a pre-condition for rural development. If the rural industry sector could be intensified, there would be some expansion of job opportunities for landless poor outside agriculture. A target oriented programme on rural industry such as small scale, cottage and agro-based industries may be intensified in the least

developed regions by promoting human resources development including productive skills. Various institutional arrangements with input support services for rural industrial development may be made particularly for the north-western and southern regions, which are poorly developed in rural industry.

(iii) Infrastructure and social services are important pre-conditions for socio-economic development through their impact on agriculture, rural industry and other development processes. Road communication, institutional facilities such as educational institutions, health care centres, banks, co-operatives etc. among others are important vehicles for development. As the hilly and north-western regions are least developed in these respects, special emphasis should be given in this sector to create multiplier effect on factors of development in these regions.

(iv) The interrelationship between education and overall development suggests that a comprehensive and viable education policy should be a part of the strategy for socio-economic development of the country in general and for the north-western region in particular where the overall literacy and adult literacy rates are relatively low. However, development may be achieved by expansion of literacy, particularly female literacy in the least developed districts through targeted planning and policy on

education sector such as vocational, informal education, adult literacy etc.

(v) Population and family planning component should be an integral part of almost every programme for development and a change from a large to small family size is an important approach for socio-economic development. Low rate of population growth should be ensured through widespread literacy and strong birth planning policy.

Limitation of the Study

The composite index provides a portrait of the development status in different sectors of each district of Bangladesh. It does not by any means capture all the dimensions of development. Important aspects of agriculture such as livestock, forestry, fishery, area under irrigation, HYV, total cropped area by districts etc. and industry particularly large scale industry, recent status of handloom by district etc. which are important for economic development could not be considered due to dearth of data by new districts. The data used in this study may conceal many other aspects that might exist in economic development. Moreover, the data for thirty-one indicators were standardized and then combined for each district giving equal weight to each indicator. However, the present study is a better and more comprehensive indicator than that based on a single measure. The CI may also be considered a yardstick for determining deprivation and disparity in development in various sectors in that it indicates which districts in the country are relatively more disadvantaged than others. To this end, it is hoped that the present analysis encourages further research in improving deficiencies and gaps in our understanding of CI for each district of Bangladesh.

Reference

1. The selection of the indicators has been influenced by availability of data. The kind of variables used by Adelman-Mirris study decades ago for cross-country study are not available and some do not show differences being within the boundary of the same country.

12

Conclusions and Strategies for Poverty Alleviation

Conclusions

Studies and discussions on poverty in Bangladesh have so far concentrated on measurement of incidence of poverty, its depth and severity. However, not much attention was given in the planning process to the development of evolving appropriate policies and programmes for poverty alleviation. But poverty alleviation has, in one way or another, occupied an important place in the list of stated objectives of all five-year plans of the country. Development of social sector, promotion of employment opportunities and reduction of income inequality have been the most talked about aims in the plans. In operational terms, these objectives received very little attention at least in the first three five year plans. Although certain broad based and growth oriented macro-economic policies were prescribed for poverty alleviation, employment generation etc., these policies did not have a favourable impact on the poor due to weak implementation process of the programmes. A well-planned programme cannot help in attaining targeted growth if it is not appropriately implemented. Thus monitoring, coordination and effective implementation are equally important in order to achieve desired effect on weaker sections of the rural society. In the absence of efficient local level institutions, planning alone is not sufficient to create positive impact on the target groups.

The last two five year plans showed greater awareness for the need of poverty alleviation programmes and more recently the government has adopted some special programmes or supplementary schemes such as Boyoska Vata, Grihayan Tahbil, Ashrayan, Karma Songsthan Bank etc. as appendages to the main development programmes. But it is not possible to eliminate poverty by merely adopting such special programmes if some of the general macroeconomic policies such as policies for income and employment generation, social sector development etc. do not have a favourable effect on the target group.

The budgetary process is very complex in Bangladesh and it is not transparent to general people. The budget is generally prepared on the incremental basis and it is not easy to assess its impact on different sections of people. For instance, the ADP allocation for social sector development increased from Tk.6830.0 million in 1990-91 to Tk.3783.0 million in 1999-2000 indicating about 453.9 per cent increase over the period. In terms of share of social sector in ADP has increased from 12.96 per cent to 24.40 per cent over the same period. Social sector development is considered to be an important vehicle for human capital development and thereby poverty alleviation. According to government official statistics, there has been a significant improvement in human capital (literacy rate, infant mortality rate, maternal mortality rate, life expectancy at birth etc.), but the low poverty reduction rate depicts a gloomy picture of development. This means that either the benefits of increased budgetary allocation for social sector development are not reaching the relatively less privileged classes of people or the development of human capital is not translating into higher income due to lack of opportunity for productive utilization of better human capital. Moreover, improvement of human capital may have taken place through improvement in the situation of the non-poor. In such circumstances, increase in budgetary allocation may not have positive impact on income of the poor and poverty alleviation. Thus, measurement of benefits in terms of budgetary allocation is very difficult if there is no scope to assess how much of the total budget is being spent for the welfare of the poor and how much of it is going to the poorer districts or areas where concentration of poor is relatively much higher.

The idea of direct attack on poverty problem through microcredit or microfinance to the poor was not considered in the early 1980s but emerged gradually and in due course it became an important objective in the last two five year plans. Up till December 1999, about Tk.92,436.50 million was disbursed by 533 NGOs as microcredit, and about Tk.63,955.50 million was distributed by 4 scheduled and 2 specialised banks and Tk.23,675.0 million was distributed by the government administrative divisions and departments. Thus, a total of Tk.180,066.0 million was disbursed to the poor for their economic development and social welfare. This figure is much higher than that of 1996, however, the proportion of poor decreased from 47.0 per cent in 1996 to 44.3 per cent in 2000 showing only 2.7 per cent point decrease over the period.

In order to increase income and employment opportunities of the disadvantaged women and extreme poor, the government allocated large sums of money from revenue budget for the safetynet programmes which include FFW, GR, TR, VGD and VGF. In 1995-96, about Tk.9610.3 million was allocated for safetynet programmes, while this figure rose to Tk.15,360.0 million in 1999-2000 showing about 60 per cent increase over the period [BER, 2000, p.112]. Women are increasingly targeted as beneficiaries of anti-poverty interventions through microcredit and safetynet programmes. The main problem is to assess how much of the total resource allocations is actually spent for the beneficiaries and how much is going to those who are linked with resource allocation and project implementation processes. It appears from different sources that almost two-thirds of the total resource goes into in the hands of these people and only one-third is spent for rural development or for the beneficiaries group. Thus, resource allocation in the government budget seems colossal but the net amount spent in the name of FFW, TR etc. is not large.

Poverty is unevenly distributed across the regions and districts. The districts of Kurigram, Nilfamari, Gaibanda, Chapai Nowabgonj, Sirajgonj, Rangpur, Mymensingh, Jamalpur, Sherpur, Shariatpur, Netrokona and Bhola have a greater proportion of their population living below the poverty line (2122 kcal/person/perday) compared to other districts. Greater care is needed while framing policies and allocating resources to attain balanced socioeconomic development and alleviate poverty in these poorer districts. In 1997 the poverty gap measure (P_1) for rural areas was estimated at 0.112. This measure has the interpretation of being an indicator for poverty alleviation by targeting transfers to the poor. Thus, minimum cost of eliminating poverty is the sum of all poverty gaps in a population. This means that every poverty gap will be filled up to the poverty line.

The actual cost needed to eliminate poverty would be equal to the total number of individuals times(P_1) times poverty line Z, ie $n.P_1.Z$. As per estimate of BBS, the poverty line income Z and total rural population were estimated at Tk.448.0 and 99.4 million. With P_1= 0.112 and Z = 448, the minimum cost of eliminating poverty using targeting transfers in a population of 99.4 million was Tk.4987.5 million in 1997. However, about Tk.37891.3 million was disbursed as microcredit by 4 large NGOs, 6 banks, Grameen bank, BRDB, PKSF and Government administrative divisions during the same period which — the minimum cost. Theoretically if the benificiaries group could earn at least Tk.5000.0 million as investment return from Tk.37871.3 million distributed among them, then the incidence of poverty would have been removed. But this was far from being the case. The incidence of poverty reduced by only 2.3 per cent from 1996 to 2000, indicating the need to develop appropriate strategies for better utilization of microcredit.

Development Strategies

In view of the large extent of poverty particularly in rural areas of Bangladesh, a wide range of development activities have been implemented and a number of strategies have been set up at the national level by the government and non-government organisations for poverty alleviation. There are many national strategy frameworks in different sectors of the economy for economic development and poverty alleviation. The primary objectives of these development efforts is to accelerate economic growth through agricultural development. The agriculture sector plays a vital role in reducing rural poverty and fostering sustainable economic growth. This is because agriculture is the major source of income and employment of the rural poor and the development of agriculture sector is still synonymous with economic development in Bangladesh. The linkage between agriculture and non-agricultural sectors in the economy are such that a given increase in production in agricultural sector usually leads to a more than proportionate increase in production in non-agricultural sectors. Thus without improvement in agriculture sector, there can hardly be any development in the rural areas and nor can there be any significant reduction of rural poverty. The main focus of the development strategy is, therefore, to alleviate poverty through high agricultural growth and generation of productive employment in both farm and non-farm activities for increasing income of the poor to meet their basic needs. Labour intensive activities such as dairy and poultry raising, fish culture, vegetable growing etc. are also important strategies for poverty alleviation in agriculture sector in rural areas. The broad development strategy of industrial sector is to maximize the contribution of this sector to GDP and to total employment generation in the country. Labour intensive growth of the economy through export-led industrialization is an important strategy to provide more benefit to the poor labourers for increasing their income and self-reliance. Small and Cottage industries are also important sub-sectors for employment generation and poverty alleviation.

Physical and social infrastructure development are a pre-requisite for agricultural development, export-led industrialization, human resources development and employment generation. Physical infrastructure includes construction of roads, canals for irrigation, rural electrification, etc. Infrastructure development, particularly in rural areas, can also make a considerable contribution to growth through job creation and improvement of access to different economic activities and social services, which lead to food security of the rural poor. The social infrastructure includes educational institutions, health care institutions, post office, banks, etc. Development of social infrastructures is directly linked to human resources development, which in turn enhances the productive capacity and skill of the poor. Human resource development also opens up opportunities for participation in and access to several economic activities.

The above indicative/interactive development and poverty alleviation strategies of the government have been operationalised through some macro and micro development programs as well as through changes in public expenditure priorities. For instance, expenditure in social sector in recent years has increased to a large extent for poverty alleviation. But there has never been a holistic and dynamic strategic framework based on different issues to combat poverty. Nor had a clearly articulated operational approach been developed to address the issues. There are some broad-based policies and strategies for poverty alleviation such as land reform policies, education policies and health policies to protect the interest of landless poor and improve their socio-economic conditions. However, the main problems lie with implementation of the process. As a result, the poor are not benefited from such strategies and they remain uncared as overall target for poverty alleviation. Thus, we need to have a comprehensive national poverty reduction strategies with a time bound framework. Some of the specific issues and strategies are briefly described below:

Issue 1: **Economic Growth and Poverty**

Economic growth is a key element in the reduction of poverty. Higher growth enhances the demand for labour which intern increases income and employment opportunities and raises workers' productivity and thereby reducing poverty economic redundant. Labour intensive growth is more effective in reducing poverty at a faster rate through trickle down process to the poorer section of people.

Strategy: Broad-based and aggressive growth of the economy is essential for reducing poverty. The annual economic growth in the 1990s averaged about 5 per cent compared to 4 per cent per annum in the 1980s. Although the growth performance in the 1990s was higher compared to the earlier decade, this was not sufficient to create a discernible impact on poverty reduction. In order to achieve rapid decline in poverty and a considerably fast growth rate (in the range of 7-8 per cent), the government needs to stimulate growth in the agricultural and industrial sectors through various policies. These include introduction of new technology and credit provision for these sectors. Accelerated growth with social justice should be encouraged through improved economic management and increased investment in agriculture, industry and social sectors.

Issue 2: Population and Poverty

There is an interrelationship between population growth and incidence of poverty. At the micro level, the poor usually have large family members with less resources. Families having more children and women are more likely to experience poverty.

Strategy: An effective national population policy can considerably reduce poverty. Integrated population and development programmes through effective family planning and MCH programmes can improve family welfare and provide the chances for better living. These programmes should encourage birth-spacing and breast-feeding to delay the next birth and consequently reduce family sizes.

Issue 3: Education and Poverty

The level of poverty is negatively associated with level of education. Higher level of education reduces household size, improves health status and increases mobility in respect of income generating opportunities. Thus, education is an important element of national development which aims at human resource development and poverty alleviation.

Strategy: Education deserves high priority for poverty alleviation and thus more attention should be given to improving its relevance, quantity, quality, as well as access of the poor to education. The rise in female participation in school reduces population growth through lower fertility. However, merely high enrolment rate at primary and secondary education levels is not enough. It is essential to maintain the quality and to link education with productive activities to enhance access to employment and income generating opportunities. The current gross enrolment rate of the female and poor at the primary and secondary levels is still lower compared to the male and non-poor. Therefore, the government should focus on creating opportunities for the female and the poor for better access to education and should encourage them to take advantage of the public investment opportunities created for education. Efforts should also be made to expand coverage of food for education and female stipend programmes.

Issue 4: Human Capital and Poverty

Human capital is the primary assets of the poor and its development is important for poverty alleviation. Human capital and poverty are closely and inversely associated. Lower the human capital, higher is the incidence of poverty. This is because human capital increases the scope of employment generation, education, skill and capacity to work.

Strategy: Strong emphasis should be given at national planning for human capital development especially vocational, skill development and occupational training in both urban and rural areas. Moreover, human capital development should be linked to the needs of the workplace, the community and the society. Efforts should be made to promote skill development training in a variety of fields in order to effectively increase participation of the poor, both in the workforce and society at large. Thus, every poor individual must have access to basic education, health care and other essential services.

Issue 5: Women Development and Poverty

Almost half of the total population are women. If this vast majority is not brought under the mainstream of development processes, the objective of poverty alleviation will not be achieved. Literacy rate, nutritional status and employment opportunities of women particularly in rural areas are very low. They are easily exposed to poverty and malnutrition. It is, therefore, important to integrate them fully into the development processes.

Strategy: Women development is expected to address the priority area of poverty by creating employment opportunities, capacity building, giving women voice, for their advancement, providing access to resources etc. Education, intensive skill development training along with provision of micro-credit create self-employment opportunities for them. Participation of women in livestock and poultry farming and small trading is an important strategy for creation of self-employment opportunities and economic development. Emphasis must be given on social sector development with adequate budgetary allocation particularly for health and education sectors to remove gender discrimination and enhance welfare of poor women.

Issue 6: Youth Development and Poverty

About one-third of the total population is youth and they are the most directive force of a nation. For economic development, they should be brought in the mainstream of national development activities. If this prospective group of people is transformed into an organised, disciplined and productive workforce, the country may move on to prosperity and consequently reduce poverty.

Strategy: Reduction of unemployment and creation of self-employment opportunities for this energetic youth force are important strategies for their economic development and poverty alleviation. Intensive training for skill development should be provided and provision of micro-credit should be made to achieve the objective of self-employment generation in different activities. Emphasis should be given on skill development training for the youth particularly on pisciculture, livestocks, poultry farming, trades, modern technologies etc.

Issue 7: Health Status and Poverty

Health is wealth, while ill health contributes to poverty through income erosion, low productivity, inability to work for longer period, and lower wages due to sickness. Sick people have less bargaining power which ultimately accentuates vulnerability by limiting their ability to work in different income generating activities.

Strategy: Improved health conditions contribute to higher income earning opportunity for the poor and reduce income erosion of the poor by increasing efficiency of human capital. Health care services both preventive and curative should be expanded to ensure easy access of the poor to these services and to improve their health status. Improved health facilities and maternity care, child care and family welfare services are essential for reducing fertility, material and infant mortality rates and getting healthy and skilled labour force. In order to achieve these goals, more public investment is required to expand health services for the poor.

Issue 8: Occupational Status, Employment and Poverty

Among the various factors, occupational status is an important element in assessing incidence of poverty. Poverty is relatively higher in households belonging to labourers, artisans and rickshaw pullers compared to households of landowner farmers, businessmen and professionals. The monthly per capita income of the former groups is also lower than in the latter groups. Lack of education as well as skill poses a major obstacle to finding good jobs. Moreover, illiterate people have less mobility with respect to income generating opportunities.

Strategy: Labour-intensive activities are important for creating demand for labour and enhancing the scope of income generating opportunities for the vast majority of the poor. A diversified export-oriented industry in both public and private sectors will lead to wider labour demand via accelerated export growth and establishment of markets for new products. Labour market reforms and facilities for skill training for unskilled labourers abundant in our country will allow the flexibility needed to adjust structural changes in the demand for labour. Skill training is one of the most important forms of skill development that increase the productivity of labour and their well being.

Issue 9: Rural Infrastructure Development and poverty

Rural infrastructure development has significant positive impacts on rural economic growth and other income and employment opportunities. It has also positive effects on agricultural and industrial productivity, education and poverty reduction. Infrastructure development enhances the flow of services and provides opportunities to the rural poor to engage themselves in different income generating activities, especially in non-farm activities.

Strategy: Large amount of resource allocation for rural infrastructure development is essential for poverty reduction. Physical infrastructure, social infrastructure and social services should be improved uniformly in all regions and districts. Emphasis should be given to health and education institutions, rural roads, rural electrification, irrigation canals, post office, banks etc. Improvement of these factors can contribute substantially to poverty alleviation through increasing employment opportunity and labour productivity.

Issue 10: Environmental Degradation and Poverty

There is a complex interrelationship between population, poverty and environmental degradation. Rapid population growth and poverty combine to create environmental problems such as land degradation, deforestation due to increased demand for natural resources and expansion of human settlement, depletion of water resources, ecological imbalance and consequently threat biological diversity due to natural habitat destruction. Environmental degradation on the other hand directly affects the quality of life, especially of the poor. As the poor have no resources to avoid environmental damages, they are easily exposed to health hazards and tend to be vulnerable to different environmental risks.

Strategy: In order to reduce environmental degradation, sustainable management of industry, forest, and water body is essential. Particularly community-based environmental management should be ensured. Special attention should be given to look for ways to reduce reliance on natural resources such as fuel wood, forestland, water etc. to minimize depletion of natural resources and to reduce pollution. Keeping in view the interaction between poverty and environment, effective steps towards reduction of environmental degradation is essential.

Issue 11: Social Protection and Poverty

Every society has vulnerable people because of age, illness, shocks from natural disasters, economic crisis, social conflicts, powerlessness, isolation and physical weakness etc. These factors also contribute to poverty and they are interlinked with each other in various ways. For instance, physically weak labourers have low productivity and they are unable to cultivate larger areas of land or to work additional hours. Physical weakness also creates isolation which in turn accentuates vulnerability. Vulnerability again relates to poverty through distress sale of assets such as land, livestocks etc.

Strategy: Effective social protection is needed to manage risks, to ensure economic security and to assist individuals, households and communities. Social protection includes old age pension, social security for unemployed, crop and disability insurance, safety net programs such as Food for Works, Test Relief, Vulnerable Group Development, Vulnerable Group Feeding etc. Targeted micro credit and safetynet programmes are essential for the poor to be self-employed in productive activities and to protect them from distress sale of assets, future labour, livestock, standing crop, land etc. Seasonal public works, seasonal credits and feeding programmes can reduce vulnerability as well as poverty. Political mobilisation and legal aid are important to protect the interest of powerless poor people.

Issue 12: Lack of Good Governance and Poverty

Governance issues of poverty arise from the nature of the state, its governance and the countries economic system. Failure to establish a framework of law and good governance conducive to development leads to weak institutions, weak financial management, arbitrary application of laws and rules, non-transparency in decision making, and failure in the implemetation of appropriate policies for development etc. The coterie of the vested interest groups makes the public institutions ineffective and they fail to bring about meaningful change in the fate of the rural poor or increase in human resources of the poor, and improvements in the welfare of the rural society. For instance, if loans are issued against collateral for agricultural development, or if the issuing of loans require certification of local political personnel, then benefits go to the ruling group. Socio-economic inequalities also increase due to indiscriminate government investment to extend patronage to the privileged groups.

Strategy: Good governance with legal framework conducive to development should be ensured. Transparency, availability, and validity of information regarding public funds and delivery of public services need to be maintained. Bureaucratic accountability, effective and efficient public sector management must be ensured. Good governance is essential to achieve good environment for economic prosperity of the country and fulfil the needs of poor people relating to health, education and other social services. Without good governance, rule of law competence and transparency, no policy or programme for poverty alleviation is likely to succeed.

Bibliography

Adelman, I and C.T. Morris (1967). Society, Politics and Development (A Quantitative Approach). The Johns Hopkins Press, Baltimore, USA.

Asaduzzaman, M. (1999). Microfinance in Bangladesh: DO Institution Matters? A Background Paper Prepared for the Conference on "Poverty Alleviation Strategies: The Next Generation" June 6-7, 1999, Dhaka.

Atkinson, (1979). Economics Inequality, Oxford University Press, London.

BBS (1995-96). Household Expenditure Survey 1995-96, Bangladesh Bureau of Statistics (Main Report), Statistics Division, Ministry of Planning, Dhaka.

BBS (1995-96). Labour Force Survey in Bangladesh, December 1996, Bangladesh Bureau of Statistics, Statistics Division, Ministry of Planning, Dhaka.

BBS (1999). Statistical Pocketbook, Bangladesh Bureau of Statistics, Statistics Division, Ministry of Planning, Dhaka.

BBS (1999). Poverty Monitoring Survey, Bangladesh Bureau of Statistics, Statistics Division, Ministry of Planning, Dhaka.

BBS (2000). National Accounting, Bangladesh Bureau of Statistics, Statistics Division, Ministry of Planning, Dhaka.

BIDS (1998). South Asia Poverty Monitor: The Bangladesh Chapter, ed. by Rahman, A. and Sen, B. (Mimeo).

Chamber, Robert (1984). Rural Development: Putting the Last First, Longman, London.

Credit and Development Forum (CDF), Microfinance Statistics of NGOs and other MFIS, Vol.9, Dhaka.

Choudhury, A.M.R. and Alam, M.A. (1997). BRAC's Poverty Alleviation Efforts: A Quarter Century of Experiences and Learning, in Wood, G.D. and Sharif, I. (ed.), Who Needs Credit?

Poverty and Finance in Bangladesh, University Press Limited, Dhaka.

CIRDAP (1997). Monitoring Adjustment and Poverty, Newsletter, December 1997.

Evans, T.G., Rafi, M. Adams, A.M., Chowdhury, A.M.R.(1995). Barriers to participation in BRAC, RDP, BRAC, Dhaka.

Haq, M. and Haq, K. (1998). Human Development in South Asia, University Press Ltd. Dhaka.

Haider, R.S. (1998). Measurement of Poverty and its Correlates, in Hussain, M.A.M. (ed.). Poverty Alleviation and Empowerment (The Second Impact Assessment Study of BRAC's Rural Development Programme), BRAC, Dhaka.

Hossain, M. and Sen, B (1992). Rural Poverty in Bangladesh: Trends and Determinants, Asian Development Review, Vol. 10, No.1.

Hossain, M.A. (1993). Programmes Under Implementation by the Ministry of Agriculture in Alleviating Poverty, in Amin, M.N. (ed.), Government of Bangladesh in Poverty Alleviation, Proceedings of a National Seminar held in Dhaka, February 17-19, 1993.

Hossain, M. (1995). Sociodconomic Characteristics of the Poor, in Hossain Zillur Rahman and Mahabul Hossain (eds.). Rethinking Rural Poverty: Bangladesh as a Case Study, Sage Publications, India, Pvt. Ltd.

Hossain, M. (1996). Income, Employment and Poverty, in Hossain Z.R and Sen, B (eds.), 1987-1994. Dynamics of Rural Poverty in Bangladesh, BIDS, (Mimeo), Dhaka.

Hossain, M. (2000). Bangladesh Agriculture at the Crossroads: Current Challenges, Dialogue in, Recent Development and Structural Changes in Bangladesh Agriculture: Issues for Reviewing Strategies and Policies (Chaper III of CPD-IRBD 2000).

Hussain, M.A.M. (ed.) (1998). Poverty Alleviation and Empowerment (The Second Impact Assessment Study of BRAC's Rural Development Program, BRAC.

Huda, S.A.T.M. (1993). Poverty Alleviation: Role of the Government, in Amin, M.N. (ed.).

Hedrick-Wong, Y. et.al (1997). Experiences and Challenges in Credit and Poverty Alleviation Programmes in Bangladesh: The Case of Bangladesh in: Wood, G.D. and Sharif, I. (ed.), Who Needs Credit? Poverty and Finance in Bangladesh.

First Five Year Plan (1973-78). Planning Commission, Ministry of Planning, Dhaka.

Second Five Year Plan (1980-85). Planning Commission, Ministry Planning, Dhaka.

Third Five Year Plan (1985-90). Planning Commission, Ministry Planning, Dhaka.

Fourth Five Year Plan (1990-95). Planning Commission, Ministry Planning, Dhaka.

Fifth Five Year Plan (1997-2002). Planning Commission, Ministry Planning, Dhaka.

GOB (1993-94). Bangladesh Economic Survey, Ministry of Finance, Dhaka.

GOB (1995). Country Paper Bangladesh. World Summit for Social Development, Copenhagen, Denmark.

GOB (1996). Food for Education Programme, Primary and Mass Education Division, Ministry of Education, Dhaka.

GOB (1997-98). Annual Development Programme, Ministry of Planning, Dhaka

GOB (1998-99). Annual Development Programme, Ministry of Planning, Dhaka

GOB (1999). Skilled Youth Force: Self-Reliant Economy, Department of Youth Development, Ministry of Youth and Sports, Bangladesh.

GOB (1999). Education for All, Primary and Mass Education Division (PMED), Ministry of Education, Bangladesh.

GOB (1999-2000). Annual Development Programme, Planning Commission, Ministry of Planning, Dhaka.

GOB (2000). Bangladesh Economic Review, Finance Division, Ministry of Finance, Dhaka.

GOB (2001). Bangladesh Economic Review, Finance Division, Ministry of Finance, Dhaka.

Khan, M.H. (1998). Role of Palli Karma Sahayak in Poverty Alleviation: An Overview, Paper to National Workshop on Sustainable Approach to Rural Development and Microcredit, 1-2 October, 1997.

Khan, M.H. (1997). Credit for Poverty Alleviation in Bangladesh: Performance of Public Sector Banks, in Wood, G.D. and Sharif, I. (ed.), Who Needs Credit? Poverty and Finance in Bangladesh, University Press Ltd.

Musfafa, S.I. Ara, et al. (1996). Impact Assessment Study of RDP, BRAC, Dhaka.

Narain, P. Rai, S.C. and Santi Sarup (1991). "Statistical Evaluation of Development on Socio-Economic Front". Journal of Indian Society of Agricultural Statistics, Vol. 43, No.3, New Delhi, India.

Narain, P. Rai, S.C. and Santi Sarup (1993). "Evaluation of Economic Development on Orissa". Journal of Indian Society of Agricultural Statistics, Vol. 45, No.2, New Delhi, India

Pearson, K. (1933). Tables of the Incomplete Beta-Function. The University Press, Combridge.

Proshad, K. (1985). Planning for Poverty Alleviation, Agricole Publishing Academy New Delhi, India.

PROSHIKA (1998-99), Activity Report. A Centre for Human Development, Dhaka.

PROSHIKA (2000). The Budget and the Poor (A Study Commissioned by PROSHIKA and Conducted by Shamunnay), The University Press Limited, Proceeding of a National Seminar held in Dhaka, February 17-19, Dhaka.

Quashem, H.A. (1993). Poverty Alleviation Programme Under the Ministry of Women's Affairs, in Amin M.N. (ed.), Government of Bangladesh in Poverty Alleviation, Dhaka.

Rahman, Pk. M. (1995). Poverty Alleviation: Government and Non-Government Organisation Interventons, in Sobhan, R. (ed.). Experiences with Economic Reform (A Review of Bangladesh Development 1995), CPD and UPL, Dhaka.

Sarker, M. (1996). Regional Disparity in Economic Well-Being of Bangladesh, Unpublished M.Sc. Thesis, Department of Statistics, Jahangirnagar University, Savar, Dhaka.

Sen, B. and Rahman, A. (1998). Bangladesh Poverty Monitor: An Overview (Based on the Report South Asia Poverty Monitor, the Bangladesh Chapter).

Sen, B. (2000). Bangladesh Poverty Analysis: Trends and Institutions, A Paper Prepared for the Seminar.

Sen, A.K. (1987). Agricultural Development and Rural Poverty, Ashish Publishing House, New Delhi, India.

Siddique, Q.I. (1993). Employment Generation and Poverty Alleviation Through Infrastructure Development Activities, in Amin, M.N. (ed.).

Sing, A.K. (1987). Agricultural Development and Rural Poverty, Ashish Publicating House, Delhi, India.

Sohrabuddin, M. (1999). Formal Sector Micro Finance in Bangladesh, Paper to International Training Course on Developing and Financing of Micro Enterprises, Organised by Bangladesh Bank and Islamic Bank, Dhaka.

UNFPA (1992). The State of World Population, Nuffield Press, Oxford, U.K.

UNDP (1996). Human Development Report, Oxford University Press, New York and London.

World Bank (1990). World Development Report: Poverty, New York, Oxford University Press.

World Bank (1990a). Poverty Reduction Handbook and Operational Directive, Washington, D.C.

World Bank (1993). Poverty Reduction, and the World Bank, Progress in Fiscal 1993, Washington, D.C.

World Food Programme (1997). Food Aid Reduces Poverty, Bangladesh.